SELECTIONS FROM THE QURAN

The Masterpiece Library of ISLAM—4

SELECTIONS FROM THE QURAN

BY

M. ABUL FAZL

ARYAN BOOKS INTERNATIONAL

NEW DELHI

Selections from the Quran

Published in 2002 By :

ARYAN BOOKS INTERNATIONAL
4378/4B, Pooja Apartments
4B, Ansari Road, Darya Ganj
New Delhi-110002 (India)

ISBN-81-7305-140-2

Printed in India at Print Perfect, New Delhi.

Contents

	Preface	*ix*
I.	The Opening Chapter	1
II.	The Cow	2
III.	The Family of Imran	43
IV.	Women	66
V.	The Table	99
VI.	Cattle	116
VII.	Al Araf	139
VIII.	The Spoils	146
IX.	Immunity	151
X.	Jonah	158
XI.	Hud	162
XII.	Joseph	164
XIII.	Thunder	166
XIV.	Abraham	171
XV.	Hijr	174
XVI.	The Bee	177
XVII.	The Children of Israel	185
XVIII.	The Cave	192
XIX.	Mary	194
XX.	T. H.	195
XXI.	The Prophets	197
XXII.	The Pilgrimage	199
XXIII.	The Believers	203
XXIV.	Light	205
XXV.	The Distinction	213

XXVI.	The Poets	218
XXVII.	The Ant	221
XXVIII.	The Story	223
XXIX.	The Spider	224
XXX.	The Greeks	226
XXXI.	Lokman	230
XXXII.	Adoration	231
XXXIII.	The Confederates	232
XXXIV.	Saba	235
XXXV.	The Creator	236
XXXVI.	Y.S.	237
XXXVII.	The Ranks	239
XXXVIII.	S	240
XXXIX.	The Troops	241
XL.	The Faithful	245
XLI.	Worship	246
XLII.	Counsel	249
XLIII.	Gold Ornaments	250
XLIV.	Smoke	251
XLV.	The Kneeling	252
XLVI.	Al Ahkaf	253
XLVII.	Mohammed	253
XLVIII.	The Victory	255
XLIX.	The Apartments	255
L.	K	257
LI.	The Scattering	259
LII.	The Mountain	260
LIII.	The Star	261
LIV.	The Moon	264
LV.	The Merciful	265
LVI.	The Inevitable	267
LVII.	Iron	268
LVIII.	She Who Pleaded	269
LIX.	The Emigration	271

LX.	She Who Is Tried	272
LXI.	Battle Array	274
LXII.	The Assembly	275
LXIII.	The Hypocrites	276
LXIV.	Mutual Deceit	276
LXV.	Divorce	278
LXVI.	Prohibition	279
LXVII.	The Kingdom	280
LXVIII.	The Pen	281
LXIX.	The Inevitable	282
LXX.	The Steps	283
LXXI.	Noah	284
LXXII.	The Jinn	285
LXXIII.	The Wrapped Up	286
LXXIV.	The Enwrapped	287
LXXV.	The Judgment Day	289
LXXVI.	Man	291
LXXVII.	The Sent	292
LXXVIII.	The News	293
LXXIX.	Who Tear Forth	294
LXXX.	He Frowned	296
LXXXI.	The Folding Up	297
LXXXII.	The Rending Asunder	298
LXXXIII.	Those Who Stint	300
LXXXIV.	The Splitting Asunder	301
LXXXV.	The Celestial Signs	302
LXXXVI.	The Night-comer	303
LXXXVII.	The Most High	304
LXXXVIII.	The Overwhelming	305
LXXXIX.	The Daybreak	306
XC.	The Soil	308
XCI.	The Sun	309
XCII.	The Night	310
XCIII.	The Brightness	311

XCIV.	The Opening	313
XCV.	The Fig	313
XCVI.	Thick Blood	314
XCVII.	Power	315
XCVIII.	Clear Evidence	316
XCIX.	The Earthquake	316
C.	The Chargers	317
CI.	The Striking	317
CII.	Desire	318
CIII.	The Afternoon	318
CIV.	The Slanderers	319
CV.	The Elephant	319
CVI.	The Koreish	320
CVII.	Religion	320
CVIII.	The Abundance	321
CIX.	The Unbelievers	321
CX.	Help	322
CXI.	Abu Lahab	322
CXII.	The Unity	323
CXIII.	The Daybreak	323
CXIV.	Men	324
	Addenda	325

Preface

In the following "Selection from the Quran" my object has been to bring together under their own Surahs all the important verses with suitable headings as may help people to form a correct estimate as to the general contents of the Sacred Book of the Mohammedan World. I have also thought fit to append some short notes to elucidite the meaning of certain verses, and have taken care not to inflict my own views upon it as far as possible.

The work has been compiled and hurried through the press in less than a couple of months' time, and I am fully conscious of my own shortcomings in the execution of this work, but I trust to the indulgence of my kind readers to overlook them.

M. Abul-Fazl.

Introduction

The word Quran comes from the verb 'karaa,' to cry,[1] and signifies properly in Arabic the revelation vouchsafed to the Prophet Mohammed, subsequently collected together into a Book which bears that name.

It is too well known that the Prophet never gave a book : be only preached and taught : whenever the Spirit moved forth 'his burning eloquence' into the ears of his countrymen and those who came to drink of the fountain which now flowed under him. These were, however, taken down by his followers on palm leaves, leather, and on such other materials as came ready to hand. And it was not till after the death of the Prophet that Omar, afterwards Caliph, turned his attention to collect the scattered fragments together, and with the help of Abu-Bakr, who was then the Caliph, succeeded in bringing out a well-authenticated recension of the whole.

An Official Recension

But so far this was a mere private endeavour, and incomplete and, in some cases, defective fragments of the Quran continued to be in use till ten years later the Caliph Osman took up the work of reproducing an authoritative recension of them with the help of the Companions of the Prophet who happened to be then living. And this recension of the Quran has stood during the last 1,300 years as a monument of the Caliph's piety to the honour of the Prophet.

The Present Arrangement

But the collection was made without regard to the chronological sequence of the subject-matter, special care being taken only with regard to their authenticity. "In fact," says a learned writer, "the age and the men were uncritical, and the only apparent rule followed was to arrange the portions of a Surah in the best way possible, and then to put the longer Surahs first in order and the shorter ones last, without any reference to chronological sequence."

Divisions

The Quran is divided into 114 larger portions of unequal length, which we call *Sowar*, in the singular *Surah*, a word which properly means a row or series, such as a line of bricks arranged in a wall, or a rank of soldiers in an army, but now exclusively used for chapters in the Quran.

Next after the title, at the head of every Surah, except only the ninth, is prefixed the solemn form, "In the name of God, the Merciful, the Compassionate."

Every Surah is sub-divided into smaller portions which are customarily called verses ; but the Arabic word is *Ayat*, in the singular *Ayat,* signifying signs.[2]

Besides these unequal divisions the Quran is also divided into sixty equal portions, in Arabic called 'Ahzab,' in singular 'Hizb,' each sub-divided into four equal parts ; but it is more usually divided into thirty equal parts only, called 'Ajza,' from the singular 'juz' each of twice the length of the former, and in the like manner sub-divided into four parts.

But the Quran naturally divides itself into two ; one consisting of the inspired utterances of the Prophet at Mecca, and the other comprising those at Medinah.

Its General Character

"The Quran," says Mr. Sale, "is universally allowed to be written with the utmost elegance and purity of language, in the dialect of the tribe of Koreish, the most noble and polite of all the Arabians, but with some mixture, though very rarely, of other dialects. It is confessedly the standard of the Arabic tongue, and as the more arthodox believe, and are taught by the book itself, inimitable by any human pen (though some sectaries have been of another opinion), and therefore insisted on as a permanent miracle, greater than that of raising the dead, and alone sufficient to convince the world of its divine origin."

"And to this miracle did Mohammed himself chiefly appeal for the confirmation of his mission, publicly challenging the most eloquent men in Arabia, which was at that time stocked with thousands whosesole study and ambition it was to excel in elegance of style and composition, to produce even a single chapter that might be compared with it.[3] I will mention but one instance out of several, to show that this book was really admired for the beauty of its composure by those who must be allowed to have been competent judges. A poem of Labid Ebn Rabia, one of the greatest wits in Arabia in Mohammed's time, being fixed up on the gate of the temple of Mecca, an honour allowed to none but the most esteemed performances, none of the other poets durst offer anything of their own in competition with it. But the second chapter of the Quran being fixed up by it soon after, Labid himself (them an idolater) on reading the first verses only, was struck with admiration, and immediately professed the religion taught thereby, declaring that such words could proceed from an inspired person only.

"The style of the Quran is generally beautiful and fluent, especially where it imitates the prophetic manner and scripture phrases. It is concise and often obscure, adorned with hold figures after the eastern taste, enlivened with florid and sententious expressions, are in many places, especially where the majesty and attributes of God and described, sublime and magnificent of which the reader cannot but observe several instances thought he must not imagine the translation comes up to the original, notwithstanding my endeavours to do it justice."[4]

Lest it be considered we are biased in our estimate of the Quran, we give the words of Samuel Johnson : "If it is not poetry, — and it is hard to say whether it be or not, — it is more than poetry. It is not history, nor biography. It is not anthology like the Sermon on the Mount ; nor metaphysical dialectics, like the Buddhist Sutras ; nor sublime homiletics, like Plato's conferences of the wise and foolish teachers. It is a prophet's cry, Semitic to the core ; yet of a meaning so universal and so timely that all the voices of the age take it up, willing or unwilling, and it echoes over palaces and deserts, over cities and empires, first kindling its chosen hearts to world conquest, then gathering itself up into a reconstructive force that all the creative lights of Greece and Asia might penetrate the heavy gloom of Christian Europe, when Christianity was but the Queen of Night."

Emanuel Deutsch calls the Quran, "a book by the aid of which the Arabs conquered a world greater than that of Alexander the Great ; greater than that of Rome, and in as many tens of years as the latter had wanted hundreds to accomplish her conquests ; by the aid of which they alone of all the Shemites came to Europe as kings, whether the Phænicians had come as tradesmen, and the Jews as fugitives or captives; came to Europe to hold up, together with these fugitives, the light to humanity; — they alone, while darkness lay around, to raise up the wisdom and knowledge of Hellas from the dead, to teach philosophy, medicine, astronomy, and the golden art of song to the West as to the East, to stand at the cradle of modern science, and to cause us late epigoni for ever to weep over the day when Grenada fell? "[5]

Elsewhere the same writer continues thus : "Those grand accents of joy and sorrow, of love, and valour, and passion, of which but faint echoes strike on our ears now, were full-toned at the time of Mohammed ; and he had not merely to rival the illustrious of the illustrious, but to excel them; to appeal to the superiority of what he said and sang as a very sing and proof of his mission."[6] The poets before him had sung of love . . . Antara, himself the hero of the most famous novel, sings of the ruin around which ever hover lovers' thoughts, of the dwelling of Abla, who is gone and her dwelling place knows her not.[7] Mohammed sang none of these. No love-minstrelsy his, not the joys of this world, nor sword nor camel, not jealousy or human vengeance, not the glories of tribe or ancestors, nor the unmeaning, swiftly and forever-extinguished existence of man, were his themes. He preached *Islam*, and he preached it by rending the skies above and tearing open the ground below, by adjuring heaven and hell, the living and the dead."[8]

Certain Difficulties With Regard To It

But after all we have seen above what does Dr. Steingass, the learned compiler of the *English-Arabic* and *Arabic-English Dictionary,* think of the Quran? He writes ; "Invited to subjoin a few further remarks on the composition and style of the Qur'an, in addition to the valuable and competent opinions contained in the above extracts, I can scarcely introduce them better then by quoting the striking words of Gothe, which Mr. Rodwell places by way of motto on the reverse of the title page of his Translation. The words seem to me so much the more weighty and worthy of attendance, as they are uttered by one who, whatever his merits of demerits in other respects may be deemed to be, indisputably belongs to the greatest masters of language of all times, and stand foremost as a leader of modern thought and the intellectual culture of modern times. Speaking of the Qur'an in his *West Oestlicher Divan*, he says, 'However often we turn to it, at first disgusting us each time afresh, it soon attracts, astounds, and in the end enforces our reverence . . . . Its style, in accordance with its contents and aim, is stern, grand, terrible — ever and anon truly sublime . . . Thus this book will go on exercising through all ages a most potent influence."

"A work, then, which calls forth so powerful and seemingly incompatible emotions, even in the distant reader — distant as to time, and still more so as to mental development — a work which not only conquers the repugnance with which he may begin his perusal, but changes this adverse feeling into astonishment and admiration, such a work must be a wonderful production of the human mind indeed, and a problem of the highest interests to every thoughtful observer of the destinies of mankind . . . . We may well say that the Qur'an is one of the grandest books ever written, because it faithfully reflects the character and life of one of the greatest man that ever breathed. 'Sincerity, ' writes Carlyle, 'sincerity, in all senses, seems to me the merit of the Quran.' This same sincerity, this ardour and earnestness in the search of truth, this never-flagging perseverance in trying to impress it, when partly found, again and again upon his unwilling hearers, appears to me as the real and undeniable 'seal of prophecy' in Muhammad.

"Truth, and above all religious truth, can only be one .

. . . But the approaches to truth are many, and he who devoted all his powers and energies, with untiring patience and self-denial, to the task of leading a whole nation by one of these approaches, from a course and effete idolatry, to the worship of the living God, has certainly a strong claim to our warmest sympathies as a faithful servant and noble champion of truth.

". . . . . Gothe, we have seen, uses such a strong word as disgust, again and again experienced by him at the very outset of its repeated reading."

"Not being an Arabic scholar himself, he knew that Qur'an only through the translations existing at the time, which follow throughout the order of the received text. Thus he was made to pass, roughly speaking, from the later to the earlier Madinah Surahs, and from these again to the Surahs given at Makkah at the various stages which mark Muhammad's ministry, while he was yet staying in his irresponsive parent town. In other words, he would have proceeded from the utterances of the worldly ruler and lawgiver to those of the inspired Divine, who had just succeeded in laying the foundation stones of a new religion, under fierce struggles and sufferings, but in obedience to a call which, in his innermost heart, the felt had gone out to him, and which he had accepted with awe, humility, and resignation. While, therefore, in the beginning of his studies, Gothe may have met with a number of details in the vast structure raised by Muhammad which appeared distasteful to the refined scion of the nineteenth century, his interest must have been awakened, his admiration kindled and kept increasing, the more he became acquainted, through the work itself, with the nature and personality of its creator, and with the purity and exalted character of the mainspring of his motives."

"Those critics, on the other hand, who view the Qur'an with regard to the chronological order of its constituents, follow the descending scale in their estimate. Speaking at first highly — nay, frequently with enthusiasm — of the earlier parts, they complain more and more of the growing tediousness and wearisomeness of the Surahs of later origin.

An Explanation

"But if we consider the variety and heterogeneousness of the topics on which the Qur'an touches, uniformity of style and diction can scarcely be expected ; on the contrary, it would appear to be strangely out of place. Let us not forget that in the books, as Muhammad's newest biographer, Ludolf Krehl (*Das Leben des Muhammed, Leipzig*, 1884), expresses it, 'there is given a complete code of creed and morals, as well as of the law based thereupon. There are also the foundations laid for every institution of an extensive commonwealth, for instruction, for the administration of justice, for military organization, for the finances, for a most careful legislation for the poor ; all built up on the belief in the one God, who holds man's destinies in His hand.' Where so many important objects are concerned, the standard of excellence by which we have to gauge the composition of the Qur'an as a whole must needs vary with the matter treated upon in each particular case. Sublime and chaste, where the supreme truth of God's unity is to be proclaimed ; appealing in high-pitched strains to the imagination of a poetically-gifted people, where the eternal consequences of man's submission to God's holy will, or of rebellion against it are pictures; touching in its simple, almost crude, earnestness, when it seeks again and again encouragement or consolation for God's messengers, and a solemn warning for those to whom he has been sent, in the histories of the prophets of old:

the language of the Qur'an adapts itself to the exigencies of every-day life, when this every-day life, in its private and public bearings, is to be brought in harmony with the fundamental principles of the new dispensation.

The Quran a Literature

"Here, therefore, its merits as a literary production should, perhaps, not be measured by some preconceived maxims of subjective and aesthetic taste, but by the effects which it produced in Muhammad's contemporaries and fellow-countrymen. If it spoke so powerfully and convincingly to the hearts of his hearers as to weld hitherto centrifugal and antagonistic elements into one compact and well-organised body, animated by ideas far beyond these which had until now ruled the Arabian mind, then its eloquence was perfect, simply because it created a civilised nation out of savage tribes, and shot a fresh woof into the old warp of history.

".... But we may well ask ourselves, What would in all probability have become of this language without Muhammad and his Qur'an? This is not at all an idle and desultory speculation. It is true the Arabic language had already produced numerous fine specimens of genuine and high-flown poetry, but such poetry was chicfly is not exclusively, preserved in the memory of the people, for the art of writing was certainly very little known, and still less practised.

"Moreover, poetry is not tantamount to literature: it may lead to it, and will always form a most essential part of it; but it will live on, and perhaps die, in solitary isolation, unless it becomes, as it were, as Brahmans say, 'twice-born,' by participating in a literary development of vaster dimensions and a more general character. Divided among themselves into numerous tribes, who were engaged in a perpetual warfare against each other, the

Arabs, and with them their various dialects, would more and more have drifted asunder, poetry would have followed in the wake, and the population of Arabia would have broken up into a multitude of clans, with their particular bards, whose love and war-songs enterprising travellers of our days might now collect, like the popular songs of the Kosaks of the steppe, or the Kalmuks and similar nationalities, vegetating for centuries in a more or less primitive state of existence.

Development of Ancient Arabic

"It seems, then, that it is only a work of the nature of the Qur'an which could develop ancient Arabic into a literary language, notwithstanding the fact that it had already been admirably handled by local poets. As this book places the national life of the Arabs upon an entirely new basis, giving it at the same time a much-needed centre and a wonderful power of expansion, it became a matter of the utmost importance, nay, of urgent necessity, that the contents of the volume should be preserved with scrupulous accuracy and undisputable conformity. This again was only possible by fixing upon *one* dialect, which by its recognised excellence commended itself to general acceptance, and also by establishing a written text.

"But not only by raising a dialect, through its generalization, to the power of a language, and by rendering the adoption of writing indispensable, has the Qur'an initiated the development of an Arabic literature; its composition itself has contributed two factors absolutely needful to this development : it has added to the existing poetry the origins of rhetoric and prose.

Creating a Literature

"But Muhammad made a still greater and more decisive step towards creating a literature for his people.

In those Surahs in which he regulated the private and public life of the Muslim, he originated a prose, which has remained the standard of classical purity ever since.

"With regard to this part, however, it has been stated, seemingly in disparagement of the later Arabic authors, that their accepting Muhammad's language as a perfect standard from which no deviation is admissible, has led them to adopt an artificial style, as unnatural 'as though Englishmen should still continue to follow Chaucer as their model, in spite of the changes which their language has undergone.' But is such a parallel justified in facts? In English, as amongst modern nations in general, the written language has always kept in close contact with the spoken language; the changes which the former has undergone are simply the registration and legislation of the changes which in course of time had taken place in the latter. Not so in Arabic. From the moment when, at the epoch of its fullest and richest growth, it was, through the composition of the Qur'an invested with the dignity of literary language, it was, by its very nature, for many centuries to come, precluded from any essential change, whether this be considered as an advantage or not.

"At the time of Muhammad this then was, apart from slight dialectical differences, the spoken language of his people. He took it, so to say, from the mouth of his interlocutors, but, weilding it with the power of a master-mind, he made in the Qur'an such a complete and perfect use of all its resources as to create a work that, in the estimation of his hearers, appeared worthy to be thought the word of God Himself.

"When a long period of conquests scattered the Arabs to the farthest West, their spoken language might deviate from its pristine purity, slurring over unaccented syllables and dropping terminations. But the fine idiom of their forefathers, as deposited in the Qur'an, remained the language of their prayer and their pious meditation, and thus lived on with them as a bond of unity, an object of national love and admiration, and a source of literary development for all times."[9]

References

1. A word from this root occurs at the commencement of Surah xcvi. 1, where the Prophet is called to receive his Mission.
2. The end of a verse is determined by the position of a small circle such as ○. The early Moslems did not agree as to the position of these circles, and so five different ways of arranging them have arisen. This accounts for a variation in the number of verses in various editions. The varieties are :
    1. Kufah verses. The Moslems in the city professed to follow the custom of Ali the son of Abu Talib. Their way of reckoning is generally adopted by the Moslems of India. They reckon 6,236 verses.
    2. Basrah verses. The Moslems of that place follow the order of Asim, son of Hajjaj, one of the earliest converts to Islam. They reckon 6,204 verses.
    3. Shami verses. The Moslems of *Sham* (or Syria) followed Abdullah, son of Omar, also one of the earliest converts. They reckon 6,226 verses.
    4. Mecca verses. According to this arrangement there are 6,219 verses.
    5. Medinah verses. This way of reading contains 6,214 verses.

    This diversity of punctuation, does not however affect the contents of the Quran.

    In each of the above varieties the auspiciatory form, 'In the name of God, the Merciful, the Compassionate,' is not reckoned. It occurs no less than 113 times in the Quran at the head of each Surah except the 9th.
3. A noble writer therefore mistakes the question when he says those eastern religionists leave their scared writ the sole standard of literate performances by extinguishing all true learning. For though they were destitute of what we

call learning, yet they were far from being ignorant or unable to compose elegantly in the own tongue, See L. Shaftesbury's Characteristics, vol. iii. p. 235.

4. George Sale, 'The Quran,' Preliminary Discourse, see, iii.
5. 'Literary Remains,' p. 123.
6. Ibid. p. 124.
7. Ibid. p. 126.
8. Ibid p. 127.
9. Hughes, 'A Dictionary of Islam.' p. 526-30.

SELECTIONS FROM THE QURAN

SURAH I. – THE OPENING CHAPTER

(Mecca.)

This is a Chapter of Prayer, and held in great veneration by the Moslems, who give it various honourable titles. They repeat it in their public and private prayers. The spirit has been admitted to be the best throughout.

In the name of God, the Merciful, the Compassionate.

Attributes of God:

1. Praise to God, Lord of the worlds.
2. Merciful, Compassionate.
3. King on the Judgment Day !

1. 'Lord of the worlds,' *i.e.*, Ruler in this world and the next; Supreme Master of the material and other kingdoms. It may also be translated 'Lord of all creatures,' animal, human, and others.
2. 'Mercy' and 'Compassion' are the chief attributes of God in Islam.
3. God is to be the Judge of all men's actions. This refers to the Islamic belief of life hereafter and a position there according to achievements here.

Prayer:

4. There we worship, and Thee We ask for help !
5. Guide us on the straight path —

6. The path of those do whom Thou art gracious,

7. With whom Thou art not angry, and such as go not astray.

4. God along is to be worshipped and prayed for help.

6, 7. Mark the 'straight path' defined here. It can also be translated: 'Of those to whom Thou art gracious , not of those with whom Thou art angry, nor of such as go astray.'

Principal Contents

God: His attributes, 1-3.

Path, the straight, 6, 7.

Prayer, 4-7.

SURAH II. — THE COW.

(*Medinah.*)

This was the first Surah promulgated at Medinah. It is the longest in the Quran. It is called 'The Cow' from an account of the sacrifice of a cow by Moses contained in verse 63.

The Quran:

1. A.L.M. That is the Book without doubt; in it is a guide to the pious.

1. A.L.M. are variously interpreted, but they are all equally farfetched. They probably indicate certain marks in the copies from which they were originally transcribed.

The word translated 'pious' literally means 'those who fear' to do evil, the God-fearing.

The Pious:

2. Who believe in secret, and observe prayer, and out of what We have given them expend.

3. And who believe in what has been revealed to thee, and what was revealed before thee, and of the Hereafter they are sure:

4. These are in guidance from their Lord, and these are the blessed.

2. 'In secret,' as opposed to 'in public,' to he seen of men. *Cf.* iv. 38; v. 95; xxi. 50; lvii. 25; lxii. 8; lxvii. 12. 'Expand,' that is, for God.

3. Belief in the goodness of the mission of Mohammed and that of the prophets before him, as also in the life to come, are here inculcated. It is an important article of Islam that of *every* people (x. 48), in their own tongues (xiv. 4), was conveyed in every age (xiii. 38), the same Divine Message of wisdom and of truth (ii. 146), through an endless succession of prophets and seers (xl. 78).

The Koreish: Their Obstinacy:

5. As to those who have disbelieved, it is equal to them whether thou warn them or do not warn them — they will not believe.

6. God has sealed up their hearts and their hearing, and over their eyes is a covering. — And for them is a severe punishment.

The Hypocrites:

7. And among men are some who say, We believe in God and in the Hereafter. — But they are not believers.

8. They seek to deceive God and those who do believe, but they deceive only themselves, — and they do not perceive it.

9. In their hearts is a weakness, and God has increased that weakness; — and for them is fearful woe, for that they lied.

Their Obstinacy:

10. And when it is said to them, Act not wickedly in the earth; they say, We are only reformers.

11. These are the evil-doers, but they do not perceive it.

12. And when it is said to them. Do ye believe as others believe; they say, Shall We believe as fools

believe? —these are the fools, but they do not know.

13. And when they meet those who believe, they say, We believe; but when they are alone with their devils, they say, We are with you, and only mock at them.

14. God will mock at them, and continue them in their transgression, blindly wandering.

15. These are they who have purchased error for guidance, but their traffic has not been gainful to them, — and they have not been guided aright.

13. 'Their devils,' who lead them astray, and command filthy actions, and sow discord and hatred among them. For the use of 'devil,' see verses 164, 204, and 271, below, and Surah v. 93.

Their Similitude:

16. Their likeness is as the likeness of him who lights up a fire, and when it has enlightened all around him, . . . God goes off with their light, and leaves them to darkness — they cannot see !

17. Deaf, dumb, and blind — they do not repent.

18. Or, like a storm-cloud from heaven, wherein is darkness and thunder and lightning, . . . they put their fingers in their ears, for fear of death. And God is round about the unbelievers.

19. The lightning almost snatches away their sight; so long as it shines upon them they walk therein, but when darkness comes upon them they stand still. And if God pleased. He would take away their hearing and their sight. God is mighty over all things.

16. After 'around him' supply 'he shuts his eyes,' which is here understood. Here the unbelieving Arabs are said to

have been in search of light, which when it appeared to them, they shut their eyes against it, and would not submit to be directed.

18. Again, they are here compared to people caught in a violent storm. The tempest here spoken of is a type of image of the Quran or law itself; the thunder signifying the truths as disagreeable contained therein; the lightning; the prospects; and the darkness, their confusion; their unwillingness to hear truths so disagreeable made them stop their cars; when bright prospects were within sight they attended with pleasure, but when it affected anything dear to them, they felt confounded, and would not stop to consider.

God: His Belief:

20. Ye People, serve your Lord who made you and those who have been before you, — that ye may fear to do evil, — who made for you the earth as a bed and the heaven as a covering, and sent from heaven water, and by it produced fruits as a sustenance for you. Then set not up an equal to God knowingly.

Of Parables:

24. God is not ashamed to set forth as well the instance of a gnat as anything beyond that, ... but the unbelievers say, What does God mean by this comparison? Many will He mislead by it, and many will He guide, but none will He mislead thereby except the wicked.

24. The above verse was occasioned by an objection made to the Quran for condescending to speak of such insignificant insects as the Ant, Bee, Spider, etc.

The Misguided:

25. Who violate the Covenant of God after the establishing thereof, and cut asunder what God has commanded to be joined, and act wickedly in the earth. — These are they who lose.

25. 'The Covenant of God:' one of these, to the Jews, is given in verses 77 and 78, below. Thus it is plainly laid down that the transgressors alone are led astray.

Belief in God:

26. How can ye disbelieve in God? Ye were dead, and He gave you life; then He will cause you to die, and again will He give you life, — then shall ye return to Him.

26. You were a dead matter, you came to life, you will die, and then pass into the world of spirits, from whence you will proceed towards God to render your accounts to Him.

Purpose in Creation:

28. When thy Lord said to the angels, Verily I am about to place a vice-gerent on earth; they said, Wilt Thou place therein one who'll do evil therein and shed blood, while we celebrate Thy praise and sanctify Thee? God said, Verily I know what ye do not know.

29. And He taught Man the names of all things.

* * *

32. And when We said to the angels, Bow down to Man; they all bowed down, except only Iblis: he disdained to do it, and became of the ungodly.

33. And We said, O Man, dwell thou and thy wife in the Garden, and eat thereof plentifully as ye will, but approach not this Tree, lest ye become of the transgressors.

34. And the devil made them slip from it, and turned them out from where they had been .....

35. And Man learned words from his Lord, and God turned towards him: for He is the relenting, gracious.

36. We said, Get ye all down from here; there will come to you a guidance from ME — whoso shall follow MY guidance, no fear shall come upon them, neither shall they grieve.

37. And those who will not believe and deny OUR evidences – these shall be the fellows of the Fire, to continue therein for ever.

28. God's purpose in creation is known to Him alone. And Man is the vice-gerent of God on earth.

29. God gave Man wisdom to understand all things.

32. Man in his original state deserved the homage of all creatures including the highest angels.

'Iblis' from Ar. *balas*, signifies a profligate, wicked person. The name is here given to Azazil, an angel of the very highest order who, only for his pride, was brought low.

33. The 'tree' mentioned here is not 'the tree of knowledge' of the Jews and Christians. It is said to be an emblem of 'sin,' whose fruits have far-reaching effects.

34. 'The devil,' see verse 13, above. It is generally understood of the baser appetites of Man.

35. 'Words,' meaning words of wisdom.

36. Though fallen by reason of his baser appetites, Man has yet the chance to rise superior to them. This is to follow the guidance of God as distinct from that of his passions. See verse 271, below.

The Jews:

38. Ye children of Israel, remember My favour wherewith I have favoured you, and perform your Covenant with Me, and I will perform My Covenant with you; Me, therefore, revere Me. And believe in what I have revealed, confirming that which is with you, and be not the first to disbelieve in it, and for a mean price do not barter My signs: Me therefore, fear by Me.

39. And clothe not the truth with a lie, and hide not the truth knowingly.

40. And observe prayer and give alms, and bow down with those who bow down.

41. Will ye enjoin upon men piety and forget yourselves? Ye read the Book: do ye not yet understand?

42. And seek help with patience and prayer; a hard duty indeed is this, unless to the humble.

43. Who believe in the meeting of their Lord, and that to Him they shall return.

44. Ye children of Israel, remember My favours wherewith I have favoured you, and that I have been bounteous to you above all peoples.

45. And fear the Day when one soul shall not make satisfaction for another soul, neither shall any intercession be accepted from them, nor shall any atonement be received, neither shall they be helped.

38. 'The Children of Israel; ' the Jews are so called, being the descendants of Jacob, 'Covenant, ' same as referred to in verse 25, above.

42. Perseverance is inculcated jointly with prayer. See also verse 182, below.

43. It is simply impossible for those who have no idea of the spiritual to be persevering in the source indicated above.

45. In this verse Intercession and Atonement are firmly discarded. The Jews believed in the Intercession of their father Abraham, and the Christians in the Atonement of Jesus. See also Surah lxxxii. 17-9.

Believers and Good Men:

59. Verily those who believe, and those who are Jews or Christians or Sabians — whose believes in God and the Hereafter and does good — theirs is a reward with their Lord, no fear shall come upon them, neither shall they grieve.

59. In work and not in the creed lies our salvation. The Sabians here mentioned are identical with the Mendaites, or Christians of St. John as they are called. These are not the same as the star-worshipping people generally known by that name.

The Wicked, the Good:

75. Yea, whoso acquires evil and is encompassed by iniquity — these are the follows of the Fire, to continue therein for ever.

76. And those who believe and do good — these are the people of Paradise — to continue therein for ever.

75. 'Acquires,' or 'earns,' evil, *i.e.,* commits evil to his own loss. The idea of Original Sin is altogether absent in Islam. 'For over,' is not to be taken literally, See Surah vi. 161.

Covenant of the Israelites:

77. And when We entered into a Covenant with the children of Israel — Worship not any but God, and be good to your parents and kindred, and to orphans and the poor, and speak what is good to men, and observe prayer, and give alms, ...

78. . . . And shed not your brother's blood, nor turn one another out of their homes.

Moses and Jesus: Their Mission:

81. And verily WE gave the Book of Moses, and WE raised up apostles after him. And to Jesus, son of Mary, WE gave clear evidences, and strengthened him with the Holy Spirit.

81. The Holy Spirit is the guardian-angel of the prophets. He is generally called Jibrail, or Gabriel.

People of the Book:

103. Many of the people of the Book desire to bring you back to unbelief after ye have believed, out

of selfish envy, even after the truth has been made plain to them. But forgive them and avoid them, till God comes in with His working. Surely, God is mighty over all things.

103. 'People of the Book', *i.e.,* those who accept the mission of the prophets, *e.g.*, the Jews and the Christians.'

Prayer and Almsgiving:

104. Be steadfast in prayer, and give alms; and what of good ye send before for your souls, ye shall find it with God. Surely, God sees what ye do.

104. The good that a man does in this world is regarded as a credit to himself in the next.

True Religion:

105. And they say, None shall enter Paradise, except such as are Jews or Christians. That is their faith. Say thou, Bring your proofs, if ye speak the truth.

106. Nay, whoso strives with his face to God, and is a doer of good — his is a reward with his Lord, — no fear shall come upon them, neither shall they grieve.

106. God regards only a man's striving for the good and his doing good, irrespective of any creed that a man holds, See verse 59, above.

Wrangling Upon Religion:

107. And the Jews say, The Christians are grounded on nothing; and the Christians say, The Jews are grounded on nothing. Yet they read the Book. So also say those who do not know, like to what these say. But God will decide between them on the Judgment Day concerning that wherein they now disagree.

107. 'The Book,' the scripture. 'Those who do not know,' the illiterates, or those who do not receive any scripture. All

disputes which are not likely to end here are referred to God in the hereafter for decision.

God's Omnipresence:

109. God's is the east and the west, then which way soever ye turn, there is the face of God. Surely God is omnipresent, omniscient.

God's Begetting A Son:

110. And they say, God has begotten a son. No! Praise to Him! His is whatever is in the heavens and the earth. All obey him.

111. Maker of the heavens and the earth! When He decrees a thing, He only says to it, Be; and it is.

110. This is a revolt against the idea of Jesus being called 'the only begotten Son of God.'

111. Without entering into any controversy with regard to his Immaculate Conception, it is simply maintained that Jesus was born by the command of God.

Jews and Christians :

114. But the Jews will not be satisfied with thee, nor yet the Christians, until thou follow their creed. Say thou, Surely the guidance of God — that is the guidance. And if thou follow their desires after the knowledge that has come to thee, then thou hast not from God a patron or help.

115. And those to whom WE have given the Book, and who read it aright — these believe therein. And whoso believes not — these are the losers.

114. The narrow-mindedness of the sectaries is here spoken of. The Moslems believe in the God of the Jews and the mission of their prophets, but the Jews still held themselves aloof from them. In the case of the Christians again, the Moslems believed in the one God preached by Jesus and himself as His prophet, but the Christians proved equally indifferent. The Moslems are here to maintain their principles unshaken.

115. Those who read aright their scriptures are said to be in guidance from their Lord.

The Jews:

116. Ye children of Israel.

117. Fear the Day when one soul shall not make satisfaction for another soul, neither shall any atonement be received from them, nor shall any intercession avail, neither shall they be helped.

117. This is a repetition of verse 45, above.

Abraham and Jacob: Their Piety:

124. And who will turn aside from the faith of Abraham, but he who has debased his soul to folly? Surely WE have chosen him in this world, and in the Hereafter he will be of the righteous.

125. When his Lord said to him, Strive after righteousness; he said, I will strive for the Lord of the worlds.

126. And this did Abraham bequeath to his children, and Jacob also — My children, God has chosen for you this religion; therefore die not unless ye are also Moslems.

127. Were ye present when Jacob was at the point of death, when he said to his sons, Whom will ye worship after Me? They said, We will worship thy God, and the God of thy fathers Abraham, and Ishmael and Isaac, —one Good — and after Him shall We strive.

128. That people have now passed away — theirs is what they earned, and yours shall be what ye earn: ye shall not be questioned as to what they did.

125. Ar. 'Aslim, ' is translated 'strive after righteousness.' It

comes from the same root as 'Islam,' *q. v.*, in Surah iii. 17.

126. 'Moslems,' followers of Islam, the religion of the prophets. See verse 130, below. It is believed that Islam is the original religion of man, since first his religious instinct has awakened. See verse 209, below.

128. The Jews depended very much for their salvation upon their father Abraham's piety. It is here stated that they shall have the reward according as they shall have individually deserved. See verses 45 and 117, above.

True Religion:

129. They say, Be ye Jews or Christians, that ye may be guided. Say thou, Nay, but the religion of Abraham, the upright man, and he was not of those who joined others with God.

129. See verses 105 and 106, above, Ar. 'Hanif,' is translated 'the upright man.' It literally means 'seeking' after truth, 'turning' from the evil.

The Creed of Islam:

130. Say thou, We believe in God, and what has been revealed to us and what was revealed to Abraham, and Ishmael, and Isaac, and Jacob, and the tribes, and what was given to Moses and Jesus, and what was given to the prophets from their Lord, — We make no distinction between any of them, — and after Him we strive.

130. A belief in the mission of the prophets is an important article in the Islamic creed. It is not confined to the prophets of the House of Israel. See notes to verse 3, above.

Acceptance of Islam :

131. If therefore they believe even as ye believe, then are they guided aright, but if they turn back, then surely they make a division; and God will suffice thee against them, for He both hears and knows.

132. The baptism of God *we have*, and who is better than God at baptising? Him We worship.

133. Say thou, Will ye dispute with us concerning God? — and He is our Lord and your Lord. We have our works, and ye have your works, and we are sincerely His.

134. Will ye say, Abraham and Ishmael, and Isaac, and Jacob, and the tribes, were Jews or Christians?

132. This was to take off an objection to the simple way of conversion in Islam, which admitted of no extra formality.

Mohammed taught that all the children of men would follow 'the straight path' appointed for them by God, were it not for the corrupting influences of their guardians, who consciously or unconsciously set an unnatural example by their way of life for their little folks to follow. He observed no peculiar rites in connexion with the conversion of people to Islam, since he only regarded it as a natural law for men to follow. All men were, according to him, born in Islam, and by virtue of their being had already 'the baptism of God.' See also Surah xxx. 29; and Surah vi. 116.

134. See also Surah iii. 60.

The Kiblah Fixed:

136. The foolish among people say, What has turned them from their Kiblah towards which they formerly turned?

138. We appointed the Kiblah towards which thou didst formerly turn merely that We might know him who follows the apostle from him who turns upon his heals, though this might seem a great matter, unless to those whom God has guided aright. But God will not waste your faith; for God is to men gracious and merciful.

139. We have seen thee turn they face to heaven with uncertainty, and We will turn thee to a Kiblah

thou dost like. Turn then thy face toward the Sacred Mosque, and wherever ye be, turn your faces towards it.

143. All have some one side to which they turn *in prayer*, but do ye hasten emulously after good works. To God is your return altogether; surely God is mighty over all things.

145. And from whatever place thou comest forth, turn they face towards the Sacred Mosque, and wherever ye be turn your faces to that part, lest men have cause of dispute against you; and as for the impious amongst them, fear them not, but fear Me, that I may perfect My favours upon you, and that ye may be guided aright.

136. 'Kiblah' is the point towards which people turn in prayer. At first, Mohammed observed no particular rite of turning his face in prayer to any certain place. As soon, however, as he reached Medinah he directed his followers to turn to the Temple of Jerusalem; but a few months after it was found more expedient to turn towards the Sacred Temple of Mecca.

138. It is acknowledged here that the 'Kiblah' was fixed merely for a uniformity in public worship.

'This might seem,' etc. This is levelled against those who appeared to have attached very great importance to this point of outward uniformity in worship.

'But God will not waste your faith' so easily, in that ye now change your Kiblah.

143. Striving to do good is insisted upon as a more important duty than any formality merely.

Apostles: There Mission:

146. And We have sent to you an apostle from among yourselves to declare OUR signs to you, and to purity you and to teach you the Book, and wisdom, and to teach you what ye did not know.

146. Such was the mission of the prophets in all ages, and among all peoples. See notes on verse 3, above.

Perseverance:

148. Ye believers, seek help with patience and prayer; surely God is with the patient.

149. And say not of those who are slain in the way of God that they are dead;—nay, they are living, but ye do not understand.

150. We will surely prove you with something of fear and hunger, and loss of wealth, and lives, and fruits; but bear glad tidings to the patient.

151. Who, when a misfortune befalls them, say, We are of God, and to Him we shall return.

152. These,—on them shall be blessings from their Lord, and mercy, and these are the rightly guided.

149. 'The way of God' has a very wide significance in Islam; it applies to all the responsibilities of a human life, from the worship of God to the minutest concerns of man in his relation to society. And all who die in the execution of their relative functions in life are esteemed 'martyrs.'

God: His Signs:

158. Your God is the one God: there is no God but He, the merciful, the compassionate.

159. Surely in the creation of the heavens and the earth, and the alternation of night and day, and in the ships that pass through the sea laden with what is useful to man, and in the rain which God sends down from heaven giving life by it to the earth after its death, and spreading over it all sorts of cattle, and in the change of the winds, and in the clouds that are pressed to service betwixt heaven and earth—are signs to people who understand.

160. Yet there are men who take to themselves others beside God, and love them with the love of God. But stronger in those who believe is the love of God. Oh! that those who act unjustly did perceive, when they see the punishment, that all power belongs to God, and that God is severe in punishing.

159. The 'signs' are the traces in Nature of an Intelligent, Conscious Being.

160. The distinction in the case of the Moslem is his intense love of God.

'Oh! that those,' etc. A deep sympathy is expressed for those who, out of ignorance, are plunged in darkness and do not understand the goodness and power of God.

The Sectaries:

161. When those who have been followed shall declare themselves clear of their followers, and shall see the punishment, and when the ties between them shall be cut asunder.

162. The followers shall say, Could we only return we would keep clear of them as they have declared themselves clear of us. And God will show them their works. Sighing shall be upon them, but from the fire they shall not come out.

161. It is here indicated that in the Hereafter the broachers or heads of new sects shall forsake or wash their hands of their disciples as if they were not accomplices in their superstitions.

162. This indicates that the followers will be held responsible for the views they hold and their works here.

'Sighing,' etc., *i.e.*, they shall sigh grievously; it will be to them a matter of great remorse.

Lawful Food:

163. Ye people, eat of what is lawful and good on earth, and follow not the steps of the devil; surely he is

your open enemy.

163. See verses 167, 168 below.

The Devil:

164. He only enjoins you evil and wickedness, and that ye should speak of God what ye know not.

Ancestral Practices:

165. And when it is said to them, Follow what God has revealed; they say, Nay, we will do what we found our fathers at.—What! and though their fathers had no sense at all or guidance?

165. Ancestral practices may not all be above reproach or criticism.

The Unbeliever's Call:

166. The unbelievers are like one who cries aloud to that which hears him not so much as his calling or crying. Deaf, dumb, blind, they do not understand.

166. 'Which hears.' etc., or, which hears not so much as his calling, or the sound of his voice.

Lawful Food:

167. Ye believers, eat of the good things which We have given you, and give thanks to God if it is Him ye worship.

168. He has only forbidden you what is dead of itself, and blood, and swine's flesh, and that on which any other name than God's has been invocated. But he who is forced by necessity, not lusting, nor transgressing: it is no crime in him. Surely God is gracious, compassionate.

168. All things which are naturally repulsive to man are here forbidden; also, all sacrificial offerings to any other than God. But in extreme necessity the rule may be suspended. See also Surah v. 4.

It is remarkable that in killing any animal for food the Mohammedans only say, 'In the name of God,' and do not add the attributes of mercy and compassion otherwise so inalienably joined in the sentence for general purposes. It points to the consciousness in Islam of the un-merciful and un-compassionate attribute in man which only leads him to sacrifice the life of a being which is in the sight of God 'a being' like himself (Surah vi. 38), in order to satisfy his animal nature. It drives the Moslem to see his ridiculous position as a believer in the merciful and compassionate Lord of the worlds, and yet feasting upon the destruction of a life.

True piety:

172. It is no good that ye turn your faces *in prayer* to the east or the west, but goodness is of him who believes in God, and the Hereafter, and the Angels, and the Books, and the Prophets; who gives of his wealth for His love to kindred, and the orphans, and the poor, and the homeless, and those who ask, and for the captives; who is steadfast in prayer and gives alms; and of those who perform their covenants when they have covenanted, and who behave themselves patiently in adversity and hardships, and in time of violence;—these are the true, and these are the pious.

172. True piety consists not in certain formalities merely, but in believing in God and striving to do most good to His creatures.

'For His love,' to please God, and not to be seen of men; see verses 266, 267, below.

'To kindred,' etc., In Islam the first attention of the charitable falls upon his poorer kinsmen, then come the orphans, then the other poor people, then the travellers and other needy people, then the slaves.

'The homeless,' *lit.*, 'sons of the road,' includes also travellers.

'Those who ask,' who might fall into trouble and have

occasion to ask your help. But the Moslem is to find out the needy himself; see verse 274, below.

'For the captives;' i.e., for their redemption.

Fasting:

179. Ye believers, a Fast is ordained you, as it was ordained to those before you, that ye may work piety.

180. A certain number of days only;—but he amongst you who is sick or on a journey, a number of other days; and as for those who are able, may redeem it by maintaining a poor man; and whoso of his own accord does a good work—it is better for him. But if ye fast, it is better for you, if ye only knew.

181. The month of Ramazan, wherein was revealed the Quran, as a guide to the people and an evidence of guidance and a distinction. Then whoso among you is present in the month, let him fast, but he who is sick or on a journey, a number of other days.

God desires for you what is easy, and desires not for you what is difficult; that ye may complete the term, and glorify God, for that He has guided you, and that ye may give thanks.

182. And when My servants ask thee concerning Me, Verily I am near; I answer the prayer's prayer whenever he prays to Me; but let them hearken to Me and believe in Me, that they may be guided aright.

183. Ye are allowed on the night of the Fast to go in to your wives;—they are a garment to you as ye are a garment to them. God knows that ye defraud yourselves therein, so He turns to you and excuses you. Now, then, go in to them and

desire what God has ordained for you, and eat and drink, until ye can discern a white thread from a black thread. Then keep the fast until night, and go not in to them, but pass your time in places of worship. These are the bounds of God, therefore draw not near to transgress them. Thus God makes His signs clear to men that they may work piety.

179. This is the third point of religious practice, and a duty of so great moment, that Mohammed was want to call it 'the Gate of Religion,' as a means of restraining the passions, by diurnal abstinence for a limited and definite period, from all the gratifications of the senses, and directing the overflow of the animal spirits into a healthy channel.

The Moslem doctors also reckon three degrees of fasting: 1. The restraining of the belly and other members of the body from satisfying their lusts; 2. The restraining of the ears, eyes, tongue, hands, feet, and other members from sin; 3. The fasting of the heart from all base thoughts and inclinations which may divert its attendance upon God. Mohammed himself said: "A keeper of fasts, who does not abandon lying and slandering, God cares not about his leaving off eating and drinking."

180. Fasting is only imposed on the able-bodied and the strong; sick persons also include the weak and all whose health would manifestly be injured by their keeping the fast, as women with child and giving such, old people, and young children.

181. It was at Hira in the month of Ramazan that Mohammed received his first message as contained in Surah xcvi.

182. God is ever near to hear prayers offered to Him, but men are to 'hearken' to Him and 'believe' in Him, for so can they be guided aright, to achieve what they desire.

183. The Fast is restricted to the day, and at night-fall the Moslems are allowed, nay, are bound, to refresh themselves, and to eat and drink, and otherwise enjoy themselves lawfully till day-break. This verse was occasioned by certain of Mohammed's followers agreeing

to oblige themselves to continual fasting and watching, and to abstain from women, in imitation of some Christian monks. Some of them actually sent away their wives to some of their people in order to be allowed to fast rigidly.

Among the recorded sayings of Mohammed is also the following: "Keep fast, and eat also; stay awake at night, and sleep also: for verily there is a duty on you to your body, not to labour overmuch, so that ye may get ill and destroy yourselves; and verily there is a duty on you to your eyes, ye must sometimes sleep and give them rest: and verily there is a duty on you to your wife, and to your visitors, and guests that call on you; you must speak to them; and nobody has fasted who fasted always; the fast of three days in every month is equal to constant fasting; then keep three days' fast in every month."

'They are a garment,' etc. A metaphorical expression to signify the mutual comfort a man and his wife find in each other.

Abuse of Wealth:

184. Consume not your wealth among yourselves in vanity, nor present it to judges, that ye might consume a part of other men's wealth unjustly, while ye know it.

184. Two things are forbidden in this verse: 1st, vain display, and 2nd, bribing, which also includes influencing by virtue of one's position the natural course of law.

Phases of the Moon:

185. They will ask thee about the moons; say thou, They show times for men, and for the pilgrimage. But there is no good in that ye enter your houses by the back thereof, but goodness is of him who fears God. So enter your houses by their doors, and fear God, that ye may be happy.

185. It was a custom of the Arabs in certain periods not to enter their houses by the old doors, but to make a hole through the back part of a passage, which practice is here condemned as foolish.

A Rule of Warfare:

186. Fight in the way of God against those who fight against you, but transgress not; surely God loves not those who transgress.

187. And kill them wherever ye find them, and turn them out from where they have turned you out; for rancour is worse than slaughter; yet fight not against them in the Sacred Mosque, until they attack you therein; but if they attack you, then kill them;—that is the punishment of the ungodly.

188. But if they desist, . . . surely God is gracious, merciful.

189. Fight therefore against them that there be no more rancour, and the religion of God come; but if they desist, then let there be no hostility, except against the transgressors.

186. This is the strict rule of all Islamic warfares; all unprovoked wars are condemned as unjust.

This and the succeeding verses were occasioned by the sudden advance in A.H. 2 upon the Moslems at Medinah of the Koreish from Mecca with a large army of 1,000 strong, mounted on 700 camels and 100 horses. Medinah is 276 miles to the north of Mecca. The Koreish had already marched fully armed. What was to be done for the preservation of the poor Moslems and the men of Medinah who had made common-cause with them? There was no time to spare. What was to be done, was to be done instantly and with effective measures. If the Koreish have the better what would be the fate of the Moslems but a universal massacre? Such were the thoughts of the Teacher of the Moslems. In this extremity came the strict in junction from Him whose apostle he was in the words of the text.

187. 'Wherever,' whether in or out of the sacred precincts of the Kaabah which were regarded as inviolate. The word translated 'rancour' in the original signifies heart-

burning with hatred, the worst type of feeling in social relation.

188. The first sentence ends abruptly, the following being understood: 'God does not allow you to kill them.'

189. 'The religion of God come,' exactly in meaning like 'the Kingdom of God come;' malice and rancour being thus rooted out religion might prevail. See also Surah iv. 77.

The Sacred Month:

190. The sacred month and the sacred precincts are safe from reprisals; but whoso transgresses against you, do ye also transgress against him as he has transgressed against you. And fear God, and know that God is with those who fear to do evil.

190. The Arabs regarded it specially unlawful for them to attack each other in certain months, but when it suited them they put off the observing of one month for another, thus leaving themselves wide margins for excursions and plunder. Standing in self-defence the Moslems were to fight *whenever* attacked.

The Cause of God:

191. And give freely in the way of God, and throw not yourselves with your own hands into ruin

191. See notes on verse 149, above.

The Pilgrimage:

192. Perform the Pilgrimage and the Visitation for the cause of God. . . .

193. The Pilgrimage is in the known months. . . . And provide for your journey, but the best provision is piety, and fear Me, ye men of understanding.

194. It is no crime in you if ye seek an increase from your Lord by commerce; and when ye pour down the Arafat, remember God near the sacred Monument, and remember Him for that He has guided you, although ye were before this of those

who go astray.

196. And when ye have finished your rites, remember God as ye remember your own fathers, or with greater reverence still.

192. This is the fourth point of religious practice in Islam, and is a great importance, as every year it renews the bond of union among the faithful, and creates a real visible Moslem Church.

Certain qualifications are also considered necessary with regard to a faithful performance of this duty. These are as follows: 1. The pilgrim must be 'free from the world' as the Moslems say, that is, all his debts must have been paid up, and his family and dependents provided for adequately during the period of his absence from home. 2. He must possess the means of transport and subsistence during his journey. 3. He must also consider the possibility and practicability of the journey. 4. He must have freely forgiven his enemies; and if he has given any one cause of offence, he must confess his fault and seek reconciliation before he sets out on his journey. 5. Finally, he must repent of every evil though, word, and deed against his fellowmen and against God.

193. The three months of the Pilgrimage are Shawwal, Zulkaadah, and Zil-Hijj.

'And fear Me;' see Surah xxii. 31. 32.

194. Whereas in pre-Islamic times it was considered a sacrilege to visit Mecca during the said months on commercial purposes.

Peace Enjoined.

204. Ye believers, enter into peace wholly, and follow not the step of the devil, for he is your open enemy.

204. Here 'peace' and 'the steps of the devil' are used in contradistinction to each other.

The Original Religion:

209. Men were of one religion, and God sent prophets with glad tidings and with warnings, and sent down with them the Book with truth, to judge

between men in what they disagreed,—and none disagreed therein but . . out of hatred among themselves.

209. The difference among the various religions is thus set forth: Men were originally of one religion, and when differences arose amongst them, God raised up prophets in their midst to guide them with truth, but people only differed among themselves out of mere jealously. Hatred alone thus explains the division among men. See Surah ii. 3, notes.

Recipients of Charity:

211. They will ask thee what they shall spend; say thou, Whatever of good ye give, let it be to parents, and kindred and orphans, and the poor, and the homeless; and what good ye do, surely God knows it.

211. In Islam, charity always begins at home; and although a man has absolute right over his property, he cannot by will devote more than one-third of his property to charity.

War Enjoined:

212. Enjoined upon you is War, but it is hateful to you. Yet it may be, that ye hate a thing while it is good for you, and it may be, that ye love a thing while it is bad for you: God knows, and ye—ye do not know.

212. After the verses 186-9, above, Mohammed was still contemplating some reconciliatory measures by which the impending battle at Badr might be averted. The orphan-child of Aminah, whose heart wept to see the miseries of this world, and whom his gentle nature had made 'womanish' (as his enemies called him), shrank back from standing up for war in self-defence as it was, till it occurred to him that he was head of the State as well as of the Church, and as in duty bound to his subjects had to defend Medinah from any aggressive attacks of the Koreish on his account; his conscience smote him, and then came the verse as in the text. Whereupon Mohammed proposed to check their advance by a rapid

march, and set out from Medinah with his little band of the faithful (300 in number).

Wine and Games:

216. They will ask thee concerning wine and games. Say thou, In both is great sin and use also for men,—but their sin is greater than their use.

216. Under 'wine' all strong and inebriating liquors are comprehended. 'Games' include all games which are subject to chance or hazard, as dice, cards, etc.

Alms-Giving:

217. They will ask thee what they shall give in alms. Say thou, What ye can spare.

217. In Islam there are two sorts of alms, *Zakat* and *Sadakah*. The one is of indispensable obligation, being commanded by the law, which directs and determines the portion which is to be given, but the other is left to every one's liberty, to give more or less as he shall think fit. The portion of the wealth to be given in alms is usually one part in forty, or two-and-a-half per cent of the value of all goods, chattels, emblements, on profits of trade, mercantile business, etc. But no alms are due for them unless they amount to a certain quantity or number, nor until a man has been in legal possession of the gift, and has sufficient for his subsistence. In the early days of Islam these alms went into the Public Treasury, and were applied to the cause indicated in Surah ix. 60.

The Orphans:

218. They will ask thee concerning orphans; say, To train them is the best.

219. And if ye interfere with them—they are your brothers, and God knows the wicked from the well-meaning; and if God please, He will surely distress you. Surely God is mighty, wise.

218. Orphans are to be educated and trained, and their concerns well-managed.

219. It is feelingly pointed out that the orphans are our

brothers, and they have as much right to our care as *our* own helpless younger brothers.

Oaths:

224. Make not God the butt of your oaths, that ye will not do good, nor be pious, nor make peace between men; surely God both hears and knows.

225. God will not punish you for a mistake in your oaths, buy He will punish you for what your hearts do, surely God is gracious, mild.

224. The *butt*, so as to swear frequently by Him. Such wicked oaths which were very prevalent amongst the Arabs, being taken in the heat of the moment, are here forbidden.

225. When a man swears inadvertently and without design. But a penance is all the same required of him. See Surah v. 91.

Divorce: Some Rules:

226. Those who swear off from their wives shall wait four months,—and if they go back, surely God is the gracious, the merciful.

227. But if they resolve on a divorce, surely God is He who hears and knows.

228. The divorced women shall wait concerning themselves until they have their courses thrice, and it is not lawful to them to hide what God has created in their wombs, if they believe in God and the Hereafter; and it will be more proper for their husbands to bring them back at this stage, if they desire a reconciliation,—and it is for the women to do to men as they would be done by them according to what is just. But the men have a degree above them. God is mighty, knowing.

229. Divorce may be twice; then either keep them with

humanity or dismiss them with kindness; but it is not allowed you to take away anything of what ye have given them, unless both fear that they cannot keep within the bounds of God. And if ye fear that they cannot observe the ordinances of God, no blame attaches to any one of them for what the wife shall herself give for her redemption.

230. But if he divorce her again, it is not allowed him to take her again, until she has married another husband; and if he divorce her, it shall be no crime in them if they return to each other, if they think they can keep within the bounds of God.

231. But when ye have divorced women, and the time to send them away is come, either keep them with humanity or put them away with generosity; but keep them not by force so as to transgress. Whoso does this, injures himself.

232. And when ye have divorced your wives, and they have waited their prescribed time, hinder them not from marrying other men, when they have agreed among themselves honourably. This is a warning for him among you who believes in God and the Hereafter. That is most proper for you and the most decent. God knows, and ye do not know.

233. Mothers when divorced shall give such to their children two full years, if the father desire that the suckling be completed; and the father shall maintain them and clothe them according to what is just. —No person shall be charged his means. A mother shall not be pressed unfairly for her child, nor a father for his child: and the same with the father's heir. But it they choose to

wean the child by mutual consent and on mutual consideration, it shall not be a fault in them, and if ye choose to provide a nurse for your children, it shall be no fault in you, in case ye pay what ye offer her, according to what is reasonable. And fear God, and know that God sees what ye do.

234. As to those of you who die and leave wives, these must wait concerning themselves four months and ten days, and when they have completed their term, it is no crime in you, for that which they shall do of themselves, according to what is reasonable. And God well knows what ye do.

235. And then no blame shall attach to you if ye make proposals of marriage to such women or hide your intention.—God knows that ye will remember these.—But make no proposals to them in private, unless ye speak honourable words.

236. And resolve not on the marriage-tie-unless the term has been completed, and know that God knows what is in your minds. Therefore, beware of Him, and know that He is gracious, compassionate.

237. It is no crime in you if ye divorce your wives before ye have completed the marriage, or settled any dowry on them. But provide what is needful for them—he who is well-off, according to his circumstances, and he who is hard-up, according to his means—according to what is reasonable,—a duty on the pious.

238. But if ye divorce them before ye have completed the marriage, and have already settled a dowry on them, give half of what ye have settled, unless they release or in whose hand is the marriage-tie: but if ye release, it will be nearer to piety.

And forget not generosity in your relations, one towards another; surely God sees what ye do.

226. This is the time given them to consider as to the desirability or otherwise of a divorce. A divorce upon a rash oath is considered reprehensible.

228. This is in order to secure a proper guardian for the child, not allowing any ground for illegitimacy. During this term the husband is to keep the divorced wife with him, and the wife is to behave towards him as she would be behaved. The whole object of this verse is to cement the attachment between the husband and the wife in the interests of the child and themselves. See Surah lxv. 1.

'It is for the women' etc. A wife is only bound to behave towards her husband as her husband would behave towards her.

'But the men,' etc. In social gradation the husband is placed above the wife, as the parents are above their children, the old people above young people, and so forth.

229. This was to prevent his followers from divorcing their wives on every light occasion, or out of an inconstant humour, as was their practice in pre-Islamic times.

230. To counteract the above practice it was made a rule that if a man divorced his wife the *third* time it was not allowed him to take her again until she had been first married and bedded by another, and divorced by such second husband. "And this precaution," observes Sale, "has had so good an effect that the Mohammedans are seldom known to proceed to the extremity of divorce, notwithstanding the liberty given them, it being reckoned a great disgrace so to do; and there are but few, besides those who have little or no sense of honour, that will take a wife again on the condition enjoined."—George Sale, *The Quran,* Preliminary Discourse, p. 104. Warne, London.

Prayer:

239. Observe prayers— and the mid-day prayer—and stand ye attent before God.

240. And if ye are in fear, pray on foot or riding when ye are safe again, remember God, how he taught

you what ye knew not.

240. Those who are in a state of war or awaiting the attacks of their enemies, are to pray standing or on horse-back. Further precautions are given in Surah iv, 102-4.

Widows:

241. And such of you as die and leave wives, shall bequeath their wives a year's maintenance, without making them quit their homes; but if they quit them, it is no crime in you for what they shall do of themselves, according to what is reasonable; and God is mighty, wise.

242. And for the divorced, let there be a reasonable provision,—a duty on those who fear God.

The Prophets' Wars:

247. Hast thou not heart of the assembly of the children of Israel after Moses, when they said to their prophet, Set up a king for us, and we will fight in the way of God. He said, May it not be that if fighting were ordained you, ye would not fight. They said, And why should we not fight in the way of God, since we and our children are turned out of our dwellings?

251. And when they went forth against Goliath and his forces,

252. They routed them by the will of God, and David slew Goliath, and God gave him the kingdom, and wisdom and taught him what He pleased,—and if God had not prevented men, the one by the other, surely the earth would have been corrupted; but God is beneficent above all the worlds.

247. This was an example from Jewish history of a defensive war which the Moslems were to follow. The prophets, according to Islam, never insisted upon an offensive war.

The Prophets:

254. These are the apostles: We have blessed some of them above the others; some of them has God spoken to, and has raised to the loftiest grade. And We gave to Jesus, son of Mary, clear evidences and strengthened him with the Holy Spirit.—And if God pleased they had not disputed at all, after the clear evidences had come to them. But into disputes they fell, some of them believed, and some remained unbelievers . . . . .

Charity

255. Ye believers, give alms out of what We have provided you, before the Day comes, when there will be no trafficking, nor friendship, nor intercession; and the ungodly, these are unjust doers.

The Throne Verse:

256. God! there is no God but He, the living, the self-subsistent; slumber siezes Him not, nor sleep; His is what is in the heavens and the earth. Who is there that can intercede with Him, but by His permission? He knows what is before them and what is behind them, yet of His knowledget they comprehend not, but what pleases Him. His Throne extends over the heavens and the earth, and it tires Him not to guard them both. And He is the high, the grand.

256. This is the Throne Verse. Regarding it Sale says: "These lines contain a magnificent description of the divine majesty and providence; but it must not be supposed the translation comes up to the dignity of the original." It is greatly esteemed by the Moslems, who also recite it in their prayers.

Compulsion in Religion:

257. There is no compulsion in religion; the right way is in itself distinct from the wrong;—whoso then denies all falsehood, and believes in God—He has caught hold of a strong handle in which is no breaking off, and God is He who hears and knows.

258. God is the patron of those who believe: He brings them out of darkness into light.

257. Compulsion not allowed in matters of religion. The firm belief is that 'the right way is in itself distinct from the wrong.' It is generally stated by European writers that this remarkable verse though promulgated at Medinah was later on cancelled by Mohammed when he stood up to preach Islam 'with sword in one hand and the Quran in the other.' Nothing can be more false. Mohammed to the end of his life never resorted to such measures. Surah v. 52. 53, 59, 73, 81, 99, 104, which is a specimen of the most enlightened tolerance, contains grand utterances of the Prophet of Islam even in his latest career.

The Charitable:

263. The likeness of those who spend their wealth in the way of God, is as a grain of corn which produces seven ears, and in each ear an hundred grains,—and God increases to whom He pleases. God is liberal, wise.

264. As to those who spend their wealth in the way of God, and then follow not what they have spent by reproaches or injury, theirs is a reward with their Lord, no fear shall come upon them, neither shall they grieve.

265. A kind speech and forgiveness is better than alms-giving followed by injury; and God is bounteous, kind.

266. Ye believers, make not vour alms void by

reproaches and injury, like him who spends his wealth to be seen of men and believes not in God and the Hereafter. The likeness of such an one is that of a rock with a thin soil upon it, on which a heavy rain falls and leaves it bare—nothing avails them of what they have earned, and God guides not the unbelieving people.

267. And the likeness of those who spend their wealth from a desire to please God, and for the insuring of their souls, is as a garden on a hill on which a heavy rain falls, and it yields its fruits two-fold, and if a heavy rain falls not on its, at least the dew does: and God sees what ye do.

268. Does any one of you desire to have a garden of palms and vines, through which rivers flows, wherein he may have all fruits, and that old age should come upon him, and that his offspring be weakly, and that then a fiery violent wind should strike it so that it is burned. . . . .

269. Ye believers, spend in alms of the good things which ye have acquired, and of that which We have produced for you out of the earth, and choose not the bad thereof to give in alms,

270. Such as ye would not accept yourselves except by connivance, and know that God is bounteous, praised.

271. The devil threatens you with poverty, and commands you filthy actions but God promises you pardon from Himself and grace, and God is generous, wise.

272. He gives wisdom to whom He will, and whoso is given wisdom, surely he has much good given him; but none will consider, except those who

have hearts.

273. And what ye give in alms, or what ye vow, truly God knows it; but for the unjust there is none to help them. If ye show your alms, it is well; but if ye hide it and give it to the poor, still better will it be for you, and will hide your faults, and God is well aware of what ye do.

274. ....And the good ye give in alms will return upon you; and give only out of a desire to please God,—and what good ye give in alms shall be repaid you, and ye shall not be wronged. To the poor who are wholely devoted to the cause of God and cannot knock about in the earth, whom those who know not think to be rich because of their modesty. Thou shalt know them by this mark—they ask not of men with importunity; and what of good ye spend, surely God knows about them.

275. Those who spend of their wealth night and day, in private and in public,—theirs is a reward with their Lord, no fear shall come upon them, neither shall they grieve.

264. 'By reproaches or injury,' *i.e.,* either by reproaching the person whom they have relieved with what they have done for him, or by exposing his poverty to his prejudice.

266. 'Rock with a thin soil upon, it,' is the heart of such a man with a thin veneer of religion, which is laid bare as soon as it is put to a strong test—a heavy rain falls upon it, as in the text.

267. 'A garden on a hill,' is the heart of the believer which when tested brings forth its internal virtues two-fold.

268. This garden is an emblem of almsgiving out of hypocrisy, or attended with reproaches (as stated in verse 266, above) which in the end blasts the hopes of the giver in the hereafter. For a time he is happy in his conceit, and enjoys it, then comes old age, an unmistakable sign of his closing life, by and by his hopes vanish; he has

perhaps a weakly offspring, and his heart burns with anguish at the thought of what he has done hitherto.

270. 'By connivance,' *i.e.,* on having some amends made by the seller of such goods, either by abatement of the price, or giving something else to the buyer to make up the value.

271. 'Threatens you with poverty,' *i.e.,* by instilling into your hearts the fear of poverty.

273. For while public giving may induce others to give, secret charity is sure to raise in the giver emotions above the average morality, which admits of good works 'to be seen of men' merely. See verse 266, above.

274. 'To please God;' lit., 'to seek the face of God,' His glory in the hereafter, the Beatific vision; thus it implies 'for the love of God.' See verse 160, 172, above.

'The poor who' etc., modest men who are workers in the cause of God, but have not the means adequately to meet the requirements of their life-work. They do not ask men importunately for help, but it is for the men to help them of their own accord.

The Usurers:

276. Those who devour usury shall only arise as he arises whom the devil has infected by his touch. This, for that they say, Truly selling is as usury;—yet God allows selling and forbids usury. Whoso then, after the warning that has come to him from his Lord, abstains, shall have pardon for the past, and his affair is with his Lord. But they who return to it—these are the fellows of the Fire, to continue therein for ever.

277. God will cancel usury, and bless almsgiving; surely, God loves not the ungodly, the impious. But they who believe and do good, and are steadfast in prayer, and give alms—theirs is a reward with their Lord, no fear shall come upon them, neither shall they grieve.

278. Ye believers, fear God, and remit what remains of usury, if ye are of those who believe.

279. But if ye do it not, hearken to war from God and His apostle: yet if ye repent, ye shall have the principal of your money. Wrong not, and ye shall not be wronged.

276. Usury is the excessive interest charged upon a man by another for having helped him out of his financial crisis. It does not include the interest charged upon any sums laid out in a commercial enterprise, but only an increase by taking advantage of other men's difficulties.

'Shall arise as he, etc., like demoniacs or possessed persons, or mad; that is, in great horror and distraction of mind. These are the earthbound spirits, who will not rise because of their greedy covetousness of wealth in this life.

279. 'Hearken to war,' *i.e.*, the violent denunciations of God and His apostle.

The Debtors:

280. And if any find difficulty, then wait till it is easy for him; but if ye remit it as alms, it is better for you, if ye did but know.

281. Fear the Day when ye shall return to God; then shall every soul have what it has earned, and they shall not be wronged.

280. If there is a debtor under a difficulty to pay, let the creditor wait till it is convenient for the debtor; but not to press him at all is the most commendable.

Debts:

282. Ye believers, when ye contract a debt for a certain time, note it down; and let the notary between you faithfully note, and let not the notary refuse to write as God has taught him, but let him write down, and let him who owes the debt dictate, and let him fear God his Lord, and not detract

anything therefrom. But if he who owes the debt is foolish or weak, or is not able to dictate himself, let his agent dictate for him with equity; and call to witness two witnesses of your people; but if there be not two men, then one man and two women of those whom ye choose for witnesses: if one of these should mistake, the other of them might put her to remembrance. And the witnesses shall not refuse whenever they are summoned. And disdain not to note it down, whether the sum is large or small, with the time of payment: this will be more proper for you in the sight of God, more suited for witnessing, and the best for avoiding doubt. But if the goods are there present, and ye pass them from hand to hand—then it is no fault in you not to note it down. But take witnesses when ye sell one to the other, and let no injury be done to the writer or the witness; it is a crime in you to do this. And fear God, and God will give you wisdom; truly God knows all things.

283. And if ye are on a journey and find no notary, let pledges be taken; but if one of you trust the other, let him who is trusted restore what he is trusted with, and fear God his Lord. And refuse not to give evidence. He who refuses has surely a wicked heart, and God knows what ye do.

282. A deed is to be executed by every debtor in favour of his creditor, in the presence of two male witnesses, or one male and two female witnesses. The reason given of two female witnesses being equal to one male witness is *not* because woman is half-man but in the ordinary walk of life she has very little opportunities to distinguish herself in business capacities, and hence the weakness referred to.

God the Knowing:

284. Whatever is in the heavens and the earth is of God; and whether ye bring forth to light what is in your minds or hide it, God will surely call you to account for it; then He will pardon whom He pleases, and whom He pleases He will punish. And God is mighty over all things.

The Faith

285. The apostle believes in what has been revealed to him from his Lord as also the believers. Each one believes in God, and His angels, and His books, and His prophets,—we make no distinction between any of His apostles. And they say, We have heard, and we obey. Thy pardon, Our Lord, for to Thee we shall return.

286. God does not oblige a soul beyond its ability: it shall have the good which it has earned, and the evil which it has earned. Our Lord, catch us not up if we forget or fall into sin. Our Lord, lay not upon us a burden which Thou hast laid on those who have been before us. Our Lord, lay not on us that which we have not strength to bear, but blot out our sins, and forgive us and have pity on us. Thou art our Master, help us therefore against the ungodly people.

285. See also verses 130 and 172, above.

'We make no distinction,' etc., *i.e.*, by believing in some and rejecting others, as the Jews do by rejecting the mission of Jesus, and the Christians that of Mohammed.

286. 'Earned,' being that for which each soul has striven. The 'Original Sin' of the Christians has therefore no place in the creed of Islam.

Principal Contents

Abraham, the upright man, 126, 129; a prophet, 130; his religion, 134.

Afflictions, a trial, 150.

Ancestral practices not above reproach, 165.

Apostles, their mission, 146; some of them named, 130; their belief insisted upon, 3, 172, 285; no distinction to be made between them, 130, 285.

Atonement discarded, 45, 117.

Charity, enjoined, 104, 255; what to give in, 217, 269, 270 its recipients, 211, 274; not to be followed by reproaches or mischief, 265, 266; in public and in private, 273, 275 certain parables, 263, 266-8,

Covenant of God, with the Jews, 77, 78.

Debtors, to be leniently dealt with, 280.

Debts, rules regarding, 282, 283.

Devil, his insinuations, 164,

Divorce, time given to consider, 226; sundry rules, 228-33, 237, 238, 242.

Evidence not to be wrested, 283.

Fasting enjoined, 179; some exempted, 180; month of Ramazan fixed for it, 181; restricted to the day, 183; not to be made rigid, 181.

Food, lawful, 163, 167, 168.

Games of chance, forbidden, 216.

God, unity of, 133, 158; belief inculcated, 20, 26; His signs, 159; His majesty and providence, 256; His knowledge, 284; His *fiat*, 111; His omnipresence, 109; has begotten no son, 110; hears prayer, 182; rewards the works of men, 284; patron of believers, 258.

Hypocrites, 7-9; their obstinacy, 10-15 their similitude, 16-9.

Intercession, discarded, 45, 117.

Islam bequeathed by Abraham, 126, 127; the creed, 130.

Jesus, a prophet, 81, 130.

Judgment Day, 45, 117, 281.

Kiblah, fixed, 139; its object, 138.

Quran, a guide, 1.

Koreish, their obstinacy, 5, 6.

Man, his place in creation, 28, 32, 33; given wisdom, 29, 35; his fall, 34; another chance given, 36; not obliged to more than he can bear, 286.

Marriage proposals, not to be made in private, 235.

Martyrs, not dead, 149.

Moon, its phases, 185.

Moses, a prophet, 81, 130.

Moslems, their faith, 130, 285.

Oaths; wicked ones, 224; on God forbidden, *ib.*; inadvertently taken, 225.

Orphans, to be brought up, 218; their concerns to be managed carefully, 219.

Parables, 24.

Patience, inculcated, 42, 148, 150.

Peace enjoined upon all believers, 204.

Piety, true, 172.

Pilgrimage, enjoined, 192; time appointed, 193; passage to be provided, *ib.*; commerce allowed during, 194.

Pious, the 2-4.

Prayer, enjoined, 239; service during danger, 240; joined to perseverance, 42, 148, 150.

Prophets, belief in all, inculcated, 3, 130, 285; their various grades, 254.

Quietism, 274.

Religion, man's by birth, 132; the original, 209; causes of difference *ib.*; of the prophets, 130; more in works, 59; true, 105, 106, 129; wrangling condemned, 107; compulsion forbidden, 257.

Sectaries, 105, 107, 114, 129, 161, 162.

Scriptures, 3,130, 115.

Usury condemned, 276-9.

War in self-defence enjoined, 186; an example from the Israelitish prophets, 247, 251, 252; enjoined at Badr, 212; its object, 187, 189.

Wealth, its abuse, 184; its use 191.

Widows, their term, 234, 236; their maintenance, 241.

Wine forbidden, 216.

Wisdom, God's greatest gift to man, 272.

Wives, their position in the social well-being, 183, 228.

Works, essential in religion, 45, 59, 106, 117, 133, 143, 172; rewarded according to individual merits, 281.

SURAH III.—THE FAMILY OF IMRAN

(*Medinah*)

This Surah was promulgated at Medinah about A.H. 3 between the victory at Badr and the defeat at Ohad. It derives its title from the mention in verse 30 of the Family of Imran, which includes all the prophets descended from Amram, as Jesus, John, Zacharias, and some others.

God:

1. A.L.M. God! there is no God but He, the living, the self-subsistent.

2. He has revealed to thee the Book with truth, confirming what was before it, and He had revealed the Law and the Evangel before it—a guide to the people, and He revealed the distinction.

4. Surely nothing is hidden from God, of that which is on earth or in heaven. He it is who formed you in the wombs as it pleased Him. There is no God but He, the mighty, the wise.

1. 'A. L. M.' See Surah ii. 1, notes.

   'God.' etc. See Surah ii. 256.

2. The Quran is a mere confirmation of the revelations of the former prophets, and its aim is primarily to restore them to their original purity.

The Quran:

5. He it is who has revealed to thee the Book; in it are some verses clear—these are the principles of the Book, and others are figurative. But they in whose hearts is a crookedness follow its figures, desiring discord in the interpretation thereof.. .

6. Our Lord, suffer not our hearts to go astray after that Thou hast guided us, and give us from before Thee mercy; for Thou art the giver.

7. Our Lord, Thou wilt surely gather mankind together on a Day of which there is no doubt . . .

5. The contents of the Quran are here distinguished into such passages as are to be taken in the literal sense, and such as require a figurative acceptation. The former being plain and unambiguous, compose the fundamental part, or, as the original express it, *the mother* of the book, and contain the principal doctrines and precepts; agreeably to and consistent with which those passages which are wrapt up in metaphors, and delivered in an enigmatical, allegorical style, are always to be interpreted.

In the latter part of this verse all attempts at disputation with regard to a certain interpretation of the figurative is condemned.

This world and the Hereafter:

12. Fair-seeming to men is the love of pleasures with women and children, and sums heaped up of gold and silver, and excellent horses, and cattle, and cornfields: this is the provision of the life of this world, but with God is the most excellent home.

13. Say thou, Shall I tell you of better things than these prepared for the pious? Before their Lord they shall be in Gardens beneath which rivers flow—to dwell therein for ever,—and their wives also purified,—and have acceptance with God;

for God regards those who serve Him.

13. The blessed shall enjoy the Beatific vision and the glory of God, in company with their wives, etc. See also Surah xiii. 23.

The Servants of God:

14. Who say, Our Lord, we have sincerely believed, pardon us our sins, and keep us from the torment of the Fire;

15. The patient, the true, the devoted, the charitable, and those who pray for pardon at day-break.

The One God:

16. God witnesses that there is no God but He; and the angels, and those who have knowledge and are steadfast in righteousness also: there is no God but He, the mighty, the wise.

The One Religion:

17. Surely the religion with God is Islam: and they to whom the Book was given before, differed only after that the knowledge had come to them, our to hatred among themselves. And whoso denies the signs of God, surely God is swift at reckoning up.

18. If they dispute with thee, say thou, I strive for the pleasure of God, as do those who follow me.

19. Say to those who have received the Book, and the illiterates, Do ye also strive? If they strive, then are they guided aright; but if they turn aside, then surely—thine is to preach only: and God regards His servants.

17. 'Islam,' coming as it does from the root 'salama,' signifies to be tranquil, at rest, to have done one's duty, to have paid up, to be at perfect peace, and finally, to strive after' righteousness with one's own strength. It means the

being at peace and living in accordance with God's words and commands, leading the life of a righteous man; the sense in which the derivatives of the Semitic 'salam' occur in early Aramaic.

Islam is said to be the Original Religion of man, and the difference between the great world-religions is attributed to mutual hatred. See ii. 130, 209; and verses 78 and 79, below.

18. 'For the pleasure of God,' *lit.*, 'as seeking the face of God. See Surah ii. 274, notes.

19. 'Illiterates,' may also be translated 'gentiles' or 'heathens,' as Jews and Christians call those who do not believe in their respective systems.

The Ungodly:

20. But those who believe not in the sings of God, and unjustly slay the prophets and those who enjoin uprightness,—announce to them a severe chastisement.

21. These are they whose works perish in this world and the Hereafter, and there is none to help them.

22. Hast thou seen those who received a portion of the Book?—they are called to the Book of God, that it might decide between them, but a part of them turn aside and withdraw.

23. This, because they say, The Fire shall not touch us, but for a number of days,—and that which they had falsely devised deceived them in their religion.

24. But how will it be with them, when We will gather them together on a Day, of which there is no doubt, and every soul shall be paid what it has earned and they shall not be wronged?

22. This refers to the Jews, who although they accepted the teachings of their prophets of the House of Israel, whom Mohammed also honoured and accepted, were yet very

violent against the Moslems. The commentators also relate the following as the occasion of this verse. Mohammed went one day into a Jewish synagogue where two Jewish priests, Naim and Haris, asked him what religion he was of. To this Mohammed answering, Of the religion of Abraham, they replied that Abraham was a Jew, Whereupon Mohammed proposed that the Pentateuch might decide the question, to which they would by no means agree.

23. Some of them actually believed that whatever their sins, they will not be punished for more than 40 days, the time during which their ancestors had worshipped the Golden Calf. Others believed that their punishment was to last but 7 days, that is, a day for every thousand years which they supposed the world was to endure. They were to be so mildly dealt with, either by reason of the intercession of their fathers, the prophets, or because God had promised Jacob that his offspring should be punished but slightly.

'That which . . . religion,' their false teachings about religion served only to lead them away from truth.

24. 'A Day' etc., the Judgment Day.

A Prayer:

25. Say, O God, King of the Kingdom, Thou givest the kingdom to whom Thou wilt, and Thou takest away the kingdom from whom Thou wilt; Thou givest honour to whom Thou wilt, and whom Thou wilt Thou dost disgrace. In Thy hand is good, and surely Thou art mighty over all things.

26. Thou dost pass the night into the day, and the day dost Thou pass into the night; Thou bringest the living out of the dead, and Thou bringest the dead out of the living, and Thou providest for whom Thou wilt, without measure.

25. The absolute rule of God is here acknowledged.

'King of the Kingdom,' in the sense of 'Lord of the worlds' as in Surah i. 1.

26. 'The living out of the dead,' etc., as a man from seed, and a bird from an egg, and vice versa.

God's Omniscience:

27. Say thou, Whether ye hide what is in your breasts, or whether ye declare it, God knows it all the same. He knows what is in the heavens and the earth; and God is mighty over all things.

28. On that Day every soul shall find what it has done of good, present; and as to what it has done of evil, it shall wish that between itself and that were a wide distance; but God warns you to beware of Himself, for God is gracious to His servants.

The Love of God:

29. If ye love God, then follow me; God will love you, and forgive you your sins, for God is gracious, compassionate.

People of the Book:

57. Say thou, Ye people of the Book, come to a proper understanding between us and you—that we'll not worship any except God, and that we'll not join anything with Him, and that the one of us take not the other for lords beside God. Then if they turn aside, say, Bear ye witness that we are believers.

58. Ye people of the Book, why do ye dispute about Abraham, since the Law and the Evangel were not revealed until after him? Do ye not then understand?

60. Abraham was not a Jew nor yet a Christian, but he was an upright man, and a Moslem, and not of those who join anything with Him.

61. The men nearest to Abraham, are those who follow him, and this prophet, and they who believe; and God is the patron of the believers.

62. A party of the people of the Book desire to lead you astray, but they only mislead themselves, and perceive it not.

63. Ye people of the Book, why disbelieve ye in the signs of God, of which yourselves have been witnesses?

64. Ye people of the Book, why clothe ye the truth with falsehood, and hide the truth knowingly?

57. The common ground upon which the followers of the different prophets are called upon to stand is here clearly given. It is: that they will not worship any except God, and that they will be true to it. *This* constitutes **Islam**, being the teaching of the prophets and seers in all ages.

60. 'An upright man;' see note to Surah ii. 129.

61. See note to verse 23, above.

Their Various Characters:

68. Of the people of the Book are some, to whom if thou trust a treasure, he will restore it to thee; and there is of them to whom if thou trust a 'dinar,' he will never restore it to thee, unless thou stand over him urgently.

69. This, because they say, We are not bound to observe faith with the gentiles; but they utter a lie against God knowingly.

70. Aye, whoso fulfils his Covenant, and fears to do evil, —surely God loves the pious.

71. But those who barter their Covenant with God, and their oaths, for a small price—there is no portion for them in the Hereafter: God will not speak to them, nor look upon them on the

Judgment Day, nor will He purify them; but for them is a painful punishment.

72. And some truly there are among them who twist their tongues in reading the Book, that ye may know it to be so in the Book, yet it is not in the Book. And they say, This is from God, although it is not from God; and they utter a lie against God knowingly.

68. 'A treasure,' or any large amount.

'A dinar,' a gold coin worth about ten shillings.

69. 'Gentiles;' see note to verse 19, above.

71. 'Who barter their convenant, *i.e.*, who break their covenant.

'Covenant with God;' see note to Surah ii. 25.

'God will not speak,' etc. He will turn His face against them, will be angry with them.

72. 'Who twist their tongues in reading, *i.e.*, who read with a wrong accent, who torture the true reading and pervert the meaning.

The Covenant of God:

73. It is not for a man, that God should give him the Book and wisdom and prophecy, and that then he should say to men, Be ye worshippers of me beside God; but rather, Be ye exclusively devoted to God, since ye know the Book and have studied.

74. God does not command you to take the angels and the prophets for Lords. What! would He command you to disbelieve after that ye have been Moslems?

75. When God accepted the Covenant of the prophets—This is the Book and Wisdom which I have given you, hereafter shall a prophet come to you to confirm what is with you; ye shall surely believe on him and ye shall assist him. He said,

Have ye resolved? and do ye receive the Covenant on these terms? They said, We have resolved. Be ye then the witnesses, and I am also a witness with you.

76. And whoso turns back after this, they are surely the transgressors.

73. 'Be ye exclusively,' etc. Sale translates it, 'Be ye perfect in knowledge and in works.'

This was in answer to the Christians who insisted that Jesus had commanded them to worship him as God. The commentators also relate the following in connexion with this verse. Two Christians named Abu-Rafi and an-Najrani offered to acknowledge Mohammed as their Lord in place of Jesus and to worship him, from which Mohammed shrank in horror, and exclaimed, 'God forbid, that we should worship any beside God.'

75. Some interpret this of the children of Israel themselves, of whose race the Semitic prophets were. But others say that the souls of all the Israelitish prophets, even of those who were not born, were present on Mount Sinai when God gave the law to Moses, and that they entered into the Covenant here mentioned with Him. This was the belief of the Jews, and in appealing to these people Mohammed made use of it, in order to reach their hearts.

The True Religion:

77. Do they seek any other religion but of God? To him submits everything that is in the heavens and in the earth, in willing or forced submission; and to Him they shall return.

78. Say thou, We believe in God, and what has been revealed to us, and what has been revealed to Abraham, and Ishmael, and Isaac, and Jacob, and the tribes, and what was given to Moses and Jesus and the prophets from their Lord,—we make no distinction between any of them,—and after Him we strive.

79. Whoso seeks any other religion than Islam, it shall not be accepted of him, and in the Hereafter he will be of those who lose.

78. This is a repetition of Surah ii. 130, *q.v.* This is the religion of Islam.

79. 'Islam,' see verse 17, above.

The Ungodly:

80. How will God guide a people who have disbelieved, after that they had believed and borne witness that they apostle was true, and after that evidences had come to them? Surely God guides not the transgressors.

81. Their reward is—that on them is the curse of God and the angels and all men.

82. Under it they shall remain for ever, their torment shall not be mitigated, neither shall God look upon them;

83. Except those who after this repent and amend; for surely God is gracious, compassionate.

84. As to those who have disbelieved after they have believed, and then increase in unbelief, their repentance shall not be accepted. Surely these are the misguided.

85. As to those who have disbelieved, and die in unbelief, the world full of gold shall not be accepted from any of them, though he should offer it in ransom: and for them is a painful punishment, and they have none to help them.

80. People who after being persuaded of the truth have returned to their old ways can never expect to be guided aright.

83. 'Repent and amend.' In the Quran these two words are used conjointly throughout. See Surah x. vi. 120. Death-bed repentance is not considered effectual, because there

is no more time for making 'amends.' See Surah iv. 21. 22.

Self-Denial:

86. Ye will never attain to goodness till ye give alms of that which ye love, and whatever ye give, surely God knows it.

86. To attain to righteousness a man has to sacrifice his own interests to those of others.

Pilgrimage:

90. The first House that was founded for men was that in Becca for a blessing and a guide to men:

91. In it are evidences, even the standing-place of Abraham, and whoso enters it is safe. There is due to God from man a pilgrimage to this House, for whoso can find his way there.

92. And as to him who does not believe—verily God is independent of the worlds.

90. 'The first House.' The Kaabah is said to have been erected by Abraham and Ishmael.

'House,' meaning Temple.

'Becca,' same as 'Mecca,' meaning 'a place of concourse.' In the Arabic usage 'M' and 'B' are often used promiscuously.

See Surah ii. 192, etc.

91. 'Evidences, i.e., traces of the prophets who first laid its foundation.

92. 'God is independent of the worlds, i.e., does not stand in need of the services of His creatures.

People of the Book:

93. Say thou, Ye people of the Book, why disbelieve ye the evidences of God? Surely God is a witness over your doings.

94. Ye people of the Book, why keep ye back from

the way of God him who believes: ye seek to make it crooked, and yet yourselves are witnesses. Surely God is not unmindful of what ye do.

The Believers:

95. Ye believers, if ye obey some amongst those who have received the Book, they will make you unbelievers, after ye have believed.

96. And how can ye disbelieve, when the evidences of God are read out to you, and His prophet is in your midst? Whoso holds fast to God, is surely guided aright.

97. Ye believers, fear God as of right He is to be feared, and die not unless ye are Moslems.

98. And hold fast the cord of God, all of you, and break not off with it; and remember the favour of God towards you, how when ye were enemies, He put love into your hearts, and by His favour ye became brothers;

99. And ye were on the brink of a pit of fire, and He kept you back from it. Thus does God show His evidences that ye may be guided aright.

95. This passage was occasioned by a quarrel excited between the tribes of Aus and Khazraj, by one Shas b. al-Kais, a Jew; who, passing by some of both tribes as they were sitting and discoursing familiarly together, and being inwardly vexed at the friendship and harmony which reigned among them on their embracing Islam, whereas they had been, for the last 120 years, most inveterate and mortal enemies, though descendants of two brothers; in order to set them at variance, sent a young man to sit down by them, directing him to relate the story of the Battle of Boas (a place near Medinah), wherein, after a bloody fight, Aus had the better of Khazraj, and to repeat some verses on that subject. The young man executed his orders; whereupon those of each tribe began to magnify themselves, and to reflect on and

irritate the other, till at length they called to arms, and great numbers getting together on each side, a dangerous battle had ensued, if Mohammed had not stepped in and reconciled them; by representing to them how much they would be to blame if they returned to their old ignorance, and revived those animosities which their new religion had composed; and telling them that what had happened was a trick of the devil to disturb their present tranquillity.

98. 'Hold fast the cord of God,' *i.e.*, believe firmly in Him, and be united in Him.

'All of you,' in a body.

'Break not off with it,' i.e., be not divided herein.

'Remember the favour of God,' etc. Instances of God's goodness in your daily life ought to bind you more strongly to Him.

The Islamic Mission:

100. And let there be among you a people who call to the good, and command what is just, and forbid what is evil,—and these are the blessed.

101. And be ye not like them who make a division and become sectaries, after that evidences have come to them;— and for them is a severe punishment.

100. 'A people' etc., a band of workers in the cause of God who are to preach and teach the truth about religion. The genesis of a missionary endeavour in the cause of Islam is here laid down.

101. 'Be ye not like them,' etc., i.e., avoid all sectarianism, and go by the principles.

'For them,' etc. All sectarianism is condemned.

The Judgment Day:

102. On the Day when faces shall turn white, and faces shall turn black, to those whose faces shall turn black—Have ye returned to unbelief after that ye had believed? Then taste the punishment, for that ye disbelieved.

103. But they whose faces shall turn white shall be in the mercy of God, therein to continue for ever.

104. These are the evidences of God: we read them to thee with truth; and God desires not injustice to the worlds.

105. God's is whatever is in the heavens and the earth: and to God belongs the decision of affairs.

102. 'Faces shall turn white,' *i.e.*, become glorious. 'Turn black,' *i.e.*, look morose and shadowy, shame settling upon their faces.

Moslems: Their Superiority:

106. Ye are the best people that have been raised up to mankind: ye command what is just and forbid what is evil, and ye believe in God. If the people of the Book believed, it were certainly better for them: there are believers among them, but most of them are transgressors.

107. Yet they shall not hurt you except a little.

108. They are smitten with vileness wherever found, unless they ally themselves with God and with men; they draw on themselves the indignation of God, and are stricken with poverty. This, because they disbelieved in the evidences of God, and killed the prophets unjustly; and this, for that they rebelled and transgressed.

106. The grounds of the Moslem's superiority are plainly laid down. It is not in belief merely but in works also that the Moslem is to emulate.

107. 'They are smitten,' etc., or, 'shame shall settle upon their faces,'

108. 'Are stricken with poverty.' Among other things, poverty also is counted upon as a sign of God's wrath upon men.

Pious Among the People of The Book:

109. Yet they are not all alike: among the people of

the Book there are some upright people; they meditate on the evidences of God in the night-time and worship;

110. They believe in God and the Hereafter, and command what is just and forbid what is evil, and zealously strive in good works.—These are of the righteous.

111. And what of good ye do, surely ye will not be denied; for God knows the pious.

109. The existence of the good and pious among the people of the Book is here acknowledged. An account also of their life is given in this and the succeeding verses.

111. All good works are acceptable to God without regard to the religion of the man doing it.

The Ungodly:

112. As to those who have disbelieved, their wealth shall not avail them, neither their children against God; these are the fellows of the Fire, to continue therein for ever.

Their Similitude:

113. The likeness of what they lay out in the life of this world is as a wind wherein is a scorching cold, which falls on the standing corn of those men who have injured their own souls, and destroys it. It is not God who wrongs them, but it is themselves they do wrong.

113. 'It is not God,' etc. It is men who by their works bring ruin upon themselves, and God does not compel them to it.

Their Hatred:

114. Ye believers, do not form intimacies among others than yourselves: they will not fail to corrupt you; they wish for your ruin. Their hatred has already appeared out of their mouths, but what their

breasts hide is still more grievous. We have already made plain to you the proofs, if ye understand.

115. Behold, ye love them, but they do not love you; ye believe the entire Book, and when they meet you they say, We believe; but when they are all alone, they bite their fingers' ends at you, out of wrath.

116. If good happen to you, it grieves them, but if evil befall you, they rejoice at it. But if ye persevere and fear God, their craftiness shall in no way harm you. Surely God encompasses their doings.

114. In this verse some Moslems who had intimate friends among the Koreish while the Moslems were yet in a belligerent condition with them, are here forbidden to be intimate with them.

116. 'But if ye persevere,' etc. Persevering steadfastly in the cause of God and fearing Him alone is enough to save the believer from all harm.

God's Judgment:

123. It is none of thy concern whether He is turned to them in kindness or chastises them; they are surely wrong-doers.

124. God's whatever is in the heavens and the earth. He spares whom He will, and whom He will He chastises; surely God is gracious, merciful.

Usury:

125. Ye believers devour not usury doubly doubled, but fear God, that ye may be happy.

126. And fear the Fire which is prepared for them that believe not, and obey God and the apostle, that ye may obtain mercy.

127. And hasten emulously for pardon from your Lord,

and Paradise vast as the heavens and the earth, prepared for the pious.

The Pious:

128. Who give alms in prosperity and adversity; who bridle their anger, and forgive men; surely God loves those who do good;

129. And who, after they committed a filthy action or wronged their own souls, remember God, and implore pardon for their sins—and who is it that will forgive sins but God?—and persist not in what they have done, knowingly.

130. As for these—their reward is pardon from their Lord, and Gardens 'neath which rivers flow, to continue therein for ever; and excellent indeed is the reward of those who work.

Perseverance:

131. There have already been before you examples. Then go through the earth, and see what has been the end of those who called it a lie.

132. This is a declaration to men and a guide, and a warning to the pious.

133. And be not faint-hearted, nor be sorrowful for ye shall rise superior, if ye are believers.

134. If a wound has befallen you, a wound like it has already befallen them: We alternate these days among men; that God may know those who believe, and that He might have martyrs from among you,—but God loves not the wrong-doers.

135. And the God may prove those who believe and destroy the ungodly.

136. Did ye imagine that ye should enter Paradise ere yet God has taken knowledge of those among you who strove and of those who steadfastly

endured?

138. Mohammed is no more than an apostle; other apostles have already passed before him: if he die therefore, or is slain, will ye turn back on your heels ? But whoso turns back on his heels, will not hurt God at all; and God will surely reward the thankful.

139. No one can die except by God's permission, according to the Book that fixed the term: and whoso chooses the reward of this world, We give him thereof; and whoso chooses the reward of the Hereafter, We give him thereof; and We will certainly reward the thankful.

140. How many prophets have combated those who had with them myriads ! and yet they were not daunted at what befell them in the way of God, nor were they weakened, nor did they basely submit. Surely God loves those who steadfastly persevere.

153. And as to the mercy of God, thou hast been mild towards them; but if thou hadst been severe and hard-hearted, they would surely have broken off with thee. But forgive them and ask pardon for them, and consult them in the affairs, and when thou hast resolved, rely upon God, for God loves those who rely upon Him.

154. If God help you, none shall overcome you; but if He abandon you, who is it that will help you against Him? In God then let the believers trust.

155. It is not the prophet that will defraud you; and whoso is defrauding shall come forth with what he has defrauded on the Judgment Day: then shall every soul be paid what it has earned and

they shall not be wronged.

156. Shall he then who has followed the goodwill of God be as he who was brought on himself wrath from God, and whose home is Hell?—truly wretched the journey thither.

157. There are grades with God; and God sees what they do.

158. Now has God been gracious to the believers, when He raised up among them an apostle out of their own people, to declare His evidences to them, to purify them, and teach them the Book and wisdom; whereas they were before in plain error.

163. And call not those slain in the way of God, dead; nay, they are alive with their Lord, richly sustained,

164. Rejoicing in what God of His bounty has vouchsafed them, filled with joy for those who follow after them but have not yet overtaken them, that no fear shall come upon them, neither shall they grieve;

165. Filled with joy at the favour of God, and at His bounty; for that God suffers not the reward of the believers to perish.

175. And let not those who are niggardly in what God has vouchsafed them of His bounty, think that it is good for them; nay, rather it is worse for them.

176. That of which they have been niggardly shall be their collar on the Judgment Day, and God's is the inheritance of the heavens and the earth, and God knows what ye do.

181. And if they treat thee as a liar, apostles before

thee have also been treated as liars, though they came with clear evidences, and law and clear book.

182. Every soul shall taste of death, and ye shall have your reward on the Judgment Day; and whoso is removed from the Fire, and is admitted into Paradise, shall be happy indeed. And the life of this world is only a deceitful provision.

183. Ye shall surely be proved in your possessions, and in your persons, and ye shall hear many hurtful things from those who have received the Book before you and those who join others with God. But if ye steadfastly endure and fear God,—surely this is a bounden duty.

184. And when God accepted the Covenant of those to whom the Book was given saying, Ye shall surely publish it to men and not hide it; they cast it behind their backs, and sold it for a small price; but woe for what they have sold it.

185. Think not that those who rejoice in what they have done, and expect to be praised for what they have done;—think not that they shall escape the chastisement: for them is a painful punishment.

186. God's is what is in the heavens and the earth; and God is mighty over all things.

187. Verily in the creation of the heavens and the earth, and the succession of night and day, are evidences to those who have hearts;

188. Who remember God standing, and sitting, and reclining, and meditate on the creation of the heavens and the earth.

189. Our Lord, Thou hast not created this in vain. Praise to Thee! Keep us from the torment of the

Fire. Our Lord, whom Thou shalt throw into the Fire, Thou wilt surely disgrace, and the wrong-doers shall have none to help them.

190. Our Lord, we have heard the voice of him that called: he called us to the Faith, saying, Believe in your Lord; and we have believed.

191. Our Lord, pardon us our sins, and drive from us evils, and make us to die with the righteous.

192. And our Lord, give us what Thou hast promised us by Thy apostles, and put not us to shame on the Judgment Day. Surely Thou wilt not fail in Thy promise.

193. And their Lord answers them,—I will not suffer the work of him among you who works to be lost, whether he is male or female: ye are the one from the other.

194. And they who have fled from their country and have been turned out of their homes, and have suffered for My sake, and have fought and fallen, I will blot out their sins from them, and I will bring them into Gardens' neath which rivers flow:

195. A reward from God,—and with God is the most excellent reward.

196. Let not the prosperity in the land of those who believe not, deceive thee. It is only a brief enjoyment. Then their home is Hell, and wretched the bed.

197. But as to those who fear their Lord—for them are Gardens neath which rivers flow, therein shall they continue for ever. This is the gift of God, and what is with God is the best for the righteous.

198. Of the people of the Book are some who believe in God, and in what has been sent down to you, and in what He has sent down to them, and are humble before God, and barter not the signs of God for a mean price.

199. These have their reward with their Lord: surely God is swift to take account.

200. Ye believers, be patient, and strive to excel in patience, and be firm, and fear God, that ye may be happy.

134. In A. H. 3, the Meccans again attacked the Moslems at Medinah with a large army of 3,000 men, including 700 mailed warriors and 200 horsemen, when Mohammed could only gather 700 men. The battle took place at Ohad, 3 miles from Medinah, in which the Moslems were defeated. See Surah iv. 80, notes. In the midst of the melee a stone from a sling struck Mohammed on the mouth, cutting his lip and knocking our one of his front teeth; he was also wounded in the face by an arrow.

136. See also Surah xxix. 1.

139. 'The Book,' is identified with 'the knowledge of God through all eternity.'

'Whoso chooses,' i.e., every man will be rewarded according as he has chosen the good or the evil in this life.

155. The prophet will not hold out false promises to those who believe.

157. 'Grades,' i.e., degrees of rewards and punishments according to the individual merits.

163. See also Surah ii. 149.

176. Mohammed is said to have declared that whoever hoarded up wealth without putting it to its proper use shall have a hideous serpent twisted round his neck on the Judgment Day.

183. See also Surah ii. 150, etc.

188. 'Standing,' etc. In postures that might be convenient to them.

A man on soldier's duty is to pray standing.

A man fatigued is to pray sitting.

And a man sick on bet to pray reclining on one side.

In fact, there is no condition of man in which he is excused from saying his prayers.

193. 'A male,' etc. In spite of such plain passages, the foolish assertion has sometimes been made by European writers that in Islam the woman has no future state of happiness.

Principal Contents

Abraham, the upright man, 60; his traces in the Kaabah, 91; people nearest to , 61.

Apostles, their mission, 158; not deceivers, 155; belief in, inculcated, 78; no distinction to be made between, *ib*.; not to be worshipped, 73, 74; their patience, 140.

Charity, true, 86.

Covenant to be fulfilled at all time, 70, 71.

Covetous, the, 175, 176.

Death, the common lot of all, 138, 182.

Gentiles, faith to be observed with, 69, 70.

God, His unity and self-subsistence, 1, 16; His knowledge, 4, 27; His power, 25, 26; His love, 98, 99: the only judge of men, 123; obedience enjoined 98; fear, 97; love, 29.

Islam, the true religion, 17; common ground with other religions, 57, 63.

Judgment Day, the 24, 28.

Quran, confirmatory of the previous scriptures, 2; its verses either plain or figurative, 5.

Life, a severe trial, 133.

Man, not to be worshipped, 73.

Martyrs not dead, 163; their happiness, 164, 165.

Missionary endeavour, 100; not to be sectarian, 101.

Mohammed, only an apostle, 138.

Moslems, the best people by virtue of their works, 106.

People of the Book, common ground with them, 57, 63; their various characters, 68, 69; their corrupt readings, 72; some good men among, 109, 110.

Perseverance, enjoined, 136. 200.

Persevering, the, 194.
Pilgrimage, enjoined, 90, 91.
Pious, the, 14, 15, 128, 129; their reward, 12, 13.
Religion, the true, 17.
Reward according to the grades of work, 157.
Unbelief, reproved, 20, 80, 84; no atonement for, 85.
Unbelievers, their hostility, 114-6; to be forgiven, 153.
Ungodly, the 20; their reward, 21.
Usury denounced, 125.
Works, good, always rewarded, 111; in man and woman, 193; emulation in good, enjoined, 127; bad punished, 185.

CHAPTER IV.—WOMEN.

(Medinah.)

This Surah was promulgated at Medinah in A.H. 4, and derives its title from the various matters relating to women treated herein, such as marriage, divorce, dower, etc.

Women: Their Respect:

1. Ye people, fear your Lord who made you from one soul, and made from it its mate, and multiplied from them two many men and women. And fear God in whose name ye beg of one another, and respect women. Verily God watcher over you.

1. 'One soul,' Ar. 'nafs,' being.

'Its mate. Ar. 'zauj.' Humanity is made up of man and woman, each being the 'mate' the other. It expresses the perfect concord that should exist between a man and wife.

'In whose name.' etc., saying, I beg of you for God's sake.

'Respect women.' *Lit.*, 'and wombs.' The meaning is understood in connexion with the main sentence, 'And fear God, . . . and wombs,' *i.e.* fear God with regard to the 'wombs' that bear you, your mothers and wives. 'Respect woman,' is the first lesson in Islam with regard to women.

'Paradise,' said Mohammed, 'is at the feet of the mother.'

'God watches,' etc., This is emphasizing the above truth.

The Orphans:

2. And give to the orphans their property, and render them not in exchange bad for good, and devour not their property with your own; for that is a great sin.

3. And if ye fear ye that cannot act equitably towords, orphans, then marry what you like of women, twos, and threes, and fours; and if ye fear that ye cannot act equitably, then one only, or what ye have already got under your hands,—that is the chief thing—that ye act not unjustly.

   And give women their dowry freely, but if of themselves they give up anything thereof, then enjoy it with satisfaction and advantage.

4. And entrust not to the incapable the substance which God has appointed you to preserve for them; and maintain them therewith, and clothe them, and speak to them in a kindly sort.

5. And teach the orphans until they reach the age of marriage, and when ye find in them a sound judgment, then hand over their substance to them; and waste it not extravagantly, or in haste.

6. For that they are growing up. And the rich shall not touch it, but he who is poor shall take of it, according to what is reasonable.

7. And when ye hand over their substance to them, then take witnesses in their presence; and God is sufficient at taking account.

2. 'Render them,' etc. i.e., take not what ye find of value among their effects to your own use, and give them worse in its stead.

3. The commentators understand this passage differently. The true meaning seems to be as it is here translated. Mohammed advising his followers that if they found they should wrong the female orphans under their care, either by marrying them against their inclinations, for the sake of their riches or beauty, or by not using or maintaining them as well as they ought, by reason of their having already several wives, they should rather choose to marry other women, to avoid all occasion of sin. Others say that when this passage was revealed, many of Mohammed's followers, fearing trouble and temptation, refused to take upon them the charge of orphans, and yet multiplied wives to a great excess, and used them ill; or gave themselves up to fornication; which occasioned this passage. And according to these, its meaning must be either that if they feared they could not act justly towards orphans, they had as great reason to apprehend they could not deal equitably with so many wives, and therefore are restricted with regard to the number of women they might marry; or else, that since fornication was a crime as well as wronging of orphans, they ought to avoid that also, by marrying so as to keep within the bounds of the law.

'Twos and threes and fours, *i.e.,* any number; it is very wrong to translate it 'two and three and four.'

'And if ye fear . . . then one only.' This is the proviso of the above law, which has to be fulfilled before marrying more than one.

'What ye have already got under your hands: ' or, 'what your right hands have already got,' *i.e.,* women over whom you have already got the mastery, a wife being considered in pre-Islamic Arabia a mere chattel, as also the slave-girl, this was said of them. While a check was put upon the polygamy of the Arabs by the above law, it was also laid down as a formal measure that they might retain the number of wives and slave-girls *already* with them.

'That is the chief thing.' The extreme importance of the above proviso is here emphasised.

'That ye act not unjustly.' Further importance of the proviso maintained.

'Give women,' etc. At marriage a certain dowry is named, part of which the husband is bound to pay to the wife on demand, the remainder being paid in the event of divorce or the death of the husband; this is the great instrument in the hand of a wife, who is also free to fix it at any sum far larger than the husband can ever expect to pay. This is paid out of the property of the husband, and does not effect the original rights of the wife upon the husband's estate. In many instances it may also curb the ape of the rich man.

4. 'The incapable,' or those who are weak of understanding; an infant, idiot, lunatic or such as are incapable of controlling their own affairs.

5. 'Teach;' *lit.*, 'try.' The guardians are also to look that they learn the management of their own affairs.

'The age of marriage,' or 'the age of discretion,' which is generally reckoned to be fifteen, though some doctors think eighteen the proper age.

6. 'For that,' etc. Because they will shortly come of age to receive what belongs to them.

'According to,' etc. No more than what shall make sufficient recompense for the trouble of their education.

7. 'God is sufficient,' etc. The expression reminds of the strict account that you will have to render to God. See Surah i. 3.

Inheritance: A Law:

8. Men have a portion of what their parents and kindred leave; and women also a portion of what their parents and kindred leave, whether it is little or much, a determined portion is theirs.

9. And when they who are of kin are present at the division, and the orphans and the poor, let them also have a share, and speak to them in a kindly sort.

10. And let them fear who if they leave behind them a weakly offspring, are solicitous for them. Let them therefore fear God, and propose what is right.

11. Surely, those who devour the substance of

orphans wrongfully shall swallow down only fire into their bellies, and shall broil in the raging Flame.

12. God commands you concerning your children: for a male the share of two females; but if they are females, more than two, then they shall have two-thirds of what they shall leave, and if she is an only daughter, she shall have the half; and the parents shall have each of them a sixth part of what he has left, if he have a child; but if he have no child, and his parents be his heirs, then his mother shall have the third, and if he have brothers, his mother shall have the sixth, after the legacies bequeathed and debts. As to your fathers or your children, ye know not which of them is of greater use to you;—the law is from God: surely God is knowing, wise.

13. And for you is half of what your wives leave, if they had no issue; but if they have issue, then a fourth of what they leave is yours, after the legacies bequeathed and debts.

14. For them also a fourth of what ye shall leave in case ye have no issue; but if ye have issue, then an eighth part of what ye leave, after the legacies bequeathed, and debts.

15. If a man or a woman is inherited by a distant relation, and he or she have a brother or sister, for each of these two a sixth; but if there are more than this, they shall be sharers in a third, after the legacies bequeathed, and debts;

16. Without loss to any one;—the ordinance of God; and God is knowing, mild.

8. This law was given to abolish the custom of the pre-

Islamic Arabs who suffered not women or children to have any part of their husband's or father's inheritance, on the ground that only those should inherit who were able to go to war.

10. 'The plain meaning is this: Take care not to wrong the orphan-children of other even as you would that others should not wrong your orphan-children if you happen to die leaving them in this helpless state.

'Propose what is right,' *i.e.,* bind yourself not down to formal measures merely, but take practical steps as to how to best benefit them.

12. This and the four succeeding verses give the rule to be followed in the distribution of the estate of the deceased.

'Females more than two.' And if there are two and no more, they will have the same share.

'She shall have the half.' And the remaining third part, or the remaining moiety of the estate, which is not here expressly disposed of, if the deceased leave behind him no son, nor a parent, goes to the Public Treasury. For its application see Surah ix. 60.

'His mother shall have the third.' And his father the other two-thirds.

'The legacies,' chiefly meaning those bequeathed to charitable purposes mentioned in Surah ix. 60; for the Moslems do not approve of a person's giving away his substance from his family and near relations on any other account.

'His debts.' The debts of the deceased claim the first attention of the law.

15. 'Inherited by a distant relation.' For this may happen by contract, or on some other special occasion.

'For each of these two a sixth.' Here and in the next case the brother and sister are made equal sharers.

Adultery: The Charge:

19. As to those of your women who are guilty of whoredom, bring four witnesses against them from among yourselves; and if they bear witness, then keep them in houses, until death release them or God makes for them a way.

20. And if two of you commit it, punish them both; but it they turn and amend, then let them be. And God is relenting merciful.

19. 'Whoredom,' either adultery or fornication.

In order to establish a charge of adultery or fornication against a women the evidences of four eye-witnesses are required, and if it is conclusively proved against her, she is not allowed to go out of her house, if the husband retains her, all her life, unless she is divorced from him.

'Keep them in houses.' The foolish inference has been drawn by some European writers on Islam that by this verse women found guilty were to be built into a wall, or that they were to be immured till they died without meat and drink. It simply points to the absence in Islam of the system of female segregation such as had only risen later under certain profligate despots and which the people had learned to copy for convenience without the sanction of their religion. For punishment of false witnesses against women, see Surah xxiv. 4, 23-5.

'God makes for them a way,' *i.e.*, if their husbands divorce them in which case they become free.

Repentance:

21. God is only obliged to accept the repentance of those who have done evil ignorantly, and then turn speedily;—these will God turn to; surely God is knowing, gracious.

22. But no repentance is accepted from those who do evil until when death presents itself to one of them, he says, Now verily I repent; nor from those who die in ungodliness;—for these We have prepared a painful punishment.

21. 'Done evil ignorantly,' i.e., without knowing that they did evil.

'Turn speedily,' as soon as the merit of the action is known.

22. In this verse death-bed repentance is said to be ineffectual.

Women: Their Rights:

23. Ye believers, it is not allowed you to be heirs of women against their will, nor hinder them in anything, that so you might take from them part of what ye have given them, unless they are guilty of a plain filthy action; but associate kindly with them; for if ye hate them, it may be ye hate a thing wherein God has placed much good for you.

24. And if ye desire to exchange a wife for another, and have also given the one of them a treasure, take not away anything therefrom. Will ye take it by slandering her, and doing her a flagrant wrong ?

25. And how can ye take it, when the one of you has gone in to the other, and they have received from you a strict bond ?

23. 'Unless they are guilty,' etc.; in which case they lose their dowry.

'But associate . . . . good for you.' This embodies a piece of sound advice to the husbands about to throw away their wives.

24. 'Exchange a wife,' etc., *i.e.*, by divorcing one, and marrying another.

'A treasure,' *i.e.*, ever so large a dower.

'Will ye take it,' etc. One of the most touching passages in the Quran.

'Slandering her,' accusing her of immodesty; which is the only excuse to keep back the settlement already made upon her. See notes on verse 23, above.

Forbidden Marriages:

26. Marry not women whom your fathers have married, except what is already past: for this is a shame, and hateful, and an evil way.

27. Forbidden to you are also your mothers, and your daughters, and your sisters, and your aunts, both on the father and mother's side, and your nieces on the brother and sister's side, and your foster-mothers, and your foster-sisters, and the mothers of your wives, and your step-daughters who are under your tuition, born of your wives to whom ye have gone in — but if ye have not gone in to them, then it is no crime in you to marry them; — and the wives of your sons who proceed out of your loins; and ye shall not marry two sisters — except where it is already past. Surely God is gracious, compassionate.

28. Also married women, except what your right hands have already possessed: this is ordained you from God. Outside this ye are allowed to seek wives by means of your wealth, with modest conduct, and without fornication. And give them for the advantage, ye receive from them their dowry, — this is the law; but it is no crime in you to make agreements over and above the law. Surely God is knowing, wise.

28. 'Except what your right hands,' etc. See notes on verse 3, above.

Slaves May be Married:

29. And whoso among you has not means enough to marry free believing women, then let him marry such of your slave-girls as ye have already got under your hands and such as believe. God well knows your faith. Ye are the one from the other; then marry them with the consent of their people, and give them their dower according to justice— living chastely with them, and not fornicating, and not taking them for concubines.

30. And if after marriage they commit adultery, then for them is a punishment half of that for free women. This is for him among you who is afraid of doing wrong, but if ye abstain, it is better for you. And God is gracious, compassionate.

31. God desires to make this known to you, and to guide you in the way of those who have been before you, and to turn to you in mercy. God is knowing, wise.

32. God desires to turn Himself to you, but they who follow their own lusts, desire that ye go wide astray. God desires to make it light to you, for man was created weak.

29. 'Ye are the one from the other,' *i.e.,* both of you come of the same stock: one of the most charming appeals of the Quran. It aims at levelling the old land-marks in Arabia of the distinction between a free-born Arab and a negro slave.

'Marry them,' etc. Slave-girls might be married lawfully, but there is absolutely no provision for concubinage in Islam.

30. 'For them a punishment,' etc. The reason of this being that they are not presumed to have so good education.

32. 'They who follow their own lusts,' are mentioned in contradistinction to those who are 'afraid of doing wrong' in verse 30, above.

'God desires to make it light to you,' *i.e.,* He only ordains such laws as ye can receive without difficulty.

'Man was created weak;' in law sufficient regard has been done to his weaknesses.

Wealth: Its Use and Abuse:

33. Ye believers, devour not your wealth among yourselves in vanity, unless there is merchandizing among you by your own consent; and kill not yourselves. Truly God is to you compassionate.

34. And whoever does this maliciously and wrongfully, We will surely cast him into the Fire,—and this is easy with God.

35. If ye avoid the deadly sins which are forbidden you, We will blot out your faults, and We will introduce you with an honourable entry.

36. Covet not the gifts by which God has raised some of you above the others: for the men is a portion of what they earn, and for the women also a portion of what they earn; therefore ask of God for His grace. Surely God has knowledge of all things.

37. To every one We have appointed kindred, as heirs of what their parents and kindred leave, and to those with whom your right hands have joined in contract. Give them their portion. Surely God is a witness over all things.

33. 'In vanity,' in foolish display.

'Kill not yourselves,' by committing mortal sins, or such crimes as will destroy yourselves.

35. 'The deadly sins,' such as associating anything with God, murder, calumniating women, wronging orphans, sacrificing principles of life-duty, disobedience to parents; some add to it pride, idleness, gluttony, lust, avarice, envy, wrath. The comentators also hold that there is no end to the number of such sins.

36. 'The gifts,' such as honour, power, riches, and other advantages. Here probably it refers to the distribution of inheritances according to the preceding ordinances, whereby some have a larger share than others.

'What they earn,' *i.e.,* they shall be blessed according to their deserts; and ought therefore instead of displeasing God by envying others, to endeavour to merit His favour by good works, and to apply to Him by prayer and perseverance.

37. 'Those whom your right hands,' etc. By this law an

intimate friend also of the deceased has a share in his estate. It is fixed at a sixth of the whole property.

'In contract, *i.e.,* of friendship.

Of Women:

38. Men are agents of women, in that God has blessed some of them above the others and for that they lay out their substance for them. The virtuous women are devoted, careful in secret, as God has taken care of them. But those, whose Perverseness ye fear, chide them, and then remove them into beds apart, and chastise them; but if they are devoted to you, seek not an occasion against them; for God is high, great.

39. And if ye fear a breach between a man and wife, then appoint a judge from his family, and a judge from her family: if they seek for reconciliation, God will effect a reconciliation between them: God is knowing, wise.

39. 'Appoint a judge,' etc. The matter is to be referred to arbitration for reconciliation as far as possible.

Some Duties:

40. Worship God, and join not anything with Him. Be good to parents, and to kindred, and to orphans, and to the poor, and the neighbour, whether of kin or a stranger, and to your companion, and to the homeless, and those whom your rights have possessed. Surely God loves not the proud, the vain boaster;

40. 'Those whom your right hands,' etc., *i.e.,* the slaves.

The Covetous:

41. Who are niggardly themselves, and bid others be niggards, and hide what God of His bounty has given them; for the ungodly We have

prepared a shameful chastisement;

42. And who spend their wealth to be seen of men, and believe not in God and the Judgment Day. Whoso has the devil for his companion, truly an evil companion he has.

43. But what if they believe in God and the Judgment Day, and give alms of what God has given them ? Surely God knows them.

44. Verily God will not wrong any one of the weight of a mite, and if it is a good action He will double it, and will reward it from His presence with a great reward.

44. 'God will not wrong,' etc., either by diminishing in the reward due to his good actions, or too severely punishing his sins. On the contrary, He will reward the former far above their deserts. See Surah vi. 161.

The Ungodly:

45. Then, how will it be with them when WE shall bring a witness out of each people, and shall bring thee a witness against them? On that Day those who have not believed and have risen against the apostle, shall wish the earth were levelled with them; and they shall not hide anything from God.

45. 'How will it be,' etc. One of the most soul-stirring passages in the Quran.

Prayer:

46. Ye believers, come not to prayer when ye are drunk, until ye understand what ye say, nor when ye are polluted, unless ye are travelling on the road, until ye have washed yourself. But if ye are sick or on a journey, or any of you come from easing nature, or have touched women, and find no water, take fine clean sand and rub your faces and your hands with it; surely God is lenient,

gracious.

51. Verily God will not pardon the giving Him an equal, but will pardon any other sin except that, to whom He pleases. And whoso associates anything with God, surely he has devised a great sin.

46. 'When ye are drink.' The reason here given against drinking is that it affects the understanding as to what a man says when standing up to pray, a thing very essential in prayer, for which reason it is here expressly forbidden.

The Covetous:

56. Do they desire a share in the kingdom who will not bestow on their fellowmen the speck in a date-stone?

60. As to those who have believed, and done good, We will introduce them into Gardens neath which rivers flow, to continue therein for ever; — for them are wives purified; and WE will lead them into perpetual shades.

61. Surely God commands you to restore what ye are trusted with, to the owners; and when ye judge between men to judge with equity; and excellent indeed is to what God exhorts you. And God both bears and sees.

56. 'The speck in a date-stone.' The original word signifies a small dent on the back of a date-stone, and is used to express a thing of no value.

The conduct of the covetous is here remarkably put forth; he will desire for a kingdom himself, but will not brook the least good that may find its way to any one beside himself.

61. This passage was revealed on the day of the Conquest of Mecca. When Mohammed proceeded to the Kaabah, and would have entered it, Osman b, Talbah, the ancient custodian, locked the door. A follower of Mohammed who

was standing close to him snatched the keys out of the old man's hand and would have given them to Abbas, an uncle of Mohammed, who was already the custodian of the well Zamzam; but the Prophet immediately caused them to be returned to the venerable officer, and so won him by his kindness that he not merely threw open the doors but actually embraced Islam.

Believers:

62. Ye believer, obey God, and obey the apostle, and those in authority among you; but if ye differ in anything, refer it to God and the apostle, if ye believe in God and the judgment Day; this is the best, and fairest way of settlement.

63. Hast thou not observed those who profess that they believe in what has been revealed to thee, and what has been revealed before thee; they seek the judgment of Taghut, though commanded not to believe in him; and the devil has seduced them into a wide error.

64. And when it is said to them, Come to what God has revealed, and to the apostle; thou seest the hypocrites turn aside from thee with great aversion.

65. But how will it be when a misfortune shall befall them for what their hands have sent before them? Then will they come to thee, swearing by God, We only intended to promote good and concord.

66. These, — God alone knows what is in their hearts; therefore withdraw from them, and admonish them, and speak into their hearts a word which may tell.

71. Whoever obeys God and the apostle, — they shall be with those to whom God has been gracious, of

the prophets, and the truthful, and the martyrs, and the good; an excellent company these.

63. 'Taghut' was an idol of the tribe of Koreish, at Mecca, whence this word is sometimes used in the Quran to mean anything worshipped beside God.

This passage was occasioned by the following incident; A certain Jaw had a dispute with a wicked Moslem, the latter appealed to the judgment of Kaab b. al-Ashraf, a principal Jew, and the former to Mohammed. But at length they agreed to refer the matter to the Prophet singly, who gave it in favour of the Jew; but the Moslem refused to acquiesce in his sentence, but would needs have it reheard by some one else of the Jews.

65. 'For what their hands,' etc., for what they have done themselves.

71. The blessed include the believers, the prophets, the truthful the martyrs in a good cause, and the good.

Precaution Taken:

73. Ye believers, take your precaution: advance in detachments, or advance in a body.

74. There is of you who would lag behind, and if a reverse befall you, he says, Verily God has been gracious to me that I was not present with them;

75. But if success attend you from God, he will say (as if there never was a friendship between you and him), Would I were with them, for then should I have acquired a great merit.

76. Let them therefore fight in the way of God who part with the life of this world in exchange for the Hereafter; for whoso fights in the way of God, whether he is slain or is victorious, WE will give him a great reward.

73. 'Take your precautions,' *i.e.*, be vigilant, and provide yourselves with arms and necessaries.

74. This is said of the easy-going people, who would hazard no danger for their principles.

75. 'As if there never was,' etc., as if there was no common interest in the cause which you espoused; he attended not to the public, but to his personal interest.

Or, these may taken as the words of the hypocrites among them insinuating that he stayed not behind in war by his own fault but was left by the other Moslems so as not to be able to participate in the glory and good fortune of the victory.

76. 'Who part with the life,' etc., who venture their persons and their wealth in the cause of God.

A Lawful War:

77. And what ails you that ye do not fight in the way of God, and for the weak among men, women, and children, who cry, Our Lord, bring us forth from this city of oppressive people, and grant us from before Thee a defender?

78. Those who believe fight in the way of God. and those who disbelieve fight in the way of Taghut; fight then against the friends of the devil; surely the craft of the devil is weak.

80. . . . If good happen to them, they say. This is from God; but if evil befall them, they say, This is from thee; say thou. All is from God. But what has come over them that they are so far from understanding what is said to them?

81. Whatever good happens to thee, it is from God, and whatever evil befalls thee, it is from thyself. And WE have sent thee to men as an apostle; and God suffices for a witness.

82. Whoso obeys the apostle, obeys God; and whoso turns back, surely WE have not sent thee to be a keeper over them.

83. And they say, Obedience; yet when they go away from thee, part of them brood by night over other than thy words; but God writes down what they

brood over; therefore let them alone, and trust in God; surely God is a sufficient protector.

84. Do not they consider the Quran? If it emanated from any other than God, they would surely have found therein many contradictions.

86. Fight therefore in the way of God, and oblige not any except thyself; and stir up the believers, that God may restrain the violence of the unbelievers; surely God is stronger and more able to punish.

77. The object of the Islamic warfare, as here given, is the defence of the weak man, inoffensive women, and children, from the oppression at Mecca, where they were left behind, being either detained there forcibly by the Koreish or for want of means to fly for refuge at Medinah.

80. 'To them,' to thy followers, the Moslems.

'From thee', addressed to Mohammed; and they forget that there own evil deeds would not go unpunished; or that it was actually the consequence of their own disobedience to the Prophet. This refers in fact to the murmuring of the Moslems at the defeat of Ohad under circumstances given below.

In A.H. 3 the Meccans under Abu-Sufyan attacked the Moslems at Medinah, with 3000 strong, and the battle of Ohad followed. At this moment Mohammed could muster only 700 men. His strict orders to his followers were not to fight but to stand firm and maintain their position, and the archers were to keep to their posts, let the battle go as it might, lest the cavalry should fall upon his rear. For a time fortune seemed to smile upon the Moslems, and the Koreish were retreating, when all of a sudden the Moslem archers forgot the commands of Mohammed and leaving their posts dispersed in search of spoil. The Koreish general at once perceived their folly and rallying the horse fell on the rear of the Moslems. The infantry of the Koreish also turned, and the Moslem troops, taken both in rear and front, had to renew the battle at fearful odds. But they lost the day.

'All is from God,' i.e., the result of your own good or evil deeds.

81. 'From thyself,' i.e. the result of thine own evil deeds.

82. 'We have not sent,' etc. It is not thine to take an account of their actions, for this is God's part; thou canst only preach and admonish.

84. It is here held that there are no contradictions in the Quran.

86. 'Oblige not any,' etc. The prophet only was under an indispensable necessity of obeying God's commands, however difficult, but others might choose, though at their peril. Restraining the 'violence of the unbelievers' is here mentioned as the object of the Islamic warfare.

Good and Evil:

87. He who shall intercede with a good intercession shall have a portion thereof; and he who intercedes with an evil intercession shall have a portion thereof; and God keeps watch over everything.

87. 'A good intercession,' *i.e.*, to maintain the right of man, or prevent his being wronged.

Salutations:

88. When ye are greeted with a greeting, greet ye with a better greeting, or return the same; God takes count of all things.

89. God ! there is no God but ! He will surely gather you together on the Judgement Day, — there is no doubt of it. And who is more true than God in what He says.

88. Whereas the pre-Islamite Arabs wished each other 'Good morning,' 'Good evening,' and so forth, Mohammed, when he had established the brotherhood among believers, taught that their chief salutation to each other ought to be 'Peace to you.'

'A better greeting,' by adding something farther, as 'the mercy of God and His blessing,' in reply to the above salutation. According to Mohammed, "he who rides must be the first to make the salute to him who walks; he who walks to him who is sitting; a small party to a large party, and the young to the old."

Homicide:

94. It is not for a believer to kill a believer, unless by mistake; and whoso kills a believer by mistake is bound to free a believer from slavery, and pay a fine to the family of the slain, unless they remit it as alms.

95. And whoso kills a believer designedly, his reward is Hell, to continue therein for ever; and God will be angry with him, and will curse him, and will prepare for him a great punishment.

96. Ye believers, when ye are on a march in the way of God, use discernment, and say not to him who salutes you, Thou art not a believer, in your greed for the life of this world; surely with God are abundant spoils. Such ye have formerly been; but God has been gracious to you; therefore use discernment; surely God is informed of what ye do.

96. The insatiable desire of the Arabs for plunder often let them to fall upon innocent Moslems under the pretext that they were unbelieving hostile people, and might therefore be warred upon in anticipation of a supposed attack from them.

The Strivers in the Way:

97. Those believers who sit still, not having any hurt, and those who exert themselves in the way of God with their substance and their persons, shall not be held equal. God has blessed those who strive with their wealth and their persons to a degree above those who sit at home. God has promised good to all. But God has blessed those who strive above those who sit still, — a great reward.

98. Degrees from Him, and pardon, and mercy; and God is gracious, merciful.

99. The angels, when they put to death those who have wronged their own souls, say, What were you in? They say, We were weak in the earth. Then will they say, Was not God's earth wide enough that ye might fly therein? — These, their home is Hell; and evil the way there; —

100. Except the weak among men, women, and children, who were not able to find means, and were not guided in the way. These will God forgive; and God is the lenient, gracious.

101. Whoso flies in the way of God, will find many in the earth forced to it, and a plenty; and whoso quits his home for God and His prophet, and death overtakes him, surely God will be obliged to reward him, for God is gracious, merciful.

97. 'Not having any hurt,' i.e., not being disabled from going to war by sickness, or other just impediment.

Easy-going people and those who have to fight the battle of life themselves will not be held equal.

100. These it was the duty of their brother - Moslems to help, and rescue. See verses 76 and 77, above.

Precautions in Prayer:

102. And when ye knock about in the earth, it is no crime in you to shorter your prayers, if ye fear the unbelievers will come upon you, surely the unbelievers are your open enemy.

103. And when thou shalt be amongst them, and shalt pray with them, let a party of them arise to pray with thee; but let them take their arms, and when they have prayed, let them, stand to your rear, and let another party that has not prayed come forward, and let them pray with you; but

let them take their precautions and their arms. The unbelievers would like that ye should neglect your arms and your baggage, that so they might turn upon you at once. It is no crime in you, if ye are inconvenienced by rain or are sick, to lay down your arms. But take your precautions. God has prepared for the unbelievers a painful punishment.

104. And when ye have ended your prayer, make mention of God, standing, and sitting, and reclining; and as soon as ye are secure complete your prayers; surely prayer is to the believers prescribed and timed.

105. Slacken not your efforts to seek out the people, for that ye suffer; and surely they suffer also as ye suffer; but ye hope from God what they cannot. Surely God is knowing, wise.

103. 'Stand to your rear,' so as to defend those who are at prayers, and to face the enemy.

104. 'Standing, and sitting,' etc., *i.e.*, in such way as ye are able.

Straightforwardness:

106. Verily We have revealed the Book to thee with truth, that thou mayest judge between men according to what God guides thee therein. But be not an advocate for the deceitful; rather ask pardon of God; surely God is forgiving, compassionate.

107. Dispute not with Us for those who deceive one another; surely God loves not him who is deceitful, criminal.

108. From men they hide themselves; but they cannot hide themselves from God, for He is with them when they contemplate by night a thing which

pleases Him not, and God comprehends what they do.

109. Ay ! ye are of those who plead for them in the life of this world, but who will plead with God for them on the Judgement Day, and who will be their patron?

110. Yet whoso has done evil, or injured his own soul, and then asks pardon of God, will find, God forgiving, compassionate.

111. And whoso commits a wickedness, commits it against his own soul. And God is knowing, wise.

112. And whoso commits a sin or iniquity, and then lays it on the innocent, shall surely bear the guilt of calumny and a manifest crime.

113. Were it not for the grace and mercy of God to thee, surely a part of them had resolved to mislead thee, but they only mislead themselves, and shall not hurt thee at all. And God has revealed to thee the Book, and wisdom, and has taught thee what thou knewest not. Surely the grace of God has been great towards thee.

114. There is no good in most of what they talk about in private, unless of him who enjoins charity, or what is right, or good-will among men: whoso does this to please God. We will surely give him a great reward.

115. But whoso separates himself from the apostle, after that the way has been made plain to him, and follows any other way than that of the believers. We will make him to obtain to what he is inclined, and east him into Hell, and evil the journey thither.

116. Verily God will not pardon the giving Him an equal, but He will pardon anything beside that to whom He pleases; and whoso associates anything with God is led wide astray.

118. ..... Whoso takes the devil for his patron beside God, he loses terribly.

119. He makes them promises, and stirs them up; but the devil only makes deceitful promises.

122. It will not be as ye will, nor as the people of the Book will; whoso does evil shall be rewarded for it, and shall not find beside God a patron or a help.

123. But whoso does good, whether male or female, and is a believer; these will enter the Garden, and they will not be wronged at all.

124. And who is better in religion than he who strives with his face to God, and does good, and follows the faith of Abraham, the upright man, and God took Abraham for His friend?

125. God's is what is in the heavens and what is in the earth; and surely God encompasses all things.

106. This and the succeeding verses were occasioned by the following remarkable incident. Toma, of the sons of Zafar, one of Mohammed's companions, stole a coat of mail from his neighbour, Kitadah, in a bag of meal, and hid it at a Jews' named Zeid; Toma being suspected, the coat of mail was demanded of him, but he denied he knew anything of it. They then followed the track of the meal, which had run out through a hole in the bag, to the Jew's, and there seized it, accusing him of the theft; but the Jew produced witnesses of his own religion that he had it of Toma. The sons of Zafar then came to Mohammed, and urging the innocence of Toma, desired him to defend the companion's reputation and condemn the Jew. But Mohammed at once saw into the facts of the case, and

condemned Toma; whereupon the sons of Zafar departed from him and relapsed into idolatry.

108. 'They contemplate by night,' etc., they secretly contrived (so it appears) means by false evidence or otherwise, to lay their crimes on the innocent Jew.

114. To enjoin charity, what is right, and good-will among men, are the greatest of virtues in the sight of God.

122. God's judgment will surely come to pass in spite of men's desires to the contrary.

'A patron,' etc. see Surah ii. 45, 117, etc.

About Women:

126. They ask thee concerning women; say thou, God instructs you concerning them, and that which is read to you in the Book concerning female orphans, to whom ye give not what is ordained them, neither ye marry them; and concerning infants, and that ye deal equitably towards orphans; and what ye do of good, surely God knows it.

127. If a wife fear ill-usage of aversion on the part of her husband, it is no crime in them both, if they should be reconciled to each other; surely reconciliation is the best. Human beings are inclined to vice; but if ye behave with kindness and fear God, — surely God is informed of what ye do.

128. And surely it is not in your power to act equitably towards women, although ye fain would do it; yet turn not with all aversion, nor leave her like one in suspense; and if ye are reconciled, and fear God, then surely God is gracious, compassionate.

129. And if they separate, God will satisfy them both of His abundance. Verily God is omnipresent, wise.

130. And whatever is in the heavens and the earth is God's. We have already enjoined those to whom the Book was given before you, and yourselves, to fear God. And if ye disbelieve, surely God's is what is in the heavens and the earth; and God is independent, praised.

131. And God's is what is in the heavens and what is in the earth, and God is a protector sufficient.

132. If He please, He can take you away, ye people, and bring others; and God has power to do it.

133. Whoso desires the reward of this world; verily with God is the reward of this world and the Hereafter; and God both hears and sees.

126. 'Concerning women,' etc., *i.e.*, as to the share they are to have in the distribution of the inheritances of their deceased relations; for it seems that the Arabs were not satisfied with Mohammed's decision on this point, against the old customs.

'God instructs you,' etc., *i.e.*, He has already, made known His will to you, by revealing the passages concerning the inheritances in the beginning of this chapter.

'Neither ye marry', etc.; or, the words may be rendered in the affirmative,' and whom ye would marry.' For the pre-Islamite Arabs used to wrong their female orphans in both instances; obliging them to marry against their inclinations, if they were beautiful or rich; or else not suffering them to marry at all, that they might keep what belonged to them.

'Concerning infants,' *i.e.*, male children of tender years, to whom the Arabs used to allow no share in the distribution of their parents' estates.

128. The proviso in verse 3, above, is here said to be impracticable; hence the argument of some doctors that polygamy is not countenanced by Islam.

Take moreover the saying of Mohammed: "Whoso has more than one wife at a time, and does not love them all equally, or otherwise carry himself equally between them, shall appear before God with half his body fallen off."

What does this point to, if not the severe importance of the justice and equity in the proviso?

'Yet turn not,' etc. To legalise the *existing* polygamy of his day, Mohammed advised his followers, that in their present cases though they could not use all their wives with equal love as required in the proviso, they ought to observe some measure of justice towards them; for if a man had already married before the operation of the law he might still act equitably so far as may be. This was a mere formal measure to defeat the evils of polygamy at this stage.

'In suspense,' *i.e.*, like one that neither has a husband, nor is divorced, and at liberty to marry elsewhere.

Justice:

134. Ye believers, stand fast to justice when ye bear witness before God, although it is against yourself, or your parents, or your kindred, whether the party is rich or poor; truly God is more worthy than them both. Therefore follow not your lust, lest ye swerve. And whether ye wrest your evidence or decline giving it, surely God is informed of what ye do.

135. Ye believers, believe in God, and His apostle, and the Book which He has revealed to His apostles, and the Book which He revealed heretofore; and whoso believes not in God, and His angels, and His Books, and His apostles, and the Hereafter, has surely gone wide astray.

136. Verily they who believed, and afterwards disbelieved, and then believed again, and after that disbelieved, and increased in unbelief. God will never pardon them or guide them into the way.

137. Announce to the hypocrites that for them is a painful punishment.

138. Those who take the unbelievers for patrons beside the believers, do they desire honour with them? But all honour is with God.

139. And He has already revealed to you in the Book. When ye shall hear the signs of God, they shall not be believed, but shall be mocked at. Therefore sit not with them unless they engage in other discourses; or ye will become like them. Surely God will gather the hypocrites and the unbelievers altogether in Hell.

The Hypocrites:

141. Verily the hypocrites seek to deceive God, but He will deceive them; when they stand up to pray, they stand carelessly, to be seen of men, and they remember God but little.

142. Wavering between the one and the other, and belonging to neither of them; and for him whom God shall lead astray, thou can find no way.

143. Ye believers, take not the unbelievers for your patrons beside the believers. Will ye furnish God with an evident argument against you?

144. Verily the hypocrites shall be in the lowest abyss of the Fire, and thou shalt not find any to help them;

145. Except those who repent and amend, and hold fast to God, and show their sincerity in religion to God alone; these shall be with the believers; and surely God will give the believers a great reward.

146. And how will God punish you if ye are grateful and believe? Surely God is grateful, knowing.

143. This is explained in Surah lx. 8, 9.

Evil-Speaking:

147. God likes not that evil be matter of public talk, unless any one has been wronged. And God both hears and knows.

148. Whether ye publish what is good, or hide it, or forgive evil, verily God is gracious, mighty.

149. And those who believe not in God and His apostle, and seek to separate God from His apostles, and say, We believe in some, and reject others; and seek to take a middle way, —

150. These surely are unbelievers, and We have prepared for the unbelievers a shameful punishment.

151. And they who believe in God and His apostles, and make no distinction between any of them: these will God give their reward; and God is gracious, merciful.

Miracles Demanded:

152. The people of the Book will demand of thee, that thou shouldst bring down to them a Book from heaven: they formerly asked of Moses a yet greater thing than this, for they said, Show us God visibly; wherefore a fire-storm from heaven caught them up, because of their iniquity.

155. And for their unbelief, and for that they spoke against Mary a grievous calumny, —

156. And for that they said, Verily we have slain Christ Jesus, son of Mary, the apostle of God, though they slew him not, neither crucified him, but they had only his likeness. And they who differed about him, were in doubt as to this, and had no knowledge thereof, but followed an

opinion merely; they did not really kill him, but God took him up to Himself. And God is mighty, wise.

155. 'A grievous calumny; ' the Jews charged Mary of immodesty.

156. 'They slew him not.' There were in the early ages of Christianity several sects of Christians who denied the crucifixion of Jesus, and Mohammed also shared their views. He refused to believe that a pious prophet, that Jesus undoubtedly was, should have suffered this humiliation at the hands of an unbelieving people.

'His likeness.' The Basilidians believed that it was one Simon of Cyrene from among the Jews, who bore great resemblance to Jesus, and whom one dark day they crucified, little knowing what they did. Thus in the wisdom of God the guilty suffered and the innocent escaped.

'God took him up,' etc. Jesus died a natural death afterwards. See also Surah xix. 34.

Some Prophets:

161. Verily We have revealed to thee, as We revealed to Noah and the prophets after him, and as We revealed to Abraham, and Ishmael, and Isaac, and Jacob, and the tribes, and Jesus, and Job, and Jonas, and Aaron, and Solomon; and to David We gave the Psalms.

162. Of some apostles We have told thee before, and of the others. We have not told thee. — And God spoke to Moses discoursing with him.

163. Apostles charged to announce and to warn, that men after that these apostles had come might have no argument against God. Surely God is mighty, wise.

162. 'Of some apostles.' Prophets have been coming in every age (xiii. 38), to all the peoples (x. 48), to teach in their own tongues (xiv. 4), the same Divine message of wisdom

and of truth (ii. 146). Names of only a few, of whom they had heard, are mentioned here and elsewhere in the Quran; but there have been others whose names have not been mentioned at all. See Surah ii. 3; also Surah xl. 78.

The Ungodly:

165. Verily they who believe not, and keep away others from the way of God have been led wide astray.

166. Verily those who believes not, and act wrongfully, God will never pardon, and never will He guide them into the way.

167. Except that to Hell wherein they shall continue for ever. And this is easy with God.

The Apostle:

168. Ye people, now has come to you an apostle with truth from your Lord; believe then, it is better for you. But if ye believe not, surely God's in what is in the heavens and the earth. And God is knowing, wise.

About Christ:

169. Ye people of the Book, he not extravagant in your religion, neither say of God beside the truth. Verily Christ Jesus the son of Mary is an apostle of God, and His word which. He conveyed into Mary, and a spirit from Him. Believe then in God, and His apostles, and say not. Three, Have done! It is better for you. God is only one God. Praise to Him above that He should have a son! His is whatever is in the heavens and the earth. And God is a sufficient guardian.

170. Christ does not disdain to be a servant to God, nor the angels who approach near to Him:

171. And whoso disdains His service, and is elated with pride. He will gather them all of Himself.

172. And to those who believe and do good. He will give them their reward, and will add to them of His grace: but those who are disdainful and proud. He will punish with a grievous punishment.

173. And none shall they find to protect or to help them against God.

174. Ye people, now has come to you an evidence from your Lord, — and We have revealed to you a clear light. And those who believe in God and hold fast to Him. He will lead them into mercy from Him, and His grace, and He will guide them on the straight path to Himself.

169. 'Extravagant in your religion,' by worshipping your own teachers and reviling the others. Some Christians who accepted the divinity of their Teacher, yet regarded 'all that ever came before' him as thieves and robbers, Cf. St. John x. 8.

'Three,' *i.e.*, the Trinity, in any shape, either of Father, Son, and the Holy Ghost; or of God, Jesus, and Mary.

About Sundry Things:

175. They will consult thee. Say thou, God gives you instructions concerning the distant kindred. If a man die childless, and he gave a sister, half of what he shall leave will be hers, and if she die childless, he shall be her heir. And if there are two sisters, two third parts of what he shall leave shall be theirs; and if there are both brothers and sisters, the male shall have the portion of two females. God declares these to you that ye err not. And God knows all things.

175. 'The distant kindred.' see the beginning of this Surah.

'Half of what,' etc., the other half going into the Public Treasury.

'Her heir,' *i.e.*, her whole substance will go to him.

Principal Contents

Adultery, charge of, to be proved, 19; its punishment, 20; of slave girls, 30.

Apostles, their mission, 162: all to be respected, 149-51; names of some, 161, 162.

Arbitration between man and wife, 39.

Believers, half-hearted, 74, 75, 80, 81, 83; the true, 76, 97.

Charity, not to be seen of men, 42.

Concubinage disallowed, 29.

Covetousness reproved, 36, 56.

Deceitful, the, 107-9, 111, 112.

Dowry, to be given to a wife, 3; not to be withheld, 24, 35.

Duties, social, 40.

Evil-speaking forbidden, 147.

God, creator of man and women, 1; all good from, 81; assigning partners with, the darkest sin, 51, 116.

Good, men, 87, 194; discourse, 114.

Heirs, 37.

Homicide, 94.

Hypocrites, 141, 142; charged, 96; their punishment, 137, 144.

Inheritance, some laws of 12-5, 175.

Jesus, an apostle of God, 169; his humility, 170; not crucified, 156; but died a natural death, *ib*.

Judgement of God not according to individual desires, 122.

Justice, to be observed always, 61: in witnessing, 134.

Quran, the, free from contradictions, 85; a straightforward rule of justice, 106.

March, precautions on a, 73.

Men, and women, their common origin, 1: incapable of doing justice between women, 128.

Miracles demanded, 152, 155.

Miser, the, 41, 56.

Orphans, to be justly treated, 2, 4-6, 9; to be trained, 5; fear of God enjoined with regard to them, 10, 11.

Prayer, precautions in, 46, 103; might be shortened on a march, 102.

Precautions against unbelievers, 103.

Prohibited degrees of marriage, 26-8.

Questions to be referred to God and the prophet, 62.

Reconciliation, between a man and wife recommended, 127.

Religion, flying for, enjoined, 99, 101; entravagance in, reproved, 169.

Repentance, acceptable, 21, 110, 145; ineffectual, 22.

Reward of good works, in excess, 44.

Salutation to be returned, 88.

Sins, mortal, 33-5.

Slave-girls, might be married, 29; concubinage forbidden, *ib*.

Suicide, 33, 34.

Trinity, the, 169.

Trusts to be restored, 61.

Ungodly, the, 45.

War enjoined, 77, 86.

Wealth, its use and abuse, 33.

Witnesses, when restoring to orphans their property, 7.

Wives, limit their number, 3; not to be disregarded, 23.

Women, to be respected, 1; their rights, 8, 23, 36; the virtuous, 38; their rewards in the Hereafter, 123; sundry laws, 126.

SURAH V. — THE TABLE

(*Medinah.*)

This is generally allowed to be the last Surah promulgated at Medinah. The title is taken from an account of the Eucharist given towards the end of the Surah.

Pilgrimage:

1. Ye believers, perform your engagements.

Allowed to you are the brute cattle other than

what are mentioned to you, — except game which is not allowed you white ye are on pilgrimage. Verily God ordains what He pleases.

2. Ye believers, violate not the rites of God, nor the sacred month, nor the offering, nor the ornaments hung thereon, nor those who are travelling to the Sacred Mosque seeking favour from their Lord and to please Him.

3. But when all is over, then take to the chase; end let not the malice of some, in that they kept you from the Sacred Mosque lead you to transgress; rather assist one another in justice and piety, but assist not one another in injustice and malice; and fear God. Surely God is severe in punishing.

1. 'Mentioned to you.' See Surah ii. 167, 168.

2. Violating the sanctity of the pilgrimage and the pilgrims during their journey, is here mentioned. In pre-Islamic times as now-a-days, the pilgrims suffered much at the hands of the marauding tribes, which is here condemned as impious.

3. 'Kept you from,' etc. In the expedition of Hodeibiyah when after six years of exile from the place of their birth Mohammed and his followers had set out for Mecca with 1400 men, all perfectly unarmed, on a pilgrimage thither, the Koreish had jealously barred the way by posting their troops under Khalid son of Walid. They would not allow the Moslems to visit Mecca, and maltreated the envoy who was sent to ask their permission to enter the city. Some even attacked the prophet with darts and arrows, and when a party of 80 men were arrested Mohammed instantly released them on merely making promises of future good conduct towards himself and his followers. Finding however that the Meccans were inexorable Mohammed contented himself with exacting a Truce from them for 10 years during which all hostilities between the Meccans and the Moslems were to cease, and the Moslems were allowed to visit Mecca in the following year and remain there for three days with their travelling arms, namely, their swords in sheaths.

Forbidden Food:

4. Ye are forbidden to eat of what is dead of itself and blood, and swine's flesh, and that on which any other name beside God's has been invocated, and that which has been strangled, or killed by a blow, or by a fall, or by goring, and that which has been eaten by a wild beast, unless ye kill yourselves, and that which has been sacrificed to idols; and also to make division by arrows is wickedness in you.

   On this day, woe to those who have disbelieved in your religion. And fear them not, but fear Me.

5. This day have I perfected for you your religion and have completed My mercy upon you, and I have been pleased to make Islam your religion.

   — But whoso is driven by hunger not lusting to transgress, surely to him God is gracious, compassionate.

6. They will ask thee what is allowed them; say thou, Such things as are good are allowed you, and the prey of beasts of chase which ye have trained like dogs, teaching them as Gold has taught you. Eat therefore, of what they catch for you, and mention the name of God thereon; and fear God; surely God is swift at reckoning up.

4. See also Surah ii, 167, 168.

   'Sacrificed to idols', *lit.*,' on blocks or shafts of stones, being those set up near their houses, and on which they slew animals in honour of their gods.

   'Division by arrows,' a sort of divination in use among the pre-Islamite Arabs.

6. 'Mention the name,' etc. In pre-Islamic times the Arabs in killing any animal for food, used to consecrate it to their idols, by saying. In the name of Allat and Al-Uzza.

Other Laws:

7. This day ye are allowed the good things, and the food of those who have received the Book is allowed you as your food is allowed them. And free believing women and free women of those who have received the Book before you, when ye have assigned them their dower, living chastely with them, and not fornicating, neither taking them for concubines. And whoso disbelieves in the faith, his works are vain, and in the Hereafter he will be of those who lose.

7. 'The food of those,' etc. Moslems might have no objection in treating with one 'who has received the scripture,' *e.g.*, the Jews, Christians, and others.

'And free women,' etc. They might also intermarry with 'the people of the Book.'

'And not taking them,' etc. Concubinage is no part of Islam.

Ablutions:

8. Ye believers, when ye prepare yourselves to pray, wash your faces, and your hands; upto the elbows, and rub your heads, and your feet to the ankles.

9. And if ye are unclean, wash yourselves. But if ye are sick, or on it journey, and if one of you has come from easing nature, or have touched women, and ye find no water, then take clean sand, and rub your faces and your hands with it. God desires not to lay a burden upon you, but He desires to purify you and to fulfil His favour upon you, that ye may be grateful.

10. And remember the favour of God upon you, and His Covenant which He has made with you, when ye said, We have heard, and will obey; and fear

God; surely God knows the secrets of the breasts of men.

8. These are necessary preparations for prayer. That his followers might be more punctual in this duty, Mohammed is said to have declared that 'the practice of religion is founded on cleanliness,' which is 'one-half of the faith,' and 'the key of prayer,' without which it will not be heard of God. At the same time he especially inculcated that mere external, or rather physical, purity does not imply true devotion.

9. 'God desires not,' etc. The ablutions have not been imposed as burdens, nor as having any mysterious merit, but merely as a measure of cleanliness.

Justice:

11. Ye believers, stand up before God as witnesses in justice, and let not hatred towards any induce you to do wrong; but act justly, — this is next to piety. And fear God, surely God is informed of what ye do.

12. God has promised to those who believe and do good, that for them is pardon, and a great reward.

13. And those who disbelieve and deny our signs, — these are the fellows of Hell.

14. Ye believers, remember God's favour towards you when certain men designed to stretch forth their hands against you, but He restrained their hands from you. And fear God, and in God let the believers trust.

14. 'Certain men designed,' etc. This was on various occasions.

At one time the Prophet in company with some of his followers went to the tribe of Koreizah (who were Jews) to levy a fine for the murder of two Moslems, who had been killed by mistake by one Amru. They desired him and his followers to sit down and eat with them, and they would pay the fine; Mohammed complying with their request, as he was sitting, they laid a design against his life, on Jew of them undertaking to throw a millstone upon him. But Mohammed abruptly left the place and departed with this followers.

On another occasion while yet in the citadel of Kheibar frequent attempts were made to assassinate the Prophet. On his entry therein a Jewess by name Zeinab, a neice of the gigantic warrior who fell at the battle that took place there, spread a poisoned repast for Mohammed and his followers. One of them died immediately after he had taken a few mouthfuls, but Mohammed and his other followers were saved.

People of the Book:

15. And God accepted the Covenant of the children of Israel, — and out of them We raised up twelve leaders, and God said, Verily I will be with you, if ye are stead-fast in prayer and give alms, and believe in My apostles, and help them, and lend God a liberal loan: I will surely put away from you your evil deeds, and I will bring you into Gardens, 'neath which rivers flow; but whoso of you disbelieves after this, has surely erred from the way.

16. Wherefore because they have broken their Covenant, We have cursed them, and have hardened their hearts: they dislocate the words from their places, and have forgotten part of what they were taught; and thou will not cease to discover deceitful practices among them, except a few of them; but forgive them and let them be; verily God loves the doers of good.

17. And of those who say, We are Christians, We have accepted the Covenant; but they have forgotten a part of what they were taught; wherefore We stirred up enmity and hatred among them, till the Judgment Day; and in the end will God tell

them what they have done.

18. Ye people of the Book, now is Our apostle come to you to clear up to you much that ye hid of the Book, and to pass over many things. Now has come to you from God a light and a clear Book, by which God guides those who follow His pleasure into the way of peace, and will bring them out of darkness into light by His will and He will guide them in the straight path.

19. Verily they have been infidels who say, Verily God is Christ the son of Mary. Say thou, And who could obtain anything from God if He pleased to destroy Christ the son of Mary, and his mother, and all who are in the earth?

20. Surely God's is the sovranty of the heavens and the earth, and what is between them. He creates what He will; and surely God is mighty over all things.

21. The Jews and the Christians say, Sons are we of God, and His beloved; say thou, Why then does He chastise you for your sins? Nay, ye are but men whom He has created. He pardons whom He pleases, and He punishes whom He pleases; and God's is the sovranty of the heavens and the earth, and what is between them, and to Him is the return.

22. Ye people of the Book, now has come to you Our apostle to clear up to you the cessation of the apostles, lest ye say. There came to us none with a promise or a warning. But now is come to you an apostle with glad tidings and with warning; and God is mighty over all things.

35. .... We have ordained to the children of Israel,

that whoso kills a being, unless it is for another being, or for wickedness in the earth, it is as though as had killed all mankind, and whose saves one, it is as though he saved the lives of all mankind.

15. 'Lend God,' etc., *i.e.*, contribute in the way of God, for which you will be rewarded by Him.

16. 'Have forgotten part,' etc. They have made a mistake in not accepting the teaching of the other and succeeding prophets to whom obedience was due by law.

17. 'They have forgotten,' etc., *i.e.*, they fell into the mistake of receiving Jesus as their Lord and God, which was not taught them by their Master.

21. This refers to the proud superiority they assert over the other people. The Jews called all besides them 'gentiles,' and the Christians called the others 'heathens.' The good old learned doctors of Islam would not suffer the others, whatever their beliefs, to be called 'Kafirs,' unbelievers, though their degenerate followers are in this respect no better than the Jews and Christians whom the Quran expressly condemns for their over-bearing attitude towards the others. See also surah iii. 69-72.

22. 'The cessation,' etc. The Arabic word signifies the intermediate space of time between two prophets, during which no revelation or dispensation was given. In the family of Ishmael Mohammed was the first prophet since the originator of this line.

35. 'Had killed all,' etc., *i.e.*, having broken the commandment which forbids the shedding of blood.

The Believers:

39. Ye believers, fear God, and desire to draw near to Him, and strive in the way of God, that ye may be happy.

40. As to those who disbelieve, if they had whatever is in the earth, and as much more withal, that they might redeem themselves from punishment on the Judgment Day, it shall not be accepted from them; and for them is a painful punishment.

41. Fain would they come forth from the Fire; but forth from it they shall not come; theirs is a lasting punishment.

45. O Apostle, let not those grieve thee who hasten to unbelief, of those who say, We believe, with their mouths, but their hearts believe not, or of the Jews — listeners to a lie, and to others, but who will not come to thee .....

46. .... But if they come to thee, then either judge between them or let them alone; and if thou leave them, they shall not hurt thee at all. But if thou judge between them, judge with equity. Verily God loves those who deal equitably.

Other Books:

47. But why should they make thee their judge, since they have the Law: in that is the judgment of God. But they turn their backs after this; and these are not believers.

48. Verily we have revealed the Law: in it is a guidance and a light; by it the prophets who excelled in piety did judge those who were Jews, and the doctors, and priests also by the Book of God, of which they were the keepers and the witnesses. Therefore fear not men, but fear me. . . .

50. And in their footsteps We made Jesus the son of Mary follow, confirming the Law which was before him; and We gave him the Evangel; in it is a guide and a light, confirming the Law which was before it, and a guide and rule to the pious.

51. That the people of the Evangel may judge according to what God has revealed therein; and

whoso judges not by what God has revealed, they are the wicked.

52. And to thee We have revealed the Book in truth, confirming the Book which was before it and restoring the same. Judge therefore between them according to what God has revealed, and follow not their desires after the truth that has come to thee.

53. To every one of you have We given a rule and an open way: and if God pleased, He would have made you one people, — but He would try you in what He has given you. Strive then to excel each other in good works: to God in your return altogether, and then He will tell you that concerning which ye now disagree.

54. Wherefore judge between them according to what God has revealed, and follow not their lusts, but beware of them, lest they lead thee astray from part of what God has revealed to thee; but if they turn back, know that God is pleased to punish them for some of their sins; and surely most of the people are transgressors.

55. Do they desire the judgment of Ignorance ? But who is a better judge than God, to people who believe ?

Apostacy:

59. Ye believers, should any of you apostatize from his religion, God will surely raise up another people to take his place, whom He will love, and who will love Him, lowly towards the believers, severe to the ungodly, striving in the way of God, and not fearing the obloquy of the detractor. This is the grace of God; He gives it to whom He pleases, And God is omnipresent, omniscience.

To Believers:

60. Verily your patron is God, and His apostle, and those who believe, and are steadfast in prayer, and give alms, and who bow in worship.

61. And whose takes God and His apostle, and those who believe, for friends — they truly are the people of God, and these are the victorious.

62. Ye believers, take not such as scoff and jest at your religion, of those to whom the Book has been given before you and the unbelievers, for your friends; and fear God, if ye are believers;

63. And who, when ye call to prayer, make a laughing-stock and a jest of it; this, because they are a people who have no sense.

People of the Book:

64. Say thou, Ye people of the Book, do ye dispute with us merely because we believe in God, and what is revealed to us and what was revealed heretofore, and because most of you are wrong-doers ?

67. Thou shall see many of them hastening to iniquity and malice, and to eat things forbidden; and woe to them for what they have done.

68. Were it not for their doctors and teachers forbidding their uttering wickedness, and their eating things forbidden, bad indeed would have been their doings.

69. And the Jews said, The hand of hand is tied up; their own hand shall be tied up, and for what they have said shall they be cursed. Nay, His hands are both stretched out: He spends at His pleasure . . . . .

70. But if the people of the Book believe and fear God, We will surely put away their sins from them, and will bring them into Gardens of delight; and if they observe the Law and the Evangel, and what has been revealed to them from their Lord, they shall surely have their fill of good things, from above them and from under their feet. There are of them a people upright; but most of them — how they do evil !

71. O Apostle, proclaim what has been revealed to thee from they Lord; and if thou do it not, thou hast not proclaimed His message at all. And God will defend thee against men; surely God guides not an unbelieving people.

72. Say thou, Ye people of the Book, ye have no ground to stand upon, until ye observe the Law and the Evangel, and what is revealed to you from your Lord . . . .

73. Verily those who believe, and those who are Jews, or Sabians, or Christians — whoso believes in God and the Hereafter, and does good — no fear shall come upon them, neither shall they grieve.

76. They are surely infidels who say, Verily God is Christ the son of Mary; for Christ said, Ye children of Israel, worship God, my Lord and your Lord. Verily whoso joins anything with God, God will forbid him the Garden, and his home is the Fire, and the transgressors shall have no helpers.

69. 'The hand of God,' etc., *i.e.,* He is become niggardly and close-fisted. These are reported to be the words of Phineas ibn Azura when the Jews were much impoverished by a dearth, and the other Jews who heard him, instead of reproving him, expressed their approbation of what he had said.

73. See also Surah ii, 59.

The Trinity:

77. They are surely infidels who say, God is the third of the Three; for there is no God but the one God; and if they refrain not from what they say, a painful punishment shall surely come upon such of them as are infidels.

78. Will they not yet be turned to God and ask pardon of Him ? And God is gracious, compassionate.

Jesus Christ:

79. Christ the son of Mary is only an apostle: apostles have also preceded him, and his mother was a truthful woman: they both ate food. Behold, how We declare to them the signs, and then behold, how they turn aside !

80. Will ye worship beside God what can neither hurt nor profit ? But God both hears and knows.

81. Ye people of the Book, be not extravagant in your religion beside the truth; neither follow the lusts of the people who have heretofore erred, and who have led many astray, and have themselves erred from the way.

79. 'A truthful woman,' i.e., she could never have pretended to partake of the divine nature, or to have been the mother of God, as she was sometimes called by the Christians.

'They both ate food,' i.e., were obliged to support their lives by the same means, and were subject to the same necessities and infirmities as the rest of mankind; and therefore, were no gods.

The Jews and Christians:

85. Of all men thou wilt find the Jews, and those who join others with God, to be the most violent in enmity against the believers; and thou wilt

surely find those most inclined to friendship with the believers, who say, We are Christians This, because there are priests and monks among them, and they are free from pride.

86. And when they hear what has been revealed to the apostle, thou seest their eyes overflow with tears at the truth they find therein, saying, Our Lord, We believe, write us down with those who bear witness.

87. And why should we not believe in God, and in the truth which has come down to us, and earnestly desire that our Lord would gather us with the righteous people ?

88. Therefore, has God rewarded them for what they said, with Gardens' neath which rivers flow, to continue therein for ever; and this is the reward of the doers of good. But they who disbelieve and deny Our signs, — these are the fellows of Hell.

God's Gifts:

89. Ye believers, forbid not the good things which God has allowed you, but transgress not; verily God loves not the transgressors.

90. And eat of what God has given you for food, things lawful and good; and fear God in whom ye believe.

89. These words refer to certain of Mohammed's companions who agreed to oblige themselves to continual fasting and watching, and to abstain from women, eating flesh, sleeping on beds, and other innocent enjoyments of life, in imitation of certain ascetic Christians; but this the Prophet disapproved, saying that he would have no monks in his religion. Regarding the Islamic view of a monastic life, see Surah lvii. 27.

Inconsiderate Oaths:

91. God will not punish you for a mistaken word in your oaths; but He will punish you for what ye solemnly swear. And the expiation of such an one is to feed the poor men with such moderate food as ye feed your families with, or to clothe them, or to free a captive. But he who has not the means shall fast three days. This is the expiation of your oaths when ye have sworn. Therefore keep your oaths. . . . .

91. See also Surah ii. 225.

Some Evil Practices:

92. Ye believers, surely wine and games and images, and divination, are an abomination of the work of the devil: therefore, avoid them, that ye may prosper.

93. The devil only seeks to sow discord and hatred among you by wine and games, and to keep you from the remembrance of God, and from prayer. Will ye not then abstain from them?

94. Obey God, and obey the Apostle, and take heed to yourselves, but if ye turn back, know that Our apostle is only bound to preach publicly.

95. It is no sin in those who believe and do good, to have tasted anything, in case they fear to do evil, and believe, and do good, and fear to do evil, and believe, and fear to do evil, and do good: surely God loves those who do good.

96. Ye believers, Kill no game while ye are on pilgrimage . . . . .

97. It is allowed you to fish in the sea and to eat, as a provision for you and for those who are on a journey; but it is unlawful for you to hunt by

land, while ye are still on pilgrimage. And fear God, before whom ye shall be gathered.

99. The apostle is only bound to preach; and God knows what ye show and what ye hide.

100. Say thou, Evil and good are not equal, though the abundance of evil pleases thee. Therefore, fear God, ye men who have hearts, that ye may be happy.

101. Ye believers, ask not of things which if they were told might only give you pain; but if ye ask concerning them when the Quran was revealed they will be told you. Yet God pardons you these; for God is gracious, mild . . . . .

102. God has not ordained anything concerning Bahirah, or Saibah, or Wasilah, or Hami; but those who disbelieved invented a lie against God, and most of them had no sense at all.

103. And when it is said to them, Come to what God has revealed, and to the apostle; they say, Sufficient for us is what we found our fathers at. What ! and though their fathers had no sense at all or guidance ?

102. 'Bahirah,' etc. These were the names given by the pre-Islamite Arabs to certain camels or sheep which were turned loose to feed, and exempted from common services, in some particular cases, having their ears slit, or with some other mark, that they might be known; and this they did in honour of their gods. Which superstitions are here declared to be no part of God's commandment, but the inventions of foolish men.

103. See also Surah ii. 165.

Believers:

104. Ye believers, take care of your souls: he who errs shall not hurt you while ye are guided: to God is

your return, then He will tell you what ye have done.

105. Ye believers, let there be witnesses between you, when death approaches one of you, at the time of the making the testament: two witnesses — just men from among you, or two others of a different tribe from yourselves — if ye are on a journey and the accident of death overtakes you . . . . .

Appearance of Jesus Before God:

116. And when God shall say, O Jesus, son of Mary, Didst thou say to men, Take me and my mother for two Gods beside God ? He shall say, Praise to Thee ! it is not for me to say what I ought not; if I had said so to them, Thou wouldst surely have known it: Thou knowest what is in me, but I know not what is in Thee; verily Thou art the knower of secrets.

117. I spoke not to them but what Thou didst did me — Worship God, my Lord and your Lord; and I was a witness of their actions so long as I stayed amongst them, but since Thou hast taken me to Thy-self, Thou hast been the watcher over them; and Thou art witness of all things.

118. If Thou punish them, they are surely Thy servants, but if Thou forgive them, Thou art the mighty, the wise.

119. God will say, This day will their truth be of advantage to the truthful, — for them are Gardens 'neath which rivers flow, to continue therein for ever: And God will be well-pleased with them, and they will be well-pleased in Him. That is the great bliss.

120. God's is the sovranty of the heavens and the earth and what is in them, and He is mighty over all things.

Principal Contents

Ablutions, before prayer, 8, 9.

Apostacy, 59.

Atonement, disallowed, 40.

Engagements, to be performed, 1.

Food, lawful, 1; unlawful, 4.

Forbidden, food, 4; things, 92, 93.

Game forbidden on pilgrimage, 96, 97.

Good, and evil, not alike, 100; things, not to be forbidden, 89.

Jesus Christ, not God, 19, 76, 77; and apostle, 79; His appearance before God, 116-8.

Justice in witnessing, 11.

Law to various peoples, 48, 50-4,, 73.

Message, to be proclaimed, 71.

Murder, its moral effects, 35.

Oaths, inadvertent, 91.

People of the Book, food and intermarriage allowed, 7; their corruption, 16-8, 64, 67-9, 72, 85.

Practices, some old, 102. 103.

Religion, extravagance in, forbidden, 81.

Reward of believers, 12.

Wine forbidden, 92.

Witnesses to be taken over a testament, 105.

SURAH VI — CATTLE

(Mecca)

This Surah derives its title from certain superstitious practices o the pre-Islamite Arabs as to cattle which are herein incidentally mentioned.

God:

1. Praise to God, who has created the heavens and the earth, and ordained the darkness and the light, Yet to their Lord the unbelievers give equals !

2. He it is who created you of clay, then decreed your term, and with Him is another prescribed term. Yet to ye doubt !

3. And He is god in the heavens and the earth; He knows what ye keep secret and what ye publish, and He knows what ye earn.

4. Never has a single evidence, of the evidences their Lord, come to them, but they turned away from it;

5. And now they have called the truth a lie when it has come to them; but in the end a message shall come to them as to what they have mocked.

6. Do they not see how many generations We have destroyed before them ? We had settled them in the earth such as We have not settled you, and We sent down the very heavens upon them in copious rains, and We made the rivers to flow under them: yet We destroyed them in their sins, and raised up other generations after them.

1. 'Ordained,' etc. Some people, like the Magians, believed that the day was made by God, whereas night was a mere creation of the devil; which is here controverted.

2. 'Then decreed,' etc. *i.e.* the term of this life.

   'Another prescribed term,' *i.e.,* life after death from this world.

3. 'Earn,' or, acquire, of good or evil; your deserts.

5. 'A message,' etc. *i.e.,* they shall be convinced of the truth which they have made a jest of, when it is too late for them to amend.

6. 'Destroyed,' etc. *i.e.,* in ungodliness. See below; also Surah vii. 82, 84, 100 etc.

Miracles Demanded:

7. And if We had sent down to thee a book on paper and they had touched it with their hands, still those who disbelieve would say, That's naught but plain magic.

8. They also say, Unless and angel is sent down to him . . . But if We had sent down an angel, the matter would have been settled, and they would have had no respite.

9. And if We had appointed an angel, We should certainly have made him a man too, and then We would have made perplexing for them what they deem perplexing now.

10. Apostles have been laughed to scorn before thee, but what they laughed to scorn encompassed the mockers among them.

7. This was a reply to the unbelieving Arabs who demanded of Mohammed such proofs, or 'miracles,' as the bringing down of a book from Heaven. The utter futility of any miracle in inducing the belief of the people is here strongly maintained. If a 'miracle' were possible the people would only rebut it as a 'magic.'

8. After 'sent down to him,' supply something like, 'we will not believe,' to complete the meaning.

'The matter,' etc., i.e., in that case they would have suffered immediate condemnation, and would not have been allowed time for repentance. For, if the angel had appeared to them, and they had not believed, they ought to have accepted the judgment of God passed upon the ungodly without being allowed respite.

9. 'A man too,' in order to make him a teacher of men.

'And them We,' etc. Or, it may also be translated, 'And then We would have clothed him before them as they are clothed.' For, though an angel, he could only appear to man as his teacher in a man's garb; which as soon as he were made to do, the unbelievers would say, 'Aha ! he is a mere man, as we are.'

10. 'What they,' etc., *i.e.*, those who mocked found out their mistakes when it was too late.

The Ungodly:

11. Say thou, Go through the earth, and see what has been the end of those who called it a lie.

12. Say thou, whose is what is in the heavens and the earth ? Say thou, God's. He has imposed upon Himself mercy; He will surely gather you together on the Judgment Day; there is no doubt of it. They who destroy their own souls are they who will not believe.

13. His is what dwells in the night in the day; and He is the hearing, the knowing.

14. Say thou, Other than God shall I take for a patron ? — Maker of the heavens and the earth; He feeds, but is not fed.

Say thou, I am commanded to be the first of those who strive; and be not thou of those who join others with God.

15. Say thou, Verily I fear if I rebel against my Lord, the punishment of the great day.

16. From whomsoever it shall be averted on that Day, He will have been merciful to him — that is the manifest bliss.

17. If God touched thee with trouble, none can take it off but He; and if He visit thee with good — He is mighty over all things.

18. And He is supreme over His servants; and He is the wise, the knowing.

19. Say thou, What is the most weighty in bearing witness ? Say thou, God is witness between me and you; and this Quran has been revealed to

me that I should warn you by it, and all whom it shall reach. Will ye bear witness that there are Gods with God. Say thou, I do not bear witness to it. Say thou, He is the one God, and I am clear of what ye join with Him.

20. They to whom We have given the Book know him even as they do their own children; but they who destroy theirs own souls are they who will not believe.

21. And who transgresses more then him who invents a lie against God, and calls His signs a lie ? Verily the transgressors will not be happy.

22. And on the Day We will gather them all together . . . . .

29. And they say, There is nothing beside our life of this world, and we shall not be raised up again.

30. O that thou couldst see when they shall be set before their Lord ! He will say, Is not this in truth ? They shall say, Yea, by our Lord ! He will say, Taste then the torment, for that ye disbelieved.

31. Now have they lost who called the meeting with God a lie, until when the Hour comes suddenly upon them, they say, Woe to us, for that we were negligent of it ! — and they shall carry their burdens on their backs. Will not that be evil with which they shall be burdened.

32. And the life of this world is but a play and a pastime, but better surely is the mansion that be in the Hereafter for those who fear to do evil. Will ye not yet understand ?

33. Now We know that what they speak grieves thee; yet they do not call thee a liar, but the ungodly deny the evidences of God.

34. And apostles before thee have been called liars, but they bore it and the wrong with patience,. till Our help came to them, for none can change the working of God. And the history of some apostles thou hast already received.

12. 'He has imposed,' etc., *i.e.*, He has laid down for himself a rule of mercy.

'They who destroy,' etc., *i.e.*, who are the authors of their own ruin.

13. 'His is,' etc., *i.e.*, to Him is due whatever happens by night or by day.

17. After 'with good,' supply such words as 'who can restrain Him from it ?'

19. 'And All,' etc. The Quran is for 'all whom it shall reach.'

20. 'Know him,' *i.e.*, recognise in Mohammed one of their own prophets.

'Who destroy, etc.,' *i.e.*, who are the authers of their own ruin with regard to spiritual development.

31. 'Their burdens,' *i.e.*, their own evil works.

In one of his apologues, Mohammed is reported to have said that a man's evil works will be represented to him under the ugliest form that he ever beheld, having a most deformed countenance, a filthy smell, and and a disagreeable voice; so that he will cry out, 'God defend me from thee, what art thou ? I never saw anything more detestable !' To which the figure will answer, 'Why dost thou wonder at my ugliness ? I am thy evil works; thou didst ride upon me while thou wast in the world, but now will I ride upon thee, and thou shalt carry me.' And immediately it shall get upon him.

33. 'They do not call,' etc., *i.e.*, it is not thou but God whom they injure by their impious gainsaying of what has been revealed to thee. It is said that Abu-Jehl once told Mohammed that they did not accuse him of falsehood, because he was known to be a man of undoubted veracity; but that they would not believe in the message which he brought them.

34. 'The working,' etc., lit., 'the words of God,' as imprinted upon His works.

Their Obstinacy:

35. But if their aversion be grievous to thee, and if thou art able to seek out a den into the earth, or a ladder up to heaven, that thou mayest show them a sign.... Yes ! but if God pleased He would bring them all to be guided aright. Therefore be not thou of the ignorant.

36. To those only who will lend an ear will He give answer; as for the dead. . . God will raise them up, and then to Him they shall return.

37. They say, Not until a sign is sent to him from his Lord. . . Say thou, Verily God alone is able to send down a sign, but most of them have no knowledge.

35. After 'a sign,' supply 'do so, if thou art able,' or some such words. This is the message to Mohammed instilling into him the utter futility of his desire to satisfy the pressing demands of the unbelieving people regarding miracles with a view to secure their conversion, As if it were said: if thou canst do the things required of thee, do it, simply for their conversion. But they will not mind these. It is not in thy power to force conviction, but if God saw any good in their conversion (for which thou art so eager), He would surely have guided them all aright. But God does what in His wisdom He esteems the best.

'Therefore be not,' etc. . . '*i.e.,* such an eager desire to secure their wholesale conversion is both foolish and unwise, and they must for bear doing this.

36. 'To those only,' etc. See Surah ii. 182.

After 'as for the dead,' supply 'thou (Mohammed) canst not raise them up by thy eagerness,' in order to be understood clearly with special reference to the context.

'Dead,' unregenerate, so called because they cannot prosper by reason of their spiritual damnation.

'God will,' etc., *i.e.,* He will enliven them by spiritual regeneration in His wisdom then their time comes.

Beasts, Birds, Etc.

38. There is no beast on earth, nor fowl which flies with its wings, but is a being like to you: We have not passed over anything in the Book,—and to their Lord they shall be gathered.

38. 'Being:' lit., 'a people.'

'Like to you;' *i.e.,* being created and preserved by the same omnipotence and providence as ye are.

'The Book,' *i.e.,* the knowledge of God. Everything is contained in the knowledge of God.

The Unbelievers:

39. They who call Our sings a lie are deaf, dumb, and in darkness: whom it pleases God, He misleads, and who He pleases He puts in the straight path.

40. Say thou, What do ye think ? If the punishment of God were to come upon you, or the Hour, will ye cry to any beside God, if ye speak the truth ?

41. Yea, to Him will ye cry: and if He please, He will save you from that which ye shall cry to Him, and ye will forget what ye joined with Him.

42. We have already sent apostles to people before thee, and We laid hold on them with troubles and adversity that so they might humble themselves;

43. Yet when Our troubles came upon them, they did not humble themselves and their hearts were hardened, and the devil made fair-seeming to them what they did.

44. And when they forgot what they were admonished, We opened to them the gates of all things, until as they were rejoicing in what had been given them, We suddenly laid hold upon

them, and lo ! they were seized with despair.

45. And the uttermost part of that impious people was cut off All praise to God, Lord of the worlds!

46. Say thou, What do you think? If God should take away your hearing and your sight, and seal up your hearts, what God beside God would restore them to you? Just see, how We show forth the signs, yet they turn aside!

47. Say, What thing Ye? If the punishment of God come upon you suddenly, or in open view, will any perish except the transgressors ?

48. We only sent Our apostles to bear good tidings and warning; and whoso believes and amends, on them shall come no fear, neither shall they grieve.

43. 'The devil,' etc. Their evil works appeared to them very fair because of their inclination towards them.

Prophet's Mission:

50. Say thou, I say not to you, mine are the treasures of God; nor that I know the unseen; I do not say to you, I am an angel: I follow only what is revealed to me. Say thou, Shall the blind and the seeing be held equal? Don't ye reflect?

51. And by it, do thou warn those who fear that they shall be gathered to their Lord, that patron or intercessor they have none beside Him,—that they may fear to do evil.

52. And turn them not out who cry to their Lord, morning and evening desiring His pleasure. It is none of thy concern to judge of their motives, as it is not for them in anything to judge of thee. If thou turn them out, thou wilt surely be of the transgressors.

53. Thus We make trial of some of them by others, that they may say, Are these among us to whom God has been gracious? Does not God know the thankful?

54. And when they who believe in Our signs come to thee, say thou, Peace upon you. Your Lord has imposed upon Himself mercy. Whoso, therefore, among you works evil through ignorance, and afterwards turns and amends. . . Surely He is forgiving, compassionate.

55. Thus have We distinctly set forth Our signs, that the way of the wicked might be made known.

52. In a time of scarcity the chief men of Mecca expelled all the poor out of their city; whereupon they all came to Mohammed and offered to embrace his religion because it condescended to ameliorate their condition, but Mohammed made some difficulty to receive them, suspecting their motive to be necessity, and not real conviction; whence this verse.

53. 'Are these,' etc. That is to say, the noble by those of mean extraction, and the rich by the poor; in that God chose to call the latter to the faith before the former.

54. Supply 'God will forgive him,' after 'and amends.'

Worship of God:

56. Say thou, Verily I am forbidden to serve those whom ye call on beside God. Say thou, I'll not follow your desires, for then I err, and not be of the guided.

57. Say thou, I act upon the evidences of my Lord, and ye call them lies. What ye desire to be hastened is not in my power; judgment is only God's. He will declare the truth; and He is the best of judges.

58. Say thou, If what ye would hasten on were in my power, the matter would have been settled

between me and you, but God best knows the wrongdoers.

58. 'What ye would,' etc., *viz.,* the Judgment of God.

59. And with Him are the keys of the secret: none knows them but He: He knows what is in the land and in the sea; and no leaf falls but He knows it, neither is there a grain in the darkness of the earth, nor a thing green nor sear, but is in the plain Book.

60. And He it is who lays you to rest at night, and knows what ye have deserved in the day: then He raises you therein, that the term prescribed may be fulfilled. They ye will return to Him, and then He will tell you what ye have done.

61. And He is supreme over His servants, and sends over you guardians, until when death overtakes any one of you, those whom We have sent receive his soul, and fail not.

62. Then are they returned to God, their true Lord. Is not judgment His ? —and He is swift at reckoning up.

63. Say thou, Who rescues you from the darkness of the land and of the sea, when humbly and in secret ye cry to Him, If Thou rescue us from this, we will surely be of the thankful ?

64. Say thou, God rescues you from them, and from every trouble; yet again ye give Him companions !

65. Say thou, He it is who has power to send on you a punishment from above you, or from beneath your feet, or to rend you with discord, and to make some of you taste the violence of others. See! how variously We show forth the signs, that

they may take wisdom.

66. Thy people have called it a lie, but it is the truth. Say thou, I am not a guardian over you: every prophecy has its time, and by and by ye shall know.

67. And when thou seest them engaged with Our signs, withdraw from them till they are engaged in some other subject; and if the devil make thee forget this, sit not after recollection with the wrong-doers.

68. Not that those who fear to do evil are to pass any judgment upon them, but to remember that they may fear to do evil.

60. 'Lays you,' etc. Lit., 'makes you dead' in sleep.

61. 'Guardians,' i.e., the guardian spirits or angels.

66. 'I am not,' etc. I am only to preach, but you are free to choose.

68. Or, 'Not that those who fear to do evil are to be held accountable for them' (the wrong-doers.)

The Ungodly:

69. And avoid those who make their religion a sport and a jest, and who the life of this world has deceived: and warn them hereby that a soul becomes liable for what it has earned, patron or intercessor beside God it shall have none; and could it atone with the fullest atonement, it would not be accepted from it. It is these who become liable for what they have earned—for them are draughts of boiling water, and a painful punishment, because they disbelieved.

About God:

70. Say thou, Shall we call upon those beside God who can neither help no hurt us ? Shall we turn

upon our heels after that God has guided us?—like him whom the devils have bewildered, wandering in the earth amazedly, though his companions call him to the guidance, saying, Come to us. Say thou, Verily the guidance of God,—that is the guidance; and we are commanded to strive for the Lord of the worlds.

71. And be steadfast in prayer, and fear Him: and He it is to whom ye shall be gathered.

72. And He it is who created the heavens and the earth in truth; and the day when He says, Be, it is.

73. His word is the truth; and His the kingdom on the Day when the trumpet shall be sounded; knower of the secret and the visible; and He is the wise, the knowing.

Some Prophets:

84. And We gave him Isaac and Jacob, and guided both aright; and We had before guided Noah, and of his prosterity, David and Solomon, and Job, and Joseph, and Moses and Aaron: thus We reward those who do good.

85. And Zacharias, and John, and Jesus, and Elias: all were righteous persons;

86. And Ishmael, and Elisha, and Jonas, and Lot: all these have We blessed above mankind:

87. And some of their fathers, and their offspring, and of their brethren: and We chose them, and guided them on the Straight path.

88. That is the guidance of God: He guides by it such of His servants as He pleases. But if they associated others with God, vain had been all that they did.

89. These are they to whom We gave the Book, and wisdom, and prophecy. . .

90. These it is whom God has guided: follow then their guidance. Say thou, I ask not of you any reward for it; verily it is only a reminder to all creatures.

84. 'We gave him,' i.e., to Abraham. 'Thus We,' etc. The good only are guided aright.

88. 'But if they,' etc. Associating anything with God is considered the blackest sin in Islam.

89. 'These,' in this and the preceding verses, refers to the prophets mentioned in verses 84-7, above.

'Prophecy,' meaning prophetship.

God: His Power:

95. Verily God causes the grain and the date-stone to put forth: He brings forth the living from the dead, and the dead from the living. That is God: why then do ye turn aside ?

96. He makes the dawn to break, and has ordained the night for rest, and the sun and the moon for a computation. That is the ordinance of the mighty, the knowing.

97. And He it is who has made for you the stars that ye may be guided thereby in the darkness of the land and of the sea. Clear have We made Our signs to people who have knowledge.

98. And He it is who has made you from one soul, and set a term and a resting-place. . .

99. And He it is who sends down water from heaven,—and We bring forth by it the springing buds of all things, and from them We bring forth the green foliage, and the close-growing grain, and palm trees with sheaths of clustering dates,

and gardens of grapes, and the olive and the pomegranate, of all sorts. Look on their fruits when they fructify and ripen. Truly herein are signs to people who believe.

100. Yet they have set up the Jinn as partners with God, though He created them; and in their ignorance they have ascribed to Him sons and daughters. Praise to Him ! and exalted be He above what they attribute to Him.

101. Maker of the heavens and the earth ! How should He have a son when he has no consort ? He created all things, and He knows them all.

102. This is God, your Lord: there is no God but He, creator of all things ! Then worship Him: and He is the guardian over all things.

103. The sight comprehends Him not, but He comprehends the sight: and He is the incomprehensible, the knowing.

104. Now has an insight come to you from your Lord: Whoso then sees it, it is for his own soul; and whoso is blind to it, his the loss; and I am not a keeper over you.

106. Follow what has been revealed to thee from thy Lord: there is not God but He; and withdraw from those who join anything with Him.

107. If God so pleased, they had not joined anything with Him. But We have not made thee a keeper over them, neither art thou over them a guardian.

98. 'Term,' i.e., of life.

'Resting-place, or 'repository,' where ye are thrown after passing from this world.

99. 'Of all sorts. 'Lit., 'Like and unlike one another.'

100. 'The Jinn.' The word signifies properly the 'genus' of rational, 'invisible' beings, whether angels, devils, or that intermediate species usually called 'genii.'

In this place some understand the angels, whom the pre-Islamite Arabs worshipped; and others the devils, because according to the Magian system, they looked on the devil (whom they named 'Ahriman') as a sort of creator, making him the author and principle of all evil, and God the author of good alone.

'Sons.' As in the Christian conception of Jesus; and the Jews of Arabia who regarded Ezra as the Son of God. See Surah ix. 30.

'Daughters.' The pre-Islamite Arabs called the angels the daughters of God. See Surah xvii. 42.

103. 'The sight,' etc. Edward Lane renders it, 'The eyes see not Him, but He seeth the eyes.'

'The incomprehensible;' or, 'the subtile.'—It might also be translated, 'the gracious.'

104. 'I am not,' etc. That is, ye are free to use your discriminating powers as best ye see, or otherwise; in which case the Lord will only demand of you your accounts, for I am only a warner.

107. 'But We have not,' etc. See note to verse 104, above.

Evil Speaking Forbidden:

108. And revile not those whom they call on beside God, for then they may abuse God openly in their ignorance. Thus have We made fair-seeming for every people their works; then to their Lord they shall return, and He will tell them what they have done.

109. They have sworn by God with a most solemn oath, that if a sign come to them they will certainly believe therein. Say thou, Verily signs are with God alone, and He teaches you not thereby, only because when they came be did not believe.

108. 'For them,' etc. To a Moslem therefore His love of God ought to make him a good companion even of a man who is a radical antagonist to his own system.

Miracles of no Avail:

111. And though We had sent down to them angels, and the dead had spoken to them, and We had gathered together all things before them, they had not believed, unless God so pleased. But most of them do not know.

112. . . . Therefore leave them and their vain imaginings.

115. And the words of thy Lord are prefect in truth and in justice: none can change His words. He is the hearing, the knowing.

111. In this passage the unbelievers are told with regard to their demand of miracles that God has not thought fit to comply with their desires, and that even if He had thought fit, yet would it have been in vain; because if they were not convinced by the Quran, they would not be convinced by the greatest miracle. Also confer St. Luke xvi, 31.

The General Practices:

116. But it thou follow most of those who are in the earth, they will lead thee aside from the way of God: they follow on opinion only, and rest on mere conjecture.

117. And thy Lord—He knows who go astray, and He knows the rightly guided.

120. And avoid iniquity, both in public and in private; verily those who have earned iniquity shall be rewarded for what they have gained.

116. 'They follow,' etc. The religion of the general people is well describe d in these words.

120. 'Iniquity,' etc. Lit., 'the outside of iniquity and its inside.

Rev. J.M. Rod well translates it, 'the semblance of wickedness, and wickedness it self.'

Rewards:

132. And for all are grades according to what they have done; for thy Lord is not unmindful of what they do.

135. Say thou, Ye people, act as best ye can; verily I will also act my part; by and by ye will know

136. Whose is the home Hereafter; but surely the wrong-doers will not be happy.

Some Idolatrous Practices:

137. They set apart to God a portion of the fruits and cattle which He has produced, and say, This is for God,—in their estimation;—and this is for what we associate with Him. But that which is for these associates of theirs, comes not to God; yet what is for God comes to their companions. How ill they judge !

138. And thus have their companions made it fair seeming to the idolaters to slay their children that so they might ruin them, and clothe their religion with ignorance. And if God pleased, they had not done this. Therefore leave them, and their devices.

139. They also say, These cattle and fruits are sacred; none shall taste thereof but whom we please—in their estimation. And cattle whose backs are exempted from labor, and cattle over which they mention not the name of God, inventing a lie against Him; and for their devices will He reward them.

140. And they say, What is in the bellies of these cattle is allowed to our males, and forbidden to our

females, but if it prove abortive then they might partake of it. God will reward them for these distinctions. Verily He is the wise, the knowing.

141. Surely they are the losers who have slain their children foolishly, and have forbidden what God had given them for food, devising a lie against God. They have surely gone astray, as were not of the rightly guided.

142. He it is who brings forth gardens of the vine trellised and untrellised, and the palm-trees, and the corn of various food, and olives and pomegrantes, of all sorts. Eat of their fruit, when they fructify, and give the due thereof on the day when ye gather it; but be not extravagant; surely God loves not the extravagant.

143. And there are the cattle for burdens and for journeys: eat of what God has given you for food, and follow not the steps of the devil, for he is your open enemy.

144. Ye have four sorts of cattle in pairs: of sheep, a pair, and of goats, a pair. Say thou, Has He forbidden the two males or the two females ? or what is in the wombs of the two females? Tell me with certainty if ye speak the truth.

145. And of camels, a pair; and of oxen, a pair. Say thou, Has He forbiddenthe two males or the two females, or what is in the wombs of the two females ? Were ye witnesses when God enjoined you this? Who then is more wicked than him who devices a lie against God without knowledge, that he may mislead people? Verily God guides not the wicked people.

146. Say thou, I find not in what has been revealed to

me anything forbidden to him who eats, except what is dead of itself, or blood poured forth, or swine's flesh: for this is unclean; or profane, being slain in the name of any other than of God: but whoso is forced by necessity, not lusting, nor transgressing; surely thy Lord is forgiving, compassionate.

148. If they treat thee as a liar, say thou, Your Lord, He is of all-embracing mercy; but His severity shall not be averted from a criminal people.

137. It was the custom of the idolatrous Arabs to set apart one portion of their fields for the Supreme God, and the other for the inferior gods represented by their idols. If any of the fruits happened to fall from the part consecrated to the idols into that consecrated to God, they restored it, but if the reverse occurred, they gave it to the idols, saying, that God was rich and could dispense with it. In the same manner, if the offering designed for God happened to be better than that designed for the idols, they made an exchange, but not otherwise. The secret of all this being that the idol's portions were reserved for the priests, whereas the share set apart for God was spent chiefly upon the poor and strangers.

138. 'To slay,' etc. In addition to the custom of the pre-Islamite Arabs that of burying their female children to the gods from each family. All this, according to the Quran, was a mere device of the priests to 'ruin' the people and 'clothe their religion with ignorance,' that they might not break it.

139. 'But whom,' etc. That is, the priests, and the male members of their family, for the women were not allowed to eat of them.

'Cattle whose backs,' etc. Which they superstitiously exempted from such services, in some particular cases, as they did the Bahirah, the Saibah and the Hami. See Surah v. 102.

'Over which,' etc. This the idolatrous Arabs did in killing any animal for food, by consecrating it, as it were, to their idols al-Lat or al-Uzza.

140. 'In the bellies,' etc. That is, the 'fætus' or embryos of the Bahirah and the Saibah, which shall be brought forth alive.

'But if it prove,' etc. For, if those cattle cast their young, the women might eat thereof as well as the men.

141. 'Who have slain,' etc. See verse 138, above.

'And have forbidden,' etc. The pre-Islamite Arabs allowed their daughters very scanty food, and some very wholesome articles of food were not allowed them at all.

142. 'Trellised,' etc., Or, as some choose to interpret the words, 'Trees or plants which are planted by the labour of man, and those which grow naturally in the deserts and on mountains.'

'Of all sorts,' See notes to verse 99, above.

'Give the due,' etc. That is, give alms thereof to the poor.

'Be not extravagant.' See Surah xvii. 31.

144. 'Four sorts of cattle.' Or, literally, eight males and females paired together; that is, four of each sex, and two of every distinct kind.

'Tell me,' etc. In this passage the Arabs are urged to see their superstitious folly in making it unlawful, one while, to eat the males of these four kinds of cattle; another while, the females; and at another time, their young.

Duties Enjoined:

152. Say thou, Come; I will rehearse to you what you Lord has forbidden you—that ye join not anything with Him; and that ye be good to your parents; and that ye kill not your children, because of poverty;—for them and for you will We provide;—and that ye draw not night to inchastity,—neither openly nor in secret;—and that ye kill not a being which God has forbidden, unless by right. This He enjoins you, that ye may get wisdom.

153. And approach not the wealth of the orphan except to improve it, until he come of age; and use a full measure, and a just balance,—We

impose upon a soul only according to its ability.—And when ye speak, observe justice, although in the case of a relative; and the Covenant of God, fulfil ye. That is what He ordains you, that ye may be reminded.

154. And this is my right way: then follow it, and follow not other ways that ye may swerve from His way. This He enjoins you that ye may fear to do wrong.

159. Do they wait for anything but that the angels should come to them, or that thy Lord should come Himself, or that some of the signs of thy Lord should come to pass ? The Day when some of thy Lord's signs shall come to pass its faith shall not profit a soul which believed not before, or did not good in its faith. Say thou, Wait ye; we also do wait.

153. 'A full measure,' i.e., of justice.

159. 'Its faith,' etc. For faith in the next life will be of no advantage to those who have not believed in this; nor yet faith in this life without good works.

Sectarianism Condemned:

160. As to those who make a division in their religion, and become sectareis, have thou nothing to do with them: their affair is with God, and He will tell them what they have done.

Works: Their Reward:

161. Whoso appears with good works, his is a tenfold recompense; and whoso appears with evil works, his is a reward like to it; and they will not be wronged.

The True Religion:

162. Say thou, My Lord has guided me into the

straight path, the standard religion, the creed of Abraham, the upright man, and he was not of the idolators.

163. Say thou, My prayers and my worship, and my life and my death, are all for God alone, Lord of the worlds. He has no partners. This I am commanded: and I am the first Moslem.

164. Shall I desire any other Lord beside God, when He is Lord of all that is ? Every soul only earns for itself: and no burdened soul shall bear the burden of another. In the end ye shall return to your God: and He will tell you concerning which ye now disagree.

165. He it is who has made you to inherit the earth and has raised some of you above others by various grades, that He might prove you by what He has given you. Verily thy Lord is swift at reckoning up, and He is also the forgiving, compassionate.

Principal Contents

Duties enjoined, 152-4.

Examples from the history of other peoples, 6, 11, 42-5.

Faith, no good without works, 159.

God, His power, 1, 2, 12, 13, 17, 18, 46, 61, 63-5, 72, 73, 95-9; His knowledge, 3, 38, 47, 59, 60, 103, 142; His mercy, 12, 54; His due, 163.

Grades of rewards, 132.

Iniquities, to be avoided, 120.

Judgment, a reality, 22, 29-31.

Man liable only for his works, 69, 164.

Miracles discarded 7-9, 35, 50, 109, 111.

Practices, some idolatrous, of the Arabs, 137-41.

Religions, other people's, not to be reviled, 108.

Sectarianism condemned, 160.

SURAH VII.—AL ARAF

(Mecca.)

The title of this Surah is taken from the mention, in verse 44, of Araf, a name given therein to the intermediate space between Heaven and Hell. It is supposed to be an indefinite region in the intermediate state, the abode of those who have had no opportunity to know the truth in this world, and who after a short process are passed over to Heaven.

The Quran :

1. A.L.M.S. The Book has been revealed to thee,—therefore let there be no doubt in thy bresat concerning it,—that thou mayest warn by it, and it may be a reminder to the believers.

1. 'A.L.M.S.' See notes Surah ii 1.

The Judgment Day :

5. We will surely call those to account to whom an apostle has been sent, and We will also demand an account of those who have been sent.

6. And We will tell them with certainty, for We have not been absent from them.

7. The weighing on that Day shall be just : and whose balances are heavy—these are the happy.

8. And whose balances are light : these it is who lose their own souls, for that to Our signs they acted wickedly.

5. The prophets and their followers will all render their accounts to God.

7. 'The weighing,' *i.e.*, of men's actions.

'Are heavy,' *i.e.*, with good works.

8. 'Our sings;' the commandments of God are here so spoken of.

God : His Gifts :

9. And now We have established you on the earth, and given there you in the supports of your life.

Yet how little are ye thankful !

25. Ye children of Man, We have sent to you the apparel to hide your nakedness, and splendid garments; but the clothing of piety,—that is the best. This is of the signs of God that they may consider.

25. 'Sent you,' etc. God has not merely provided the proper materials, but also the ingenuity of mind and dexterity of hand to make use of them.

God's Commands :

27. And when they commit a filthy action they say, We found our fathers at it, and God commands us to do it. Say thou, God commands not filthy actions. Will ye speak of God what ye do not know?

28. Say thou, My Lord has commanded me justice : then turn your faces to every place where He is worshipped, and call upon Him in sincere religious esteem. As He made you, so shall ye return.

Some has He guided aright, and some there are upon whom is error justly due, for that they have taken the devils for their patrons beside God, and imagine that they are guided aright.

29. Ye children of Man, wear your decent apparel at every place of worship; and eat, and drink, but be not extravagant; verily He loves not those who are extravagant.

30. Say thou, Who has forbidden the decent apparel of God which He has produced for His servants, and the good things for food? Say thou, These are for those who believe, in the life of this world, but peculiarly in the Hereafter.

31. Say thou, Verily my Lord has forbidden filthy actions whether open or secret, and iniquity, and unjust violence, and to associate with God what He has sent you down no authority for, and to speak of God what ye know not.

27. 'What ye do not,' etc. Or, 'against your consciences.'

28. 'In sincere religious esteem;' lit., 'exhibiting to Him your sincerity in religion.'

29. This was chiefly to reprove the immodest custom of the idolatrous Arabs, who used to encompass the Kaabah in perfect nudity during the pilgrimage.

'Be not extravagant.' Habits too rich and sumptuous are here condemned; such as clothes adorned with gold, etc.

31. 'What ye know not;' or, 'against your consciences.'

The Ungodly :

38. Verily those who treat Our signs as a lie, and in their pride turn away from them, the gates of Heaven shall not be opened to them, neither shall they enter the Garden, until the camel passes through the eye of the needle. And this is the reward of the criminal.

39. Theirs the couch in Hell, and above them coverings of Fire. This is the reward of the wrongdoers.

38. 'Until the camel,' etc. Which is an impossibility and out of question altogether.

The Pious :

40. And those who have believed and done good,— We impose not upon a soul but according to its ability.—These are the people of the Garden, therein to continue for ever.

41. And We will remove all grudges from their bosoms,—rivers running beneath them. . . .

41. 'We will remove,' etc. So that, whatever the differences

or animosities in the life of this world, they will all be forgotten, and give place to sincere love and amity. This is an important idea in the conception of the Moslem Hereafter.

God : His Power :

52. Verily your Lord is God, who created the heavens and the earth; and then ascended the Throne : He makes the night to cover the day : it pursues it incessantly; and the sun and the moon and the stars are pressed into service by His command. It not all creation and command His? Blessed be God, Lord of the worlds !

A Rule Given :

53. Call upon your Lord humbly and in secret; verily He loves not the transgressors.

54. And commit not disorders in the earth, after its reformation; and call upon Him with fear and desire. Surely the mercy of God is nigh to the righteous.

53. 'The transgressors;' who behave themselves arrogantly in their prayers; who are proud of their piety in public.

'Humbly and in secret.' These are the necessary conditions of prayer.

54. 'After its reformation.' That is, after that God had from time to time raised up prophets for the regeneration of men.

'With fear and desire.' The fear to do wrong and an inward disposition of the soul are among the essentials of prayers.

Some Examples :

58. Of old We sent Noah to his people, and he said, My people, worship God : ye have no God but Him : . .

63. And to Ad, their brother Hud. He said, My people, worship God, Ye have no God but Him. . .

71. And to Samud, their brother Salih. He said, My people, worship God : ye have no God but Him. . .

78. And Lot, when he said to his people, Do ye commit this filthy deed wherein no creature has gone before you ?

83. And to Midian their brother Shoeib. He said, My people, worship God : ye have no God beside Him.

101. Then after them We sent Moses with Our signs to Pharaoh, and his nobles, who treated them unjustly; but see, what was the end of the evil-doers !

171. And when thy Lord brought forth their posterity from the loins of the sons of Adam and took them to witness against themselves, saying, Am not I your Lord ? They said, Yea, we bear witness. This, lest ye should say on the Judgment Day, Truly we were ignorant of this.

172. Or, lest ye should say, Our fathers indeed joined others with God before this, and we their posterity after them. . .

63. Ad was a tribe of the ancient Arabs, long since lost. Hud is supposed by some to be the same as the Eber of the Bible.

71. Samud was another of the tribes of the Arabs long since extinct. Salih is supposed to be the Peleg of Genesis xi. 16.

83. The prophet Shoeib is perhaps the Jethro of the Bible.

171. The object of his verse is to impress that the Unity of the Godhead is a principle ingrained in the human nature.

The Evil-Doers :

173. And relate to them the history of him to whom We brought Our signs, and who departed from them; wherefore the devil followed him, and he became of the seduced.

174. If We pleased, We had surely exalted him thereby, but he inclined to the earth and followed his own lust. And his likeness is as the likeness of a dog which lolls out his tongue, whether thou drive him away or leave him alone. Such the likeness of those who call Our signs a lie. Tell them then this tale, that they may reflect.

175. Evil the likeness of those who call Our signs a lie ! and it is themselves they lose.

176. And We have made many of the Jinn and men for Hell : hearts they have, but by them they understand not; and eyes they have, but by them they see not; and ears they have but by them they hear not.—These are like brutes; yea, they go more astray : these are the heedless.

177. God's are most excellent titles : then call on Him by the same; and avoid those who use His titles perversely : they will be rewarded for what they do.

180. And of those whom We have created there are a people who guide with truth, and act justly in accordance therewith.

184. . . . In what declaration will they believe after this?

173. 'The history,' etc. Of Balaam, who though he knew the scriptures, yet allowed himself to be seduced for some little gifts against Moses.

174. God would have guided him into the right way but for his 'inclining to earth and following his own lust,' as expressed in the text. Such people are bound to be lead astray.

176. The heedless alone who will not use their senses are doomed.

The Judgment :

186. They will ask thee of the Hour,—when 'its coming. Say thou, Verily the knowledge thereof is with my Lord alone : and He will manifest it in its time : it is the burden of the heavens and the earth, and it will only come upon you suddenly.

187. They will ask thee as though thou wast informed of it. Say thou, The knowledge thereof is with God alone; but most people do not understand.

188. Say thou, I have no control over what may be of help or hurt to me, but as God pleases. If I knew the secret, I should surely have much of good, neither should evil befall me; but I am only a warner, and a herald of glad tidings to those who believe.

186. 'The Hour,' referring to the Judgment Day.

'The burden,' etc. That is, it weighs heavily on the hopes and fears of all accountable creatures.

God : The Creator :

189. He it is who created you from one soul, and from it brought forth its mate, that he might dwell with her. . .

190. Yet when He had given them a good child, they joined partners with Him, for that which He had given them. But high is God above what they join with Him !

191. What ! will they join with Him what cannot create, but themselves are created, who to help them have no power, nor can help themselves ?

194. Have they feet, to walk with ? Or, have they hands, to hold with? Or, have they eyes, to see with ?

198. Use indulgence, and enjoin what is just, and withdraw from the ignorant.

203. And when the Quran is chanted, attend thereto, and keep silence; that ye may obtain mercy.

204. And meditate on thy Lord within thine own soul, with humility and fear, and without loud speaking, evening and morning; and be not of the negligent.

190. 'A good child.' In Arabic 'Salihan;' meaning thereby a virtuous offspring. This refers to the Islamic belief of all children being born in virtue, who unless they are perverted by the example and education of their guardians or parents, would only be virtuous. Hence the standard religion is defined in the Quran as 'the constitution whereon God has constituted men.' See Surah xxx. 29.

198. 'Use indulgence;' that is, take men and their actions as they are, and make all due allowances.

204. See notes on verses 53 and 54, above.

Principal Contents

Actions, filthy, not commanded by God, 27; forbidden by Him, 31.

Apparel, to hide nakedness, 25; decent, for prayer, 29.

Blessed state, the, 40, 41.

God, the creator, 189, His ordinances in natures, 52; has most excellent titles, 177.

Indulgence to be given, 198.

Judgment Day, men's actions on, 7; known to God alone, 186.

Justice alone commanded by God, 28.

Quran, a warning and a reminder, 1.

Ungodly, the, their fate, 38, 39.

SURAH VIII.—THE SPOILS

(Medinah.)

This Surah is so called from certain directions in verse 42, regarding the distribution of spoils taken at the Battle of Badr, a dispute having arisen between the young men who had fought and the old men who had stayed under the ensigns; the former insisting that they ought to have the whole, and the latter that they deserved a share. To end the contention, Mohammed divided the booty among them equally, having first taken thereout a fifth part for the purposes mentioned herein.

The Believers :

2. Verily the believers are those whose hearts thrill with fear when God is mentioned, and whose faith increases at each recital of His signs, and who trust in their Lord;

3. Who are steadfast in prayer, and of what We have given them expend.

4. These are the true believers : for them are grades with their Lord, and pardon and an honourable provision.

15. Ye believers, when ye meet the marshalled hosts of unbelievers, turn not your backs to them :

16. Whoso turns his back to them on that day, unless it is to fight, or to rally to some other troop, shall incur the wrath of God. And his home is Hell, and evil the journey thither !

18. This, that God might bring to nought the craft of the ungodly.

19. If ye desire a decision, now has the decision come to you; and if ye desist, it will be better for you. But if ye return to it, we will also return; and your forces shall avail not, great in numbers though they be. Surely God is with the believers.

20. Ye believers, obey God and His apostle, and turn not away from Him, now that ye have heard.

21. And be not like those who say, We hear, while they hear not;

22. For, the vilest beasts in the sight of God are the deaf, and the dumb, who will not understand.

23. If God had known any good in them, He would certainly have made them hear. . .

24. Ye believers, answer God, and His apostle, when he calls you to what gives you life; and know that God goes between a man and his heart, and that to Him shall ye be gathered.

25. Beware of discord; it will not come upon the evil-doers alone among you; and know that God is severe in punishing.

26. And remember when ye were few, and reputed weak in the land : ye feared lest men should pluck you away; then He took you in and strengthened you with His help, and supplied you with good things, that ye may give thanks.

27. Ye believers, deceive not God and His apostle, and be not false to your engagements knowingly.

28. And know that your wealth and your children are a trial; but with God is a great reward.

29. Ye believers, if ye fear God, He will grant you a distinction, and will put away your sins from you, and will pardon you. Surely God He is of unbounded grace.

39. Say to the unbelievers that if they desist, what is already past shall be forgiven them; but if they return to it, they have already before them the punishment of the past.

40. Fight therefore against them until there is no more discord, and the religion is of God. But if they desist, surely God sees what they do.

41. And if they turn back, know that God is your

patron, an excellent patron, and an excellent help.

16. 'Turns his back,' so as to endanger the lives of the Moslems consequent upon a defeat by the unbelievers.

19. This and verse 39, were an offer made to the people of Mecca after their defeat of Badr.

39. See notes, verse 19, above.

The Spoils :

42. And know that when ye have got a booty, a fifth part thereof is God's and the Apostle's, and his kindred, and the orphans, and the poor, and the homeless. . .

42. According to this direction four-fifths of the spoils belong to the troops, and the remaining one-fifth divided into three equal portions for the relief of orphans, the feeding of the poor, and the entertainment of travellers.

War : Some Directions :

47. Ye believers, when ye meet a party of enemies, stand firm , and remember God frequently, that ye may be happy;

48. And obey God and His apostle, and dispute not, lest ye lose heart, and your success depart from you; but endure with patience; surely God is with those who steadfastly endure.

55. . . . Verily God will not change what is in men, unless they change what is in themselves. . .

58. They who enter into a league with thee, and then violate it at every opportunity, and fear not God;

59. If thou take them in war, then by the example of their fate, scatter those who follow them, that they may be warned :

60. Or, if thou fear treachery from any people throw back to them their like; surely God loves not the treacherous.

62. Therefore prepare against them what force ye are able, and strong squadrons, whereby ye may strike terror into the enemy of God and your enemy, and into others beside them whom ye know not, but whom God knows. . .

63. And if they incline to peace, do thou also incline thereto; and put thy trust in God; for He is the hearing, the knowing.

64. But if they seek to betray thee, God suffices thee against them.

He it is who has strengthened thee with His help, and with the believers, and has united their hearts. If thou hadst spent whatever is in the earth, thou couldst not have united their hearts; but God has united them; and He is mighty, wise.

Believers : Their Relation :

73. Verily, they who have believed, and fled their homes, and striven with their wealth and their lives in the way of God, and those who have taken them in, and have assisted them,—these are of kin to one another. And those who have believed, and fled not, have no rights of kindred with you at all, unless they too fly their homes. Yet if they seek help from you on account of religion, ye are bound to help them, except against a people between whom and yourself is a treaty. And God sees what ye do.

74. Those who disbelieve are of kin to each other; unless ye do the same there will be a strife in the land and a general disorder.

75. And those who have believed and fled their homes and striven in the way of God, and those who have taken them in and helped them,—these

are the true believers; for them is pardon and an honourable provision.

76. And they who have believed since, and have fled their homes, and have striven with you,—there are of you. And those who are united by blood are the nearest of kin, one to another, in the Book of God. Verily God is informed of all things.

73. 'They are of kin,' etc. And shall consequently inherit one another's substance, preferably to their relations by blood. And this was practised for some time, the Refugees of Mecca and the Helpers of Medinah being judged heirs to one another, exclusive of the deceased's other kindred, till there was no longer any need of perpetuating it, the Moslems having settled down in peace, when verse 76 was given to regulate the law of natural propinquity.

74. 'A strife,' etc. With regard to the inheritance.

Principal Contents

Believers, true 2, 3, 75.

Discord, to be rooted out, 25, 40.

Fighting, some directions in, 15, 16, 40, 41, 47, 48, 58-64.

God, His favours to believers, 26, 64.

Peace, offered to the unbelievers, 19, 39.

Refugees and Helpers, bond between them, 73,

Spoils, their distribution, 42.

Unbelievers, stubborn, 22, 23.

Wealth and children, a trial, 28.

SURAH IX.—IMMUNITY

(Medinah.)

This Surah is named from the first important word at the beginning. It was revealed after the conquest of Mecca in A. H. 9.

It is remarkable that this Surah alone has not the usual auspiciatory form, 'In the name of God,' etc.

The Immunity :

1. An Immunity from God and His Apostle to those

with whom ye are in league among the polytheists.

2. Go ye, therefore, at large in the land four months, and know that ye shall not weaken God; and that the unbelievers will God put to shame;

3. And a Proclamation on the part of God and His apostle to the people on the Day of the Greater Pilgrimage, that God is clear of the polytheists, and His apostle also. Wherefore if ye repent, it will be better for you, and if ye turn back, know that ye shall not weaken God; and to those who believe not, announce thou a painful punishment;

4. Except those of the polytheists with whom ye are in league, and who since have not failed you in any way, nor helped any against you; wherefore perform your engagements with them until the end of time; surely God loves those who fear to do wrong.

5. And when the sacred months are passed, kill the polytheists wherever ye find them, and seize them, and besiege them, and lay wait for them, in every ambush; but if they repent, and observe prayer, and give alms, then let them go their way; surely God is forgiving, compassionate.

6. And if any of the polytheists seek an asylum of thee, give him an asylum, so that he may hear the word of God : then let him reach his place of safety. This, for that they are a people who have no sense.

1. Some understand this sentence of the immunity therein granted to the idolatrous people for the space of four months; but others think that the words properly signify that Mohammed is here declared to be absolutely free and discharged from all truce or league with them,

(subject, of course, to verses 4, 8, and 10,) after the expiration of that time.

4. 'Who since,' etc. For instance, the tribes of Damra, Kinanah, and a few others.

5. 'The sacred months.' Shawwal, Zul-kaadah, Zil-Hijj, and Moharram, which the ancient Arabs considered inviolate. See also notes under Surah ii. 190.

'The polytheists.' This refers to those only who have taken the initiative. See Surah ii. 186, etc.; also lx. 8, 9.

6. 'Let him reach,' etc. That is, you shall give him a safe conduct, that he may return home again securely, in case he shall not think fit to accept Islam.

The Unbelievers :

7. How can the polytheists be in league with God and His apostle, except those with whom ye have already entered into a league at the Sacred Mosque ? So long as they are true to you, be ye true to them also; surely God loves those who fear to do wrong.

8. And how ? Since if they prevail against you they will not regard in you either ties of blood or faith. They will please you with their mouths, but their hearts are averse; and most of them are wicked doers.

11. Yet if they repent, and observe prayer, and give alms, then are they your brothers in religion.

12. But if, after their league, they break their oaths and revile your religion, then fight with the leaders of infidelity—for then no oaths are binding with them—that they may desist.

13. What ! will ye not fight against a people who break their oaths and conspire to expel the apostle, and who begin the fight themselves ?

17. It is not for the polytheists to visit the Mosques

of God while they are witnesses against their own souls of infidelity. These ! their works are vain.

18. But he only shall visit the Mosques of God who believes in God and the Judgment Day, and observes prayer, and gives alms, and fears God alone. These perhaps are of the rightly guided.

7. 'So long,' etc. This explains the relation between the Moslems and polytheists.

13. 'Conspire,' etc. As did the Koreish in assisting the tribe of Bakr against those of Khozaah, and laying a design to ruin Mohammed and his followers without any just provocation; and as several of the Jewish tribes did, by aiding the enemy, and endeavouring to oblige the prophet to leave Medinah, as he had been obliged to leave Mecca.

18. 'These perhaps,' etc. These words are to warn the believers from having too great a confidence in their own merits.

The Believers :

20. They who have believed, and fled their homes, and striven with their wealth and their lives in the way of God, have the highest grades with God; and these are the blessed.

23. Ye believers, take not your fathers, or your brothers, for your friends if they love infidelity above faith; and whoso of you takes them for friends, surely these are the unjust.

24. Say thou, If your fathers, and your sons, and your brothers, and your wives and your relations, and the wealth which ye have acquired, and merchandize which ye fear may not be sold off, and pleasure-houses, be dearer to you above God and His apostle, and striving in His way, then wait till God comes with His command; and surely God loves not the wicked people.

The Jews and Christians :

30. The Jews say, Ezra is the son of God; and the Christians say, Christ is the son of God. That is their saying in their mouths : they imitate the saying of those who believed no before. God fight them ! How are they misguided !

31. They take their priests and their monks for Lords beside God, and Christ, son of Mary; although they are commanded to worship only one God. There is no God but He ! Praise to Him above what they join with Him !

34. Ye believers, verily many of the priests and monks devour the wealth of men in vanity, and turn them from the way of God. But those who treasure up gold and silver, and expend it not in the way of God,—announce to them a painful punishment.

40. If ye assist not, . . . verily God assisted him formerly, when the unbelievers drove him forth second of two, when they were both in the cave, when he said to him companion, Be not distressed; surely God is with us. . .

30. 'Ezra.' This refers to the Jews of Medinah, who transferred to this restorer of their Law all the veneration with God.

31. 'Take their priests,' etc. By taking their words as those of God, as in the case of absolutions etc.

34. 'Devour the wealth,' etc. By taking money for dispensing with the commands of God, and by way of commutation.

40. 'If ye assist not,' i.e., the prophet.

'Drove him forth,' etc. That is, having only Abu-Bakr with him.

Almsgiving :

60. And alms are only for the poor and the needy,

and those who work for them, and for those whose hearts are to be won over, and for the captives, and those in debt, and in the way of God, and the homeless;—an ordinance from God; and God is knowing, wise.

60. 'The poor and the needy.' The commentators make a distinction between these two words in the original, 'fakir' and 'miskin'; one, they say, signifies him who is utterly destitute both of money and means of livelihood; the other, one who has fallen in distress and needs relief.

This is the rule regarding the distribution of charitable funds. See also notes, Surah ii. 217.

68. The hypocritical men and the hypocritical women are the one from the other : they command what is evil, and forbid what is just, and shut up their hands; they forget God, wherefore He forgets them. Verily the hypocrites are the wicked doers.

71. Have they not been told the history of those who were before them? . . . Their apostles came to them with clear evidences : and it was not God who wronged them, but it was themselves they did wrong.

The Believers :

72. The believers, men and women, are friends one to another : they command what is just, and forbid what is evil, and they are steadfast in prayer, and give alms, and they obey God and His apostle. These,—on them will God have mercy. Verily God is mighty, wise.

73. God has promised to the believers, men and women Gardens beneath which rivers flow, to dwell therein for ever; and goodly mansions in the Gardens of Eden; and best of all, the pleasure of God,—that is the great bliss.

98. The Arabs of the desert are most stubborn in unbelief and discord, and it is easier for them to be ignorant of the ordinance which God has sent to His apostle; and God is knowing, wise.

105. Do not they know that God accepts the repentance of His servants; and that He receives alms; surely God, He is relenting, compassionate.

106. Say thou, Work ye; surely God sees your works, and His prophet, and the believers, and ye will surely be brought before Him who knows the secret and the manifest, and He will tell you what ye have done.

72. Mark this definition of 'believers.'

Opposition Mosque Condemned :

108. There are those who have built a Mosque for mischief, and for infidelity, and to divide the believers, and for an asylum for him who fought against God and His apostle in time past. And they swear, We intended only good; but God witnesses that they certainly do lie.

109. Never set thou foot in it : there is a mosque founded in piety from its first day. It is more worthy that thou shouldst stand up therein : therein are men who love to be purified; and God loves the pure.

108. About the time of the Prophet's flight Banu Amru b. Auf had built a mosque at Koba, which Mohammed opened; this excited the envy of another party, who also built a mosque, but which Mohammed condemned saying that it was an opposition mosque.

109. 'There is a mosque,' etc. That of Kobah.

The Believers :

112. Verily God has bought of those who believe their lives and their wealth for the Garden prepared

for them : they fight in the way of God, whether they slay or are slain, —His promise in the Law, and the Evangel, and the Quran.

120. Ye believers, fear God, and be with the sincere.

129. Now has an apostle come to you from among yourselves : your iniquities press heavily upon him; to the believers he is kind, and full of compassion.

130. If they turn away, say thou, God suffices me; there is no God but He : in Him I trust, and He is the Lord of the mighty Throne.

Principal Contents

Alms, Its distribution, 60

Believers, defined, 72; their relative duties to unbelievers, 7; their reward, 20, 73.

Hypocrites, 68.

Jews and Christians, 30, 31, 34.

Mosque, an opposition, condemned, 108, 109.

Sacrifice of self, enjoined, 112.

Unbelievers, their attitude to Moslems, 8, 13.

SURAH X—JONAH

(Mecca.)

The Prophet Jonah is mentioned in verse 98.

Sincerity :

2. . . . And bear glad tidings to those who believe, that on the merit of their sincerity they have an interest with their Lord.

God's Providence :

5. He it is who has ordained the sun to shine, and the moon for the light, and has ordained her

stations, they ye may learn the number of years, and the computation thereof. God has only created all this in truth. He explains His signs to those who understand.

6. Verily in the alteration of night and day, and in what God has created in the heavens and the earth, are sings to people who fear to do wrong.

5. 'In truth,' with a purpose, and not in frivolity.

The Believers :

9. As to those who believe and to good, their Lord will guide them because of their faith : rivers shall flow beneath them in Gardens of Pleasure.

10. Their cry therein is, Glory to Thee, O God and their salutation therein, Peace;

11. And the end of their prayer is, Praise to God, Lord of the worlds!

The Ungodly :

13. When evil befalls a man, he cries to Us, on his side, or sitting, or standing; and when We deliver him from his affliction, he passes on as though he had never called on Us against the evil which had befallen him. Thus are the deeds of the transgressors prepared for them.

14. And of old we destroyed generations before you, when they had acted wickedly, and their apostles had come to them with clear evidences, and they would not believe. Thus We reward the criminal people.

15. Then have We made you to succeed them in the earth, that We might see how ye would act.

24. Ye people, verily the violence which ye commit against your own souls, is only an enjoyment of

the life of this world; then to Us will ye return, and We will tell you what ye have done.

25. Verily the likeness of the life of this world is only like as water which We send down from heaven, and wherewith the produce of the earth are mixed, of which men eat, and cattle also, until the earth has received its vesture, and is adorned; the dwellers on it imagine that they have power over it, but Our command comes to it by night or by day, and We make it as if it were mown down, as though it had not abounded yesterday. . .

26. God calls to the abode of Peace, and guides whom He pleases into the straight path.

27. For those who do good is excellence, and an abundance; . . .

31. There shall every soul have what it has sent before it, and they shall be brought before God, their true Lord, and what they have falsely imagined shall vanish from them.

God : His Power :

32. Say thou, Who provides you food from heaven and earth ? or who has power over the hearing and the sight ? and who brings forth the living from the dead, and the dead from the living? and who rules all things ? . .

33. This God then is your true Lord : and what remains after truth but error ? How then are ye turned aside ?

37. But most of them follow an opinion only, and a mere opinion attains not to any truth. Verily God knows what ye do.

42. If they yet call thee a liar, then say, My work is

for me, and for you is your work : ye are clear of that which I do, and I am clear of that which ye do.

His Goodness :

45. Verily God will not wrong men in anything, but men do wrong themselves.

48. Every people has its apostle. . .

58. Ye people, now has come to you a warning from your Lord, and a balm for what is in your bosoms, and a guide and mercy to believers.

99. But if thy Lord pleased, verily all who are in the earth would have believed together. What ! wilt thou then compel men to become believers ?

48. Mark this verse.

True Religion :

104. Say thou, Ye people, if ye are in doubt as to my religion, verily I worship not what ye worship beside God; but I worship God alone . . .

105. And set thy face steadfast in religion as an upright man, and be not of the polytheists.

108. Say thou, Ye people, now has the truth come to you from your Lord : whoso then is guided, it is for his own soul, and whoso errs, errs only against it. And I am not a keeper over you.

109. And do thou follow what it revealed to thee, and persevere steadfastly, till God judges; and He is the best of judges.

Principal Contents

Apostle for every people, 48.

Believers, their reward, 9-11.

Evil redounds to the doer, 24.

God, His providence, 5, 6, 32.

Quran, its true nature, 58.
Perseverence inculcated, 109.
Religion, the true, 104, 105; not to forced upon people, 99.
Reward according to works, 27, 31, 45, 108.
Sincerity, its value, 2.
Ungodly, the, 13-5.

SURAH XI.—HUD

(Mecca.)

This Surah derives its title from the story of Hud, the prophet of the Adites, which is here repeated. Examples from the history of other prophets are also given to show that the ungodly have been invariably visited with divine chastisement. The matter is much the same as that contained in Surah VII.

The Quran :

1. A.L.R. A Book the verses whereof are established in wisdom, and again set forth with clearness—from the wise, the knowing.

1. A.L.R. See notes, Surah ii. 1.

Its Object :

2. That ye worship none but God.—Verily I come from Him as a warner and a bearer of glad tidings;

3. And that ye seek pardon from your Lord, and be turned to Him. Excellent enjoyments will He give you until a prescribed time, and to every one who has merit, will He give of His grace.

God's Knowledge :

5. Do they not doubly fold up their breasts, that so they may hide themselves from Him ?

6. And when they cover themselves with their garments, does not He know what they hide and what they show ?

7. For He knows the very inmost of their breasts.

His Providence :

8. There is no moving thing on earth, but with God is its food : He knows its retreat, and where it is laid up : all is in the plain Book.

113. And surely every one of them will thy Lord repay for their works; verily He is informed of what they do.

Some Duties :

114. Be steadfast therefore as thou art commanded, thou and he who turns with thee, and transgress not; He certainly sees what ye do.

115. And incline not to those who act wickedly, lest the Fire touch you, and ye have no one to protect you against God, neither be ye helped.

116. And be steadfast in prayer, morning and evening, and at night-fall; for certainly good works drive away evils. This, a reminder to those who remember.

117. And persevere steadfastly; surely God wastes not the reward of those who do good.

The Ungodly :

118. . . But those who were wicked followed what they enjoyed, and were criminals.

119. And thy Lord would not destroy the cities unjustly, while their inhabitants were righteous.

122. And say to those who believe not, Do your part, we will do ours; and wait ye, and we also will wait.

123. God's is the secret of the heavens and the earth; and all command is with God : then worship Him,

and trust in Him; surely thy Lord is not unmindful of what ye do.

Principal Contents

Evil, to be avoided, 115, always punished, 119.

God, His knowledge, 5-7; His providence, 8; His power, 123.

Quran, the, 1; its aims, 2, 3.

Perseverence inculcated, 114 , 117.

Prayers, their object, 116.

SURAH XII.—JOSEPH

(Mecca.)

This Surah treats throughout of the history of Joseph. An abstract is here subjoined to elucidate the object of this Surah.

Joseph, son of Jacob, was the best beloved son of the patriarch, and thus incurred the jealousy of his brothers, who contrived by a stratagem to get Joseph to a distance from his father and threw him into a well. He was taken out by somes travellers and sold to an Egyptian. By the mere dint of his character he subsequently rose to a high eminence in the government of the country, and finally his brothers submitted to him saying, 'By God ! Now has God chosen thee above us, and we have been sinners.' But Joseph received them with open arms, and said, 'There is no blame on you this day : God forgive you; surely He is the most merciful of those who show mercy.' (vv. 91 and 92.)

The moral of it all to Mohammed was that God's help is always nigh to the righteous, as put forth in verse 110, below.

This Surah was revealed at Mecca, at a time of life when Mohammed was in daily peril of his own life and the lives of His followers. And it bears a glorious testimony to the intensity of Mohammed's faith in the final success of his cause. In time his hopes were fully realised : he got an asylum at Medinah 276 miles away from Mecca, and after twelve years or even more he had the pleasure to enter as a Conqueror the city of his birth from which he had been estranged by the persecutions of his fellow-men who had turned his bitterest enemies and whom he now freely forgave all the years of sorrow and cruel scorn they had inflicted on him and his followers in the self-same words of Joseph quoted above. Could faith in a living God and a high ideal of forgiveness go further ?

The Quran :

1. A.L.R. These are the verses of the plain Book.

2. We have sent down the Quran in Arabic, that ye might understand.

108. Say thou, This is my way; I call you to God by a clear evidence: I and whoso follows, me; and thanks to God ! I am not of the polytheists.

1. 'A.L.R.' See notes to Surah ii. 1.
2. 'That ye might understand.' See also Surah xiv. 4.

Examples of Former Days :

109. We never sent before thee any but men inspired, out of the people of the cities. Will they not journey through the earth, and see what has been the end of those who have been before them ? But the home in the Hereafter is better for those who fear to do wrong. Will they not yet take wisdom ?

110. When at last the apostles lost all hope, and thought they were taken as liars, Our help came to them, and We delivered whom We pleased; and Our vengeance was not averted from the criminal people.

111. Certainly in their stories is an example for those who have hearts. This is not a newly-invented fiction, but a confirmation of what was before it, and an explanation of all things, and a guide, and mercy, to people who believe.

Principal Contents

Examples of former days, their use, 111.

Quran, in Arabic, its object, 2.

Prophets, all were under divine providence, 110.

SURAH XIII. — THUNDER

(Mecca)

This Surah takes its title from verse 14, where the word occurs incidentally.

God : His Power :

2. God it is who raised the heavens without pillars thou canst see; then mounted His Throne, and pressed into service the sun and the moon : each runs its appointed course. He rules all things . . . . .

3. He it is who has spread the earth, and placed on it firm mountains, and rivers; and of every fruit He has ordained two kinds; and He makes the night to cover the day. Surely herein are signs to people who consider.

4. And in the earth are tracts ordering each other; and also vine-yards, and corn, and palm-trees single and clustered. They are watered by the same water; yet some of them We make more excellent than others to eat : verily herein are signs to people who understand.

5. If thou dost wonder, surely wonderful is their saying, What ! when we are dust, shall we again be raised a new creation ?

6. These are they who believe not in their Lord : these ! — collars shall be on their necks, and these are the fellows of the Fire, to continue therein for ever.

3. 'Two kinds.' As sweet and sour, black and white, small and large.

4. 'Tracts,' meaning various tracts; some fruitful and others barren, some plain and others mountainous, some proper for corn and others for trees, etc.

6. 'Collars,' The 'collar' here mentioned is an engine

something like a pillory. Some understand this passage figuratively, of the ungodly being bound in the chains of error and obstinacy.

Miracles Demanded :

7. They ask thee to hasten evil rather than good, although there have already been examples before them. And surely thy Lord is endued with grace to men, despite their sins; but thy Lord is also severe in punishing.

8. And those who believe not say, If a sign is not sent to him from his Lord .... Thou art a warner only, and to every people a guide.

8. Supply 'we will not believe,' after 'from his Lord.'

The Guardian Angels :

12. Each has those mutually succeeding ones, before him and behind him : they watch over him by God's commands. Verily God will not change what is in men unless they change what is in themselves. And when God wills evil on a people, there is none to avert it : neither have they beside God a patron.

12. 'Those mutually succeeding ones.' This refers to the guardian-angels who invariably accompany men. See also Surah 1. 16.

God : His Power :

13. He it is who makes the lightning to shine to you, for fear and hope, and who brings up the laden clouds.

14. And the thunder celebrates His praise, and the angels also, for fear of Him; and He sends the thunderbolts, and smites therewith whom He will, while they dispute about God. And surely He is mighty in power.

15. He ought of right to be called on; but those whom they call beside Him give them no answer, otherwise than as he who stretches forth his hands to the water that it may reach his mouth, when it cannot reach it : the prayer of the ungodly is only delusive.

16. And to God does all in the heavens and the earth low down, willingly or by force; and their shadows also, morning and evening.

17. He sends down rain from heaven, and the torrents follow in their measure, and the floods bear along a swelling foam. And from what they melt in the fire, to make ornaments and vessels, a like scum arises.

Thus God sets forth truth and vanity : as to the foam it is quickly gone, and as to what is useful to man remains on the earth. Thus God puts forth parables.

For those who respond to their Lord are excellent things, but those who respond not, if they had all that is in the earth, and as much more, they would surely give it for their ransom. Evil their reckoning ! and their home Gehenna ! and wretched the bed !

13. 'Hope.' Thunder and lightning being the sign of approaching rain.

14. 'Celebrates His praise,' Or it testifies to His greatness.

'While they dispute,' etc. This alludes to the following incident. Amir b. at-Tofeil and Arbad b. Rabiyah went to Mohammed with an intent to kill him; and Amir opened a discussion with him regarding certain doctrines, while Arbad taking a compass, went behind him to despatch him with his sword. The Prophet who was alone perceived his design, and implored God's protection; and immediately Arbad was struck dead by lightning; whereupon his companion fled.

The Godly :

19. . . . . Only those who have hearts will consider;

20. Who fulfil their Covenant to God, and break not; their compact.

21. And who join what God has commanded to be joined, and who fear their Lord, and fear an ill account;

22. And who persevere from a desire to seek the Face of his Lord, and are steadfast in prayer, and give alms of what We have given them, in secret and in public, and who turn away evil by good; these ! for them is the reward of the Abode.

23. Gardens of Eden, wherein they shall enter, and whoever has been upright, of their fathers, and their wives, and their posterity, and the angels, shall go in to them by every portal with —

24. Peace upon you ! for that ye have persevered. How excellent the Home hereafter !

27. . . . He will guide to Himself him who turns to Him;

28. And those who believe, their hearts resting securely on the thought of God; — and do not all hearts rest securely on the thought of God ? — They who believe and do good, for them is bliss, and the excellent Home.

29. . . . Say thou, He is my Lord : there is no God but He : in Him I trust, and to him is my return.

21. 'To be joined.' By believing in God and joining thereto the continual practice of their duty both towards God and man.

22. 'The Face of God,' This refers to the Beatific Vision in the Hereafter.

23. The Moslem Heaven includes the idea of a happy Home, amidst family and children.

The Ungodly :

30. And though it were a Quran by which the mountains could be moved, and the earth cleft, and the dead made to speak . . . ! But all command is with God. Do then those who believe deny that if God pleased He would certainly guide all men aright ?

30. 'Deny'; lit., 'despair.' After 'made to speak,' supply 'they will not believe.'

Various Dispensations :

38. And We have sent apostles before thee, and We gave them wives and children; and no apostle came with a sign but by the permission of God.

39. For every age is a book : God abolishes what He pleases, or confirms; and with Him is the Original Book.

40. And whether We make thee see a part of what We have denounced to them, or whether We take thee hence; verily thine is to preach only, and Ours to take account.

42. And those who have been before them, devised plots, but all plots were mastered by God : He knows what every soul earns, and the ungodly shall know whose is the Home hereafter.

43. And those who believe not, say, Thou art not of those sent. Say thou, God suffices for a witness between me and yourselves, and whoso has knowledge of the Book.

39. This shows that each dispensation varied with each age, and that no law, however best, could be always equally applicable.

'Original Book;' lit., 'Mother of the Book.'

Principal Contents

God, His power, 2-5, 13, 14, 16, 17.
Godly, the, 19-24, 27, 28.
Guardian-angels, 12.
Miracles demanded, 7, 8.
Reward of evil, 17.
Scriptures for each age, 39.
Ungodly, the 30.

SURAH XIV. — ABRAHAM
(Mecca.)

This Surah takes its name after the patriarch mentioned in verse 38. Some other prophets are also mentioned; and the aim of it all is to warn the unbelieving Arabs of a day when they shall be called to account before God.

The Quran :

1. A.L.R. A. Book have We revealed to thee that thou mayest bring men out of darkness into light, by the permission of their Lord, into the path of the mighty, the glorious.

2. God, whose is whatever is in the heavens and in the earth; and woe to the ungodly for their terrible punishment !

The Ungodly :

3. Who love the life of this world above the Hereafter, and turn aside from the way of God, and seek to make it crooked. These are in a wide error.

4. And We have not sent any apostle but with the language of his people, that he might explain to them . . .

God : His Power :

22. Seest thou not that in truth has God made the

heavens and the earth ? If He please, He can make you pass away, and make a new creation come.

A Good Word :

29. Seest thou not how God strikes forth the parable of a good word ? It is like a good tree, its roots firmly fixed, and its branches reaching up to heaven.

30. Yielding its fruits in all seasons, by the permission of God. And God strikes forth the parable to men that they may consider.

An Evil Word :

31. And the likeness of an evil word is as an evil tree torn up from the face of the earth, and has no stability.

God : His Power :

32. God will establish those who believe, by the steadfast word, in the life of this world and in the Hereafter; and God misleads the wicked; surely God does what He pleases.

37. He gives you of everything which ye ask Him, and if ye would reckon up the gifts of God, ye shall not be able to count them. Surely man is unjust, ungrateful.

32. With regard to the guidance of people it is here put forth that 'God misleads the wicked.' All the passages therefore which make mention of God's will to lead people must be construed accordingly. See also Surah ii. 24, 25.

The Judgment Day :

43. Think not that God is unmindful of what the ungodly do : He only respites them to the day when all eyes shall stare up;

44. And they shall hasten forward, their heads upraised, their looks riveted, and their hearts a blank. Warn them therefore of the Day when the punishment shall overtake them.

45. And when the wrong-doers shall say, Our Lord, respite us yet a little while;

46. To Thy call will we make answer, and we will follow Thine apostles.

47. Did not ye swear heretofore that no reverse should befall you ? Yet ye dwelt in the dwellings of those who wronged their ownselves, and it was made plain to you how We had dealt with them, and We held them up as examples to you : they devised plots, but God did master their plots even though their plots could move mountains.

43. 'Shall stare up,' etc. These are signs of excessive terror in men, for now are they to be judged for what they have done.

45. 'A little while;' lit., 'to a term near at hand.'

47. 'Did not,' etc. Spoken by God.

'In the dwellings,' etc. This refers to the ancient Arabs, the Adites, Smudites, etc., who were now extinct by reason of their iniquities.

Promise of Success :

48. Think not then that God will fail His promise to His apostles. Verily God is mighty at avenging.

The Judgment Day :

49. The day the earth is changed into another earth, and the heavens also, shall men come forth before God, the one, the mighty.

50. And thou shalt see the wicked on that day bound down in chains;

51. Their garments of pitch, and their faces covered

with fire — that God may reward every soul for what it has earned; verily God is swift at reckoning up.

52. This is a message to people, that they may be warned thereby, and that they may know that there is only one God, and that those who have hearts may consider.

49. 'The day,' refers to the Judgment Day, a glowing picture of which is here given in the succeeding verses.

Principal Contents

Apostles, their language, 4.

God, His power, 22, 32, 37.

Judgment Day, its stern reality, 43-5; 49-51.

Quran, the , 1; its aim, 52.

Success of truth insured, 48.

Ungodly, the, 3.

Wicked, the, misled, 32.

Word, good, 29, 30; evil, 31.

SURAH XV. — HIJR

(Mecca.)

This Surah is named after Hijr, a territory in the province of Hijaz, between Medinah and Syria, where the Samudites dwelt, whose story is mentioned towards the end of the Surah. The date of this Surah is somewhere about the seventh year of Mohammed's ministry.

Promise of Success :

2. Many a time will those who disbelieve wish that they had been Moslems.

3. Let them feast and enjoy themselves, and let hope beguile them, but by and by shall they know !

4. We never destroyed a city, but a prefixed term was granted them :

5. No people can forestall or retard their fate.

2. This fact came out true, for during the lifetime of Mohammed all Arabia had accepted Islam.

Miracle Demanded :

6. They say, O thou to whom the reminder is sent down, thou are surely possessed of a Jinn;

7. Wouldst not thou have come to us with angels, if thou wert of those who spoke the truth ?

8. We send down angels only on urgent occasions; for then they should not have been respited.

9. We have sent down the reminder, and We will certainly preserve the same.

10. We have already sent apostles before thee among peoples of old;

11. And there came no apostle to them, but they laughed him to scorn.

14. Even were We to open a gate in the Heaven above them, and all the while they were climbing into it,

15. They would still say, It is only our eyes are dazzled; nay, we are a people enchanted.

16. We have set in the heaven towers, and adorned and decked them forth for those who see,

19. And the earth We have spread forth, and thrown thereon the mountains, and made everything to spring forth in the same in just proportion;

20. And We have provided therein sustenance for you, and for him whom ye do not sustain.

21. There is not one thing but with Us are its store-houses; and We send not the same but in a fixed measure.

8. 'On urgent occasions.' Lit., 'in truth;' not to gratify the curiosity merely of the people.

16. 'Towers.' These are the signs of the Zodiac.

The Pious :

45. Verily the pious shall be in Gardens, and amidst fountains :

46. Enter ye therein in peace and security;

47. And We will remove all grudges from their bosoms; as brothers they shall sit, face to face, on couches :

48. No worry will touch them there, nor shall they be thrown out.

God : His Ways :

49. Announce thou to My servants that I am the gracious, the compassionate;

50. And My chastisement — that is a painful chastisement.

85. We have not created the heavens and the earth, and what is between them, but for a purpose. And the Hour shall certainly come : wherefore do thou forgive them with a kindly grace.

86. Verily thy Lord, He is the creator and does know.

88. Cast not thine eyes on what We have given some of them : neither be thou grieved on their account; rather lower thy wing to the believers.

85. 'For a purpose.' Lit., 'in truth,' not in play or vain amusement.

88. It is not for thee to judge whether God should have given them these advantages; the prophet's duty only lies in humbling himself before all who believe.

The Prophet :

89. And say thou, I am a plain warner :

90. And We will punish those who foster divisions,

91. Who break up the Quran into parts.

92. For, by they Lord ! We will surely demand an account from them all,

93. Of what they have done.

94. Wherefore publish what thou hast been commanded, and withdraw from the polytheists.

95. Verily We suffice thee against the scoffers,

96. Who set up Gods with God; by and by they shall know :

97. Now We know that thy heart is distressed for what they say;

98. But do thou celebrate the praise of thy Lord, and be of those who worship,

99. And serve thy Lord until the certainty does come to thee.

90. 'Who foster,' etc., who become sectaries.

91. Who accept a part, and ignore the other.

97. 'They say,' i.e., in derision.

99. 'The certainty,' here refers to death.

Principal Contents

God, His power, 16, 19-21; His ways, 49, 50, 85.

Miracles demanded, 6-11, 14, 15.

Pious, the, their reward 45-8.

Sectarianism condemned, 90 4.

Success, promise of, 2.

SURAH XVI. — THE BEE

(Mecca.)

The Bee is mentioned in verse 70; hence the title of the Surah.

God : His Power and Providence :

1. The sentence of God will surely come; wherefore do not thou hasten it. Glory to Him ! and exalted is He above what they join with Him.

4. He has created man from seed, yet behold, and open disputer is he !

5. And the cattle, He created them for you : from them ye have warm garments, and other uses; and of them ye eat :

6. And they are a credit to you when ye drive them home and when ye lead them forth to pasture;

7. And they carry your burdens to lands which ye could not otherwise reach unless with great difficulty to yourselves : truly your Lord is kind, compassionate.

8. And horses, and mules, and asses, that ye may ride them, and for your ornament and things which ye have no knowledge has He created.

9. God's is to point out the way, and from it some do turn aside; but if He pleased, He would certainly have guided you all aright.

10. He it is who sends down from heaven water, whereof ye drink, and from which grow plants by which ye pasture.

11. By it He causes the corn, and the olives, and the palm trees, and the grapes, to spring forth for you. Surely herein are signs to people who reflect.

12. And He has pressed into your service the night and the day; and the sun, and the moon, and the stars also, subject to His bidding. Herein are signs to people who understand.

13. And all of varied hues, that He has created for you in the earth : surely herein are signs to people who consider.

14. And He it is who has subjected the sea to you, that ye may eat fresh flesh thereout, and take from thence ornaments to wear; and thou seest the ships ploughing its waves, that ye may seek of His grace; and that ye might give thanks.

15. And He has thrown upon the earth firm mountains, lest it move with you, and rivers, and ways, that ye may be guided.

16. And way-marks : and by the stars too are they guided.

17. . . . . Will ye not yet consider ?

18. And if ye would reckon up the favours of God, ye could not count them. Verily God is gracious, compassionate.

14. 'Fresh flesh,' *i.e.*, the fish; as being naturally more fresh, and sooner liable to corruption, than the flesh of birds and beasts. The expression is thought to have been made use of here the rather, because the production of such fresh food from salt water is an instance of God's power.

'Ornaments;' *e.g.*, pearls and coral.

'Seek of His grace,' *i.e.*, by means of commerce.

The Ungodly :

23. Your God is one God : and they who believe not in the Hereafter, their hearts are given to denial, and they are full of pride.

27. That on the Judgement Day they may bear their own entire burden, and the burden of those whom in their ignorance they misled. Is not that evil which they shall bear ?

35. What can they expect but that angels should

come upon them, or that a sentence of thy Lord take effect ? So did those who were before them; and it was not God who did wrong them, but it was themselves they did wrong;

36. And the evils which they had done, recoiled upon them, and what they had scoffed at encompassed them round about.

36. 'What;' *i.e.,* the Judgment of God.

The True Believers :

43. As to those who have fled their homes for God after that they had been unjustly persecuted, We will surely provide them an excellent home in this world, and the reward of the Hereafter is greater, did they but know ! —

44. They who steadfastly endure, and in their Lord do trust.

The Ungodly :

47. What ! Are they then who have plotted evil sure that God will not cleave the earth with them, or that a punishment will not come upon them from whence they do not expect ?

48. Or, that He will not seize upon them in their comings and goings, while they shall not be able to resist Him ?

49. Or, that He will not seize them with some slowly-wasting scourge ?

50. Do they not see the things which God has created, how they turn their shadows, right and left, worshipping God in all abasement ?

51. And whatever moves in the heavens and in the earth, God does worship and the angels also; and they are not elated with pride :

52. They fear their Lord above them, and do what they are commanded.

Female Infanticide:

59. They ascribe daughters to God. Glory to Him ! But to themselves they desire not.

60. For, when any of them is told the good news of a female child, his face turns black, and he is distressed :

61. He hides himself from the people, because of the ill tidings : should he keep it with disgrace, or bury it in the dust ? How ill they judge !

60. This and the following verses refer to the pre-Islamite custom of the Arabs of burying their female children alive.

Their manner of doing this varied with different tribes. Sometimes when a woman was ready to fall in labour they dug a pit on the brink whereof she was to be delievered, and if the child happened to be a daughter, they threw it into the pit, but if a son, they saved it alive. Others, however let her live till she was six or nine years of age, when her mother having perfumed her and adorned her, the father led her to a well or pit dug for that purpose, and having bid her look down into it pushed her in headlong, as he stood behind her, and then filling up the pit, levelled it with the rest of the ground.

God : His Mercy and Providence :

63. If God were to punish men for their iniquity. He would not leave on earth a moving thing; but He respites them to a fixed term; and when their time comes, they shall not be respited an hour, nor shall they be fore-stalled.

68. And for you in cattle is an example. We give you to drink of what is in their bellies, between digested dregs and blood—pure milk—the pleasant beverage of those that quaff it.

69. And of the fruits of palm-trees, and of grapes, ye get wine and healthy nutriment : herein are signs to people who understand.

70. And thy Lord has inspired the bee—Provide thee houses in the mountains, and in the trees, and in what houses men do build :

71. And feed on every fruit, and walk in the beaten paths of thy Lord. From its belly comes forth a fluid of varying hues, which yields medicine to man : verily herein are signs to people who reflect.

72. God has created you, and He will hereafter take you to Himself; and some of you will be carried on to a decrepit age, when all that once was known is known no longer . . .

73. And God has blessed some of you above others as regards provisions, yet those who are blessed among them do not give of their provisions to those whom their right hands have possessed, that they may share alike ! What ! will they yet deny the beneficence of God ?

74. And God has made for you wives from among yourselves, and from your wives has He given you sons and grandsons, and has provided you with good things.

76. Make therefore no comparison with God . . .

77. God strikes forth the parable of a slave, the property of his lord, who has no power over anything, and another whom We have supplied with a good provision, and who expends of it in private and in public. Shall they be held equal ? All praise to God alone ! but most of them do not know.

78. And God strikes forth the parable of two men; one of them is born dumb who has no power over anything, and is a burden to his lord : send him where he will, he comes not back with success; shall he and the man who commands what is just, and keeps to the straight path be held equal ?

79. God has brought you forth from the wombs of your mothers : ye knew nothing, and He gave you hearing, and sight, and heart, that ye might give thanks.

80. Do not they look at the birds subjected in the vault of heaven : none does hold them in but God ! Verily herein are signs to people who believe.

81. And God has given you houses to dwell in, and He has given you tents of the skins of cattle, which ye find light when ye shift your quarters, or when ye halt; and of their wool, and soft fur and hair, He has supplied you with furniture and goods for a season . . .

83. But if they turn aside; surely thine is only to preach publicly.

Justice Enjoined :

92. Verily God commands justice and the doing of good, and the giving to kindred their due; and He forbids you wickedness, and iniquity, and oppression. He warns you that ye might consider.

93. And fulfil your covenant with God, when ye have covenanted; and break not your oaths after ye have covenanted; and break not your oaths after ye have pledged them; for now ye have made God stand surety for you. Verily God knows what ye do.

94. And be not like to her who undoes what she has spun, untwisting it after she had twisted it strongly, taking your oaths among you deceitfully, because one party is more numerous than the other party. God only tries you therein, and on the Judgment Day He will clear up to you that concerning which ye now disagree.

96. Therefore take not your oaths among yourselves deceitfully, lest your foot slip after that it is firmly fixed, and ye taste evil, for that ye have turned aside from the way of God, and great be your punishment.

98. What is with you will pass away, but what is with God will endure. And We will reward those who steadfastly persevere with a reward meet for their best deeds.

100. When thou readest the Quran, have recourse to God against the devil cast away :

101. For no power has he over those who believe, and trust in their Lord.

102. But his power is only with those who take him for their patron, and those who join gods with Him.

108. Whoso disbelieves in God, after he has believed, — unless he is forced, his heart resting secure in the faith — and opens his breast to infidelity, on these is the indignation of God, and for them is a severe punishment.

110. These it is whose hearts has God sealed up, and their hearing, and their sight; and these are the heedless. Without doubt, in the hereafter they shall lose.

126. Call to the way of thy Lord with wisdom and kindly exhortation, and dispute with them in the kindest manner : verily thy Lord, He knows who errs from His way, and He knows who are the rightly guided.

127. And if ye take vengeance, take a vengeance equal to the wrong that has been done you, but if ye steadfastly endure; surely best it will be for the patiently enduring.

128. Endure then with patience, but thy patience is only in God. And be not thou grieved on their account, neither be thou troubled for their craftiness. Verily God is with those who fear to do wrong and who are doers of good.

Principal Contents

Devil, patron of the ungodly, 101, 102.

God, His power, 4-18, 50-2, 68-74; His mercy, 63; His greatness, 76, 77, 79-81.

Indulgence allowed to believers, 108.

Infanticide, female, condemned, 60, 61.

Judgment Day, inevitable, 1.

Justice enjoined, 92.

Oaths to be kept, 93-6.

Perseverance inculcated, 43, 44, 98, 128.

Preaching with persuasion enjoined, 126.

Ungodly, the, 23, 27, 35, 36; their fate, 47-9.

Vengeance only equal, 127.

SURAH XVII. — THE CHILDREN OF ISRAEL
(Mecca.)

The title is taken from verse 4, when a certain account is given of the Children of Israel.

God : His Glory :

1. Glory to Him who carried His servant by night from the sacred Mosque to the furthest Mosque, whose precincts We have blessed, that We might show him of Our signs. Verily He is the hearer, the seer.

1. 'His servant,' *i.e.,* Mohammed.

   This refers to the celebrated Vision of Ascension which Mohammed had at Mecca some time before his flight to Medinah. It was a time when the Prophet and his followers were in the worst plight, but the work still went on as usual, and it evinces the ardent spirit of Mohammed in the cause with which he had begun.

Man's Fate :

12. May prays for evil as he prays for good; for man is hasty.

14. Every man's fate have We fastened about his neck : and on the Day of Judgment We will bring forth to him a book which shall be proffered to him wide open :

15. Read thy Book; thine own soul is enough to take account against thee this day.

16. Whoso is guided aright it is only for his own soul, and whoso errs, errs only against it, and no burdened soul shall bear the burden of another . . .

12. 'Man prays,' etc., That is, out of ignorance, mistaking evil for good; or making wicked imprecations on himself and others, out of passion and impatience.

    'Man is hasty;' or inconsiderate not weighing the consequence of what he asks.

14. 'Fate.' Lit., 'the bird,' which is here used to signify a man's fortune or success; the Arabs as well as the Greeks and the Romans taking omens from the flight of birds, which they supposed to portend good luck, if they flew from the

left to the right, but if from the right to the left, the contrary; similar omens they took when certain beasts passed before them.

'About his neck;' *i.e.*, like a collar, which he cannot by any means get off.

Duties Enjoined :

24. Thy Lord has ordained that ye worship none beside Him, and that ye be good to your parents, whether the one or both of them attain to old age with thee; and say not to them, Uff; neither reproach them, but speak to them in respectful sort;

25. And defer humbly to them, out of tenderness, and say, Lord, have mercy on them both, even as they nursed me when I was little.

28. And give to him who is of kin his due, and to the poor, and the homeless;

29. But waste not wastefully, for the wasteful are brothers of the devils, and the devil was ungrateful to his Lord.

30. But if thou turn away from them to seek the mercy of thy Lord for which thou hopest, at least speak to them in kindly sort.

31. And let not thy hand be chained to thy neck, nor yet stretch it out right open, or thou wilt sit down in reproach and destitution.

33. Kill not you children for fear of want : for them and for you will We provide. Verily the killing them is a great sin.

34. Come not near to inchastity, for it is a foul thing and an evil way;

35. And kill not the being which God has forbidden you to kill, unless by right; and whoso it killed

unjustly, to his heir We have given power, but let him not transgress in putting the murderer to death, for he too is assisted.

36. And come not near to the wealth of the orphan, unless it is to improve it, until they come of age. And perform your engagements, verily the engagements shall be inquired into.

37. And give full measure when ye measure, and weigh with a just balance. This is better, and fairest for settlement.

38. And follow not that whereof thou hast no knowledge; verily the hearing, and the sight, and the heart, each of these shall be inquired into.

39. And walk not proudly in the earth, for thou canst not cleave the earth, neither shalt thou reach to the mountains in height.

40. All this is evil; abominable to thy Lord.

41. This is of the wisdom which thy Lord has revealed to thee. Set not up another god with God, or thou wilt be thrown into Hell, reproved and cast away.

46. The seven heavens praise Him, and the earth, and all who are therein; neither is there a thing but does celebrate His praise, but ye understand not their celebration. Verily He is mild, gracious.

55. Speak to My creatures, that they speak in kindly sort. Verily the Devil would sow discord among them; for surely the devil is man's avowed enemy.

80. Observe prayer at sunset, till night-fall, and the day-break chanting — for the day-break chanting is witnessed.

81. And watch to it in the night : as an excess in

service for thee; it may be that thy Lord will raise thee to an honourable position.

82. And say thou, Lord, make me to enter with a right entry, and make me to come forth with a right coming forth, and give me from Thy presence a helping power.

86. Say thou, Each one does after his own manner : but your Lord well knows who is guided aright in the way.

87. And they will ask thee about the soul; say thou, the soul is at the command of My Lord, but ye have no knowledge given you except a little.

24. 'With thee;' that is, receiving their support and maintenance from thee.

'Uff,' a slight token of vexation

25. 'Defer humbly,' etc. Lit., 'Lower the wing of humility.'

28. 'His due;' that is, friendship and affection, and assistance in time of need.

29. 'Waste not.' See Surah ii. 184.

30. 'If thou turn away,' etc. If thy present circumstances will not permit thee to assist others, defer thy charity till God grants thee better ability.

31. That is, Be neither niggardly nor profuse, but observe the mean between the two extremes, wherein consists true liberality.

33. This is as against the practice of female infanticide prevalent amongst the Arabs.

35. 'Unless by right.' See Surah v. 35.

'Power,' *i.e.,* to retaliate.

'Transgress not,' by retaliating in too cruel a manner, or by revenging the murder on any other than the person who actually killed him; for the Arabs under such circumstances rose against a whole tribe any played havoc with them. See also Surah xvi. 127.

'Is assisted,' *i.e.,* by law.

38. 'Whereof thou hast,' etc. That is, vain and uncertain opinions, which thou hast not any good reason to believe true, or at least probable.

Some interpret the words, 'Accuse not any of a crime whereof thou hast no knowledge;' supposing they forbid the bearing false witness, or the spreading or giving credit to idle reports of others.

81. 'Excess in service,' a work of supererogation.

87. 'The soul,' It might also mean the 'Spirit.'

Miracles Demanded :

92. And they say, We will not believe on thee, until thou cause a spring of water to gush forth for us out of the earth.

93. Or, thou have a garden of palm trees and vines, and thou cause rivers to spring forth therein in abundance;

94. Or, thou make the heaven to fall down upon us, as thou has given out, in pieces; or thou bring God and the angels to vouch for thee;

95. Or, thou have a house of gold; or, thou climb up into the heaven; and we will not believe in thy climbing there until thou make a book to come down to us which we may read. Say thou, Glory to my Lord ! Am I more than a man, an apostle ?

96. And what hinders men from believing when the guidance has come to them, but that they say, Has God sent a man as His apostle ?

97. Say thou, If angels walked on earth familiarly, We had surely sent down to them from heaven an angle as an apostle.

98. Say thou, God is witness enough between me and you. Verily His servants He knows and sees.

102. If ye held the treasures of the mercy of my Lord,

ye would certain refrain from them for fear of spending them; for man is covetous.

106. .... In truth have We sent it down and in truth has it come down, and We have only sent thee to announce and to warn.

107. And We have divided the Quran into sections, that thou mightest recite it to men by degrees, and We have revealed it gradually.

110. Say thou, Call upon God, or call upon the merciful, whichever name ye invoke him by : He has most excellent names.

And be not loud in thy prayer, nor yet pronounce it too low, but follow between them a way.

111. And say thou, Praise to God who has not begotten a child, who has no partner in the Kingdom, nor any to protect Him from weakness. And magnify Him by proclaiming His greatness.

107. The Quran was revealed in 23 years time of Mohammed's ministry, from the fortieth year of his life till the close of his career at sixty-three. It is well known that it was not given as a book complete, but only in pieces as occasion required.

Principal Contents

Chastity inculcated, 34.

Duties, some, 24, 25, 28-31, 33-41.

God, His unity 111.

Infanticide condemned, 33.

Justice enjoined, 37.

Man, hasty, 12; his fate, 14.

Miracles demanded, 92-8.

Murder forbidden, 35.

Parents, duty to, 24, 25.

Pride reprehended, 39.

Soul, about, 87.
Thrift inculcated, 29, 31.

SURAH XVIII. — THE CAVE

This Surah is so named from the Cave mentioned in verse 8, in which the seven Christian youths who had fled to escape the persecution of the Emperor Decius hid themselves and whose account is given in the succeeding verses.

The Quran :

1. Praise to God, who has revealed to His servant the Book, and has not put therein any crookedness,

2. But made it straight, that he should warn them of a grievous punishment from Him, and announce to the believers who do good, that for them is an excellent reward, wherein they shall continue for ever;

3. And that it may warn those who say, God has begotten a son.

4. And they have no knowledge, nor their fathers. A grievous saying it is to come out of their mouths : they speak only a lie.

6. Verily We have made all that is on earth as its ornament, that We might make trial of them to see which does the best of actions.

26. Read what has been revealed to thee of the Book from thy Lord — none can change His words, — and thou hast no refuge beside Him.

Perseverance Enjoined :

27. And persevere steadfastly with those who call upon their Lord, morning and evening, seeking His Face, and let not thine eyes be turned away from them in quest of the pomp of the life of this

world, and obey not him whose heart We have made careless of the remembrance of Us, and who follows his own lusts, and whose ways are unbridled.

28. And say thou, The truth is from you Lord : let him then who will, believe; and let him who will, not believe . . . .

29. And as to those who believe and do good, — verily We will not deny the reward of him who does good.

44. Wealth and children are the ornament of the life of this world, but good works, which are enduring, are better to they Lord as to reward, and better as to hope.

27. 'His Face,' *i.e.*, His pleasure.

The Judgment Day :

45. And the Day when We will cause the mountains to pass away, and thou shalt see the earth a levelled plain, and We will gather them together and not leave of them any one.

46. And they shall be set before thy Lord in ranks; — Now are ye come to Us even as We created you at first, but ye thought We should not make good to you the promise.

47. And the Book shall be produced, and thou shalt see the wicked in great terror at what is therein, and they shall say, O woe is us ! What is this Book ? it leaves nothing small nor great unnoted; and they shall find what they have done present, and thy Lord will not wrong any one.

103. Say thou, Shall we tell you who they are that have lost their works ?

104. — Whose efforts in the life of this world is mistaken, and who think that they do the right.

105. These are they who believe not in the signs of their Lord, or that they shall meet Him : wherefore their works are lost, and We will not allow them any weight on the Judgment Day.

109. Say thou, Were the sea to become ink to write the words of my Lord, the sea would surely fail ere the words of my Lord would fail, though We brought its like in aid.

47. 'The Book,' *i.e.,* of men's actions. This is generally understood of the knowledge of God.

The Prophet : His Mission :

110. Say thou, I am only a man like to you : it is but revealed to me that your God is only one God : let him then who hopes to meet his Lord do good and not join anything in the worship of his Lord.

Principal Contents

Judgment Day, a strict account of men's actions, 47.

Quran, a straight rule, 1, 2.

Perseverance enjoined, 27.

Prophet, his mission, 110.

SURAH XIX. — MARY

(Mecca.)

This Surah derives its name from the Mother of Jesus, several circumstances relating to whom are mentioned herein.

God has not Begotten a Son :

91. They say, The Merciful God has begotten a son. Now have ye uttered an impious thing !

92. It wants little but that the heavens be rent thereat, and the earth cleave asunder, and the mountains fall down in pieces;

93. For that they ascribe to the merciful God a son, when it becomes not the Merciful God to beget a son.

94. Verily there is none in the heavens and the earth, but shall approach the Merciful God as a servant. He encompasses them, and numbers them with number.

95. Ana all shall come to Him on the Judgment Day alone.

96. Verily those who believe and do good, — to these will the Merciful God give love.

97. Verily We have made it easy in thine own tongue, that by it thou mayest bear glad tidings to the pious, and that thou mayest warn the contentious people.

98. How many generations We have destroyed before them ! Canst thou search out one of them ? or canst thou hear a whisper from them ?

91. This refers to the Christian conception of Jesus as "the only begotten of the Father."

98. The utter destruction of the impious people of old is here urged as a lesson to all generations.

Principal Contents

Believers, their reward, 96.

God has begotten no son, 91-5.

Ungodly, the, destroyed in their sins, 98.

SURAH XX. — T. H.

(Mecca.)

The name of the Surah is taken from verse 1.

The Quran : Its Aim :

1. T. H. We have not revealed the Quran to thee

that thou shouldst be unhappy.

2. But as a warning for him who fears God, —

3. Sent down from Him who created the earth and the lofty heavens.

4. The Merciful God sits on His Throne :

5. His is what is in the heavens and the earth, and what is between them both, and what is beneath the earth.

6. If thou raise thy voice, — verily He knows the secret and the more hidden still.

7. God ! there is no God but He ! His are most excellent names.

1. See notes on Surah ii. 1.

The Judgment Day :

15. Verily the Hour comes : I will surely manifest it,

16. That every soul may be rewarded for what it has striven.

17. And let not him who believes not therein, and who follows his lust, turn thee aside from it, lest thou lose.

15. 'The Hour;' that is, the Judgment hour.

Some Directions :

130. Put up then with what they say, and celebrate the praise of thy Lord before the sun-rise and before its setting, and do thou praise Him sometime in the night, and the extremes of the day, that thou mayest be well-pleased.

131. And cast not thine eyes on what We have given to many of them — the splendour of the life of this world —that We might prove them thereby. And the provision of thy Lord is better and more enduring.

132. Enjoin prayer on thy family, and persevere therein. We ask not of thee to find provision : We will provide for thee, and the happy issue shall attend on piety.

135. Say thou, All await the end : wait then ye, and ye shall surely know hereafter who are the company in the straight way, and who are the rightly guided.

135. 'The end,' that is, the judgment of God according as they have deserved.

Principal Contents

Judgment Day, inevitable, 15, 16, 135.

Quran, its aim, 1, 2.

Prayer enjoined, 130, 132.

SURAH XXI. — THE PROPHETS

(Mecca.)

The Surah has its name from some particulars regarding several of the ancient prophets described herein.

The Judgment Day :

1. Their account draws nigh to the people, yet in carelessness they turn aside !

2. There comes to them no admonition from their Lord, but they only hear to make a jest of it;

3. Their hearts set on lusts. And those who act wickedly say in private discourse, Is he any more than a man like yourselves ? What ! will ye accede to sorcery knowingly ?

5. And they say, It is a medley of dreams; nay, he has forged it; nay, he is a poet. . . .

7. We sent none before thee but men to whom We revealed Ourselves. . . .

8. We gave them not a body which could dispense with food, and they were not to live for ever.

16. We created not the heaven and the earth and what is between them, for sport :

3. It appears that Mohammed's wonderful eloquence had a magical effect upon his audience : whence he was sometimes looked upon a sorcerer.

5. Mohammed's ardent preaching regarding the Judgment of God was taken as an idle dream by the unbelieving Meccans.

16. God must have some purpose in creation.

God : His Unity :

17. If We pleased to find a pastime, We had surely found it in Ourselves, if We did it.

18. Nay, We will hurl the truth at falsehood, and it shall smite it, and lo ! it shall vanish. And woe to you for what ye utter !

22. If there were in them both gods beside God, both would surely have been corrupted. But glory to God alone, Lord of the Throne, above what they utter !

25. We sent no apostle before thee but We revealed to him that there is no God beside Me; wherefore worship Me.

26. Yet they say, The Merciful God has begotten a son. Glory to Him ! they are but His honoured servants.

27. They cannot precede Him in speech, and they do His bidding.

35. Never have We given to man a life permanent : if thou die then, will they live for ever ?

36. Every soul shall taste of death, and We will prove you with evil and with good, and to Us ye shall return.

22. 'Them both,' *i.e.*, the heaven and the earth.

25. The mission of all the prophets has been to restore the Unity of the Godhead.

27. To precede one in speech is considered the height of incivility and in subordination.

The Unity of Religion :

92. Verily this your religion is one religion, and I am your Lord; wherefore serve Me.

93. But they have made a division in their affairs among themselves; all will return to Us.

94. Whoso then does good, and is a believer, his efforts shall not be disowned, and We will surely write it down for him.

105. And now have We prescribed in the Psalms, after the Law, that My servants the righteous shall inherit the earth.

92. The unity of religions is most emphatically taught in this verse.

93. Sectarianism is discountenanced throughout the Quran.

Principal Contents

God, His unity, 22, 25.

Judgment Day, its reality, 1.

Prophets, all from men, 7, 8, 35.

Religion, its unity, 92.

Sectarianism discountenanced, 93.

Truth to prevail, 18.

Ungodly, the, 3, 5.

SURAH XXII. — THE PILGRIMAGE

(Medinah.)

Certain regulations regarding the Pilgrimage being mentioned in this Surah give it the title it bears.

The Judgment Day :

1. Ye people, fear your Lord. Verily the shock of the earthquake of the Hour will be a terrible thing.
2. On the Day when ye shall see it, every suckling mother shall forget her sucking babe, and every one that is with young shall cast her burden, and thou shalt see men drunken, though not drunk; and the punishment of God shall be severe !

17. Verily those who believe, and those who are Jews, and the Sabians, and the Christians, and the Magians, and those who are polytheists, — verily God will decide between them on the Judgment Day. Surely God is witness over all things.

2. These are signs of excessive terror in men because of the great Judgment that is to overtake them for what they shall have done.

Pilgrimage :

28. Proclaim to the people a Pilgrimage : let them come to thee on foot and on every fleet camel, arriving from every distant way;
29. That they may be witnesses of its benefits to themselves, and may commemorate the name of God on the appointed days for the brute beasts which He has provided them : wherefore eat thereof and feed the needy and the poor; . . . .

31. . . . . But avoid the abomination of idols, and avoid the speaking of falsehood;
32. Upright towards God, and not of the polytheists; for whoever is polytheistic is like that which falls from heaven and the birds snatch away, or the wind wafts it to a distant place.
33. This do; and whoso respects the ordinances of God; verily these are from the piety of hearts.

35. And to every people We have appointed rites that they may commemorate the name of God on the brute beasts which He has provided them. And your God is the one God : strive then after Him.

38. By no means does their meat reach to God, nor yet their blood, but your piety alone will reach to Him . . . .

28. See Surah ii. 192, etc.; iii. 90, 91.

31. Pilgrimage is enjoined but divested of all idolatrous rites.

32. Because he who falls into idolatry sinks from the height of faith into the depth of infidelity, has his thoughts distracted by wicked lusts, and he is thus hurried into the most absurd errors.

38. Mark this verse.

War Permitted :

40. Permission is given to those who fight for that they have been unjustly persecuted; (and verily God has power to help them);

41. Who have been turned out of their homes wrongfully, only because they said, Our Lord is God. And if God had not repelled some men by others surely monasteries, and churches, and synagogues, and mosques, wherein the name of God is frequently mentioned, would be utterly destroyed. And him who helps God will God sure help; verily God is powerful, mighty.

42. Those who, if We establish them in the earth, will observe prayer, and give alms, and did what is just and forbid what is evil. And God's is the end of affairs.

66. To every people have We appointed certain rites which they observe. Wherefore let them not dispute with thee concerning the matter, but call them to thy Lord; for thou art in the right guidance;

67. But if they dispute with thee then say, God best knows what ye do.

68. God will judge between you on the Judgment Day as to that wherein ye disagree.

40. See Surah ii. 186, etc.

Idolatry :

72. Ye men, a parable is set forth to you, wherefore hearken to it. Verily they whom ye call on beside God cannot create a fly, though they were all assembled for it, and if the fly snatch away anything from them, they cannot recover the same from it. Weak is the petitioner and the petitioned.

73. They esteem not God as is His due; surely God is mighty, powerful.

76. Ye believers, bow down and worship, and serve your Lord, and do good, that ye may be happy.

The True Religion :

77. And strive for God as is His due. He has chosen you, and has not put upon you any hindrance in religion, the religion of your father Abraham; He has named you Moslems.

78. Heretofore and in this; that the apostle may be a witness against you, and that ye may be a witness against mankind.

Wherefore be steadfast in prayer and give alms, and hold fast by God : He is your master, an excellent master, and an excellent help.

Principal Contents

Idolatry to be avoided, 31, 32.

Judgment Day, its terrors, 1,2.

Pilgrimage enjoined, 28.

Religion, true, 77, 78.
Sacrifice not accepted of God, 38.
Sectarians, God alone to judge between them, 17.
War permitted, 40, 41.

SURAH XXIII. — THE BELIEVERS
(Mecca.)

The title is taken from the opening verses of the Surah relating to a description of Believers.

Believers :

1. Now are the believers happy,
2. Who humble themselves in prayer,
3. And who eschew vain words,
4. And are doers of charity,
5. And who preserve their modesty,
8. And who tend well their trusts and their covenants.
9. And in their prayers are steadfast :
10. These are the heirs,
11. Who will inherit Paradise, and continue therein for ever.

The Unity of Religion :

54. This your religion is one religion, and I am your Lord : wherefore fear Me;
55. But they have divided the affairs among themselves and become sectaries : every party rejoice in what they have.
56. Wherefore do thou leave them for a time in their ignorance.

55. See Surah vi. 160.

The Godly and the Ungodly :

57. What ! do they think that what We hasten to them of wealth and children,

58. We hasten to them for their good? Nay, they do not understand.

59. Verily those who stand in awe, for fear of their Lord,

60. And who believe in the signs of their Lord,

61. And who join not anything with their Lord,

62. And who give what they give, their hearts thrilling with fear, for that to their Lord they shall return :

63. These hasten after good, and are the first to attain it.

64. And We oblige not a soul but according to its ability; and with Us is a Book which speaks the truth, and they shall not be wronged.

72. . . . But most of them do hate the truth;

73. And if the truth had followed their desires, verily the heavens and the earth and what is therein would have been corrupted. . .

Polytheism :

93. God has not begotten a son, neither is there a God with Him, or every God has surely gone off with what he had created, and some would have surely raised themselves above the others. Glory to God above what they say !

94. Knower of the secret and the manifest; far be He above what they join with Him !

Good For Evil :

98. Turn aside evil with what is best : We best know what they say.

118. And say thou, Lord, pardon, and have mercy; for thou art the best of the merciful.

98. See Surah xli. 34, 35.

Principal Contents

Believers this conduct, 1-5, 8, 9, 59-63.

Forgiveness inculcated, 98.

Polytheism, 93.

Religion, the Unity of, 54.

SURAH XXIV.—LIGHT.

(Medinah.)

The title of this Surah is taken from an allegorical comparison made between light and God, in verse 35.

Whoredom : Its Punishment :

2. The adulterer and the adulteress, scourge each of them with an hundred stripes; and let no compassion towards them keep you from the judgment of God, while ye believe in God and the Hereafter; and let a party of the believers witness their punishment.

2. See also Surah iv. 19, 20.

False Charge Against Women :

4. And those who accuse chaste women, and then bring not four witnesses, scourge them with eighty stripes, and receive not their testimony for ever; and these it is who are the wicked. . .

18. Verily those who love that calumnies should go forth against those who believe;— for these is a painful punishment.

19. In this world and the Hereafter; surely God knows, and ye do not know.

Forgiveness Inculcated :

22. And let not those who are fortunate among you and able, swear that they will not give to their kindred, and the poor, and those who have fled in the way of God : rather let them pardon and pass over. Don't ye desire that God should pardon you? Surely God is forgiving, compassionate.

Slanderers of Women :

23. Verily they who accuse chaste women, careless but believing, are cursed in this world and the Hereafter; and for them is a terrible punishment.

24. The Day their tongues shall bear witness against them, and their hands, and their feet also, of what they did.

25. On that day shall God give them their just due, and they shall know that God is the plain truth.

Privacy of Houses :

27. Ye believers, enter not into houses, except your own houses, until ye have asked leave, and saluted the family thereof : this is better for you, that ye may remember.

28. And if ye find no one therein, yet enter not them until leave is given you; and if it is said to you, Go ye back, do ye go back : this is more decent for you. And God knows what ye do.

29. It is no crime in you, that ye enter houses not inhabited, wherein is provision for you; and God knows what ye do openly and what ye hide.

27. To enter suddenly or abruptly into any man's house or apartment, is reckoned a great incivility among the

Moslems.

29. 'House not inhabited;' that is which are not the private habitation of a family; such as public inns, shops, sheds, etc.

Modesty of the Sexes :

30. Speak to the men who believe, that they cast down their looks, and preserve their modesty; that is more pure for them : verily God is informed of what they do.

31. And speak to the women who believe, that they cast down their looks, and preserve their modesty, and that they display not their ornaments, except what appears thereof, and that they throw their kerchiefs over their bosoms and not make a display of their ornaments, unless to their husbands, or their fathers, or their husbands' fathers, or their sons, or their husbands' sons, or their brothers, or their brothers' sons, or their sisters' sons, or their women, or what their right hands have possessed, or to such men as attend them, and have no desire, or to children who mark not the nakedness of women. And let them not beat with their feet that their hidden ornaments might be known. And be ye all turned to God, Ye believers, that ye may be happy.

Marriage, and Emancipation of Slaves :

32. Marry those who are single among you, and the pious among your servants and your maid-servants : if they are poor, God will enrich them of His grace : surely God it all-embracing, knowing.

33. And let those who cannot find a match keep

chaste, until God enriches them of His grace.

And of those whom your right hands have possessed and who desire a deed, write for them, if ye know any good in them, and give them of the wealth of God which He has given you.

And compel not your maid-servants to prostitute themselves while they are willing to lively chastely, seeking the casual pleasure of this world; and whoso compels them, verily God will be forgiving, compassionate, to them after their compulsion.

32. 'Single;' that is, those who are unmarried of either sex; whether they have been married before or not.

33. 'Those whom,' etc. That is, the slaves.

'Dead;' that is, one allowing them to redeem themselves on paying a certain sum.

'If ye know good,' etc. That is, if ye have found them faithful, and have reason to believe they will perform their engagement.

'And give them,' etc. Either by bestowing something on them of your own substance in order to enable them to redeem themselves, or by abating them a part of their ransom. Some suppose these words are directed, not to the master only, but to all Moslems in general; recommending it to them to assist those who are willing to redeem themselves from slavery on making the promised payment.

'And compel not,' etc. In pre-Islamic Arabia female slaves were compelled to prostitute themselves, the price of prostitution being appropriated by the owners.

God And Light :

35. God is the light of the heavens and the earth : His light is as a niche in which is a lamp,—the lamp is in glass, the glass is, as it were, a shining star. It is lit from a blessed tree, an olive neither of the east nor of the west : its oil would well-

nigh give light though no fire touched it. Light upon light. God guides to His light whom He pleases.

35. The commentators explain this allegory, and every particular of it, with great subtlely; interpreting the 'light' here described to be the 'light' revealed in the revelation of the prophets, or God's 'enlightening grace' in the heart of man; and in a variety of ways.

The Ungodly :

39. And those who disbelieve, their works are as the vapour in a plain which the thirsty thinks to be water, until when he comes to it he finds it to be nothing, but he finds God with him, and He fully pays him his account; surely God is swift to take account;

40. Or, as the darkness in a deep sea covered by waves upon waves, above which are clouds : darkness one above the other: when he stretches forth his hand he cannot nearly see it ! And whom God gives no light, no light at all has he !

39. 'Vapour in a plain.' The original word, 'sarab,' signifies that false appearance which, in the eastern countries, is often seen in sandy plains about noon, resembling a large lake of water in motion, and is occasioned by the reverberation of the sunbeams. It sometimes tempts thirsty travellers out of their way, but deceives them when they come near, either going forward (for it always appears at the same distance), or quite vanishing.

'He finds God,' etc. That is wherever he is he cannot escape the eye of God.

God : His Power :

41. Hast thou not seen that all in the heavens and the earth praise God, and the birds also as they spread their wings ? Each one knows his prayer and his praise; surely God knows what they do.

42. God's is the kingdom of the heavens and the earth, and to Him will they return.

53. Say thou, Obey God, and obey the apostle, but if ye turn back, upon him is his duty and upon you is your duty, and if ye obey him ye will be guided; but the apostle's is only to preach publicly.

The Believers :

54. God promises to such of you as believe and do good, that He will make them to inherit the earth as He made those to inherit who were before them, and that He will establish for them their religion well-pleasing for them, and will change for them after their fear security. They will serve Me and not join anything with Me, and whoso disbelieve after this, are surely wicked.

55. Be steadfast in prayer, and give alms, and obey the apostle, that ye may have mercy.

56. Think not that those who disbelieve will conquer in the earth.

54. 'After their fear,' their present state of persecution at the hands of the Arabs.

Rules of Privacy :

57. Ye believers, let those whom your right hands have possessed, and those of you who have not come of age, ask leave of you three times a day,—before the morning prayer, and when ye lay aside your garments at mid-day, and after the evening prayers,—three times of privacy for you. It is no crime in you or in them after these to go your rounds of visit to one another.

58. And when your children come of age, let them

ask leave in the same way as those who were before them asked it. . .

59. As to such women who are past child-bearing and have no hope of marriage, it is no crime in them if they lay aside their garments not showing their ornaments : but if they abstain, it is better for them; and God is the hearing, knowing.

57. 'Ask leave of you.' Because there are certain times when it is not convenient, even for a domestic, or a child, to come in to one without notice.

'Before the morning prayer;' which is the time of people's rising from their beds, and dressing themselves for the day.

'At mid-day.' That is, when ye take off your outer garments to sleep at noon; which is a common custom in the east, and all warm countries.

'After the evening prayer.' That is, when ye undress yourselves to prepare for bed. The commentators add a fourth time, when permission to enter must be asked, namely, at night; but this follows of course.

Some Superstitions Condemned :

60. It is no crime in the blind, or in the lame, or in the sick, or in yourselves, that ye eat in your houses, or in the houses of your fathers, or the houses of your mothers, or in the houses of your brothers, or the houses of your sisters, or the houses of your uncles on the father's side, or the houses of your aunts on the mother's side, or the house of your aunts on the mother's side, or the keys whereof ye possess, or of your friend. It is not crime in you whether ye eat together or apart.

61. And when ye enter any houses, salute one another as from God with a welcome and blessed greeting. . .

64. Is not what is in the heavens and the earth God's ? He knows what ye are about, and the day they shall return to Him He will tell them what they have done; surely God knows all things.

60. 'Your houses.' That is, where your wives or families are; or in the houses of your sons, which may looked on as your own.

This passage was intended to remove some scruples or superstitions of the Arabs in Mohammed's time; some of whom thought their eating with maimed or sick people defiled them; others imagined they ought not to eat in the house of another, though ever so nearly related them, or though they were entrusted with the key and care of the house in the master's absence, and might therefore conclude it would be no offence; and others declined eating with their friends though invited, lest they should be a burden. The whole passage seems to be no more than a declaration that the things scrupled were perfectly innocent.

'Eat together or apart.' Certain tribes thought it unlawful for a man to eat alone; and some never ate but in company with some guests; so there were others who refused to eat with any, out of a superstitious caution lest they should be defiled, or out of a hoggish greediness.

Principal Contents

Believers, 54.

Forgiveness inculcated, 22.

God, His power, 41, 42; a comparison with light, 35.

Houses, privacy of, 27-9; some rules, 57-9.

Marriage recommended, 32.

Modesty enjoined upon men and women, 30.

Slaves, a provision for their emancipation, 33.

Slave-girls not to be compelled to prostitute themselves, 33.

Superstitions, some condemned, 60.

Ungodly, their works, 39, 40.

Whoredom, its punishment, 2.

Women, false charges against them, 4, 18, 19; slanderers against them, 23-5.

SURAH XXV.—THE DISTINCTION.

(Mecca.)

The Surah takes it name from the word which occurs in the first verse.

The Quran :

1. Blessed is He who has revealed the Distinction to His servant, that to all creatures he may be a warner.

The Apostle :

8. And they say, What an apostle is this ? He eats food and walks in the streets : unless an angel is sent to him to be a preacher with him,

9. Or, a treasure is thrown down to him, or he have a garden whereof the may eat, . . . And the ungodly say, Ye follow only a man enchanted.

10. See what they liken thee, to, but they err and cannot find a way.

22. We have not sent before thee any apostles but they ate food and walked through the streets. And We make some of you a trial to others. . .

23. And those who hopes not to meet Us say. Unless an angel is sent down to us, or we see our Lord.— These behave themselves proudly, and transgress most perversely.

24. On the Day they shall see angels there will be no glad tidings for the wicked, and they shall say, Away, away with thee !

25. And We will go on to the works which they have done.

27. The Day when the heaven with its clouds shall be cleft asunder, and the angels shall be sent down descending.

28. The Kingdom on that day shall of right be of the Merciful God, and the day shall be terrible to the ungodly.

8. The Meccans were acquainted with Mohammed and with his circumstances and way of life, too well to change their old familiarity into the obedience due to an apostle of God : for a prophet is not honoured in his own country.

9. After 'He may eat,' add 'we will not believe.'

10. 'Cannot find a way,' that is, they do not find a better reason to reject thee.

22. 'Ate food,' etc. Being subject to the same wants and infirmities of nature, and obliged to submit to the same low means of supporting himself and his family, with ourselves.

23. 'Those who hope not,' etc. That is, those who do not believe in the hereafter when they shall be called to God to render their accounts of what they did in the life of this world. It refers to the unbelievers.

'They behave themselves,' etc. Because they have no thought of any responsibility to God for their doings here.

24. 'The Day;' it refers to the Judgment Day.

'They shall say,' etc. They shall wish the angels had not appeared at all.

25. 'And We will go on, etc. God will demand from them an account of their actions.

The Quran : Its Revelation Gradual :

34. And those who disbelieve say, Unless the Quran is revealed to him all at once, . . . But it is so, that We might establish thy heart thereby, and We have dictated to thee gradually in parcels.

43. And when they see thee, they only receive thee with scoffing—Is this he whom God has sent as an apostle ?

44. . . . But in the end they shall know, when they shall see the punishment, who has erred from the way.

45. Hast thou seen him who takes his lust for his God ? Canst thou be a guardian over him ?

46. Dost thou imagine that most of them do hear, or take wisdom ? These are only as brute beasts; nay, they err more from the way.

34. 'Unless the Quran,' etc. The Quran is composed of the inspired utterances of Mohammed which extended for about 23 years of the prophet's ministry. It was not given in a book form all at once. Hence the objection on the part of the unbelievers of Mecca.

'That We might establish,' etc. The inspired utterances were made during the troubled days of Mohammed's greatest crises, as occasion required, or to meet the passing exigencies of the day or related to the circumstances and requirements of a primitive and archaic society. Hence the Islamic doctors have held that there is no eternal law as regards human actions, and that the Divine ordinances which regulate the conduct of men are results of growth and development, and that the whole world is in a process of evolution.

45. 'Takes his lust,' etc. Who follows his lust as men ought to follow God alone.

'A guardian;' that is, thou canst not control his desires.

God : His Power :

47. Hast thou not seen how thy Lord lengthens out the shadow ? If He pleased, He could have kept it the same.—But We made the sun its cause;

48. Then We draw it in to Us drawing easily.

49. He it is who has ordained the night as a garment, and sleep for rest, and has ordained the day for waking up.

50. He it is who sends the winds as the forerunner of His mercy, and has sent down from heaven

pure water,

51. That We may revive thereby a dead land, and give to drink thereof to what We have created numerous cattle and men;

52. And We spent it between them, that they may consider; but most men refuse only out of ingratitude.

54. Wherefore do not thou obey the ungodly; but strive with them by it with a great strength.

55. And He it is who has let loose the two seas, this fresh, sweet; and that salt, bitter; and has put between them a barrier and a bound they cannot pass.

60. And put thou thy trust in Him that lives and dies not, and celebrate His praise.

61. When it is said to them, Worship the merciful God, they say, And who is the merciful God that we should worship at thy bidding? And it increases their hatred.

62. Blessed is He who has placed in the heavens signs, and placed therein a lamp, and the moon which shines.

47. 'Lengthens out the shadow;' that is, at sunrise.

63. 'Signs;' that is, of the Zodiac.

The Servants of the Merciful God :

64. The servants of the merciful God are those who walk humbly in the earth; and when the ignorant speak to them, they say, Peace;

65. And who pass the night adoring their Lord, and standing up;

66. And who say, Our Lord, keep away from us the

torment of Hell, for the torment thereof is lasting; it is indeed an ill abode and a resting place;

67. And who, when they spend, are neither lavish nor niggard, but keep the mean;

68. And who call not other gods with God; nor kill a being, which God has forbidden unless by right, and who commit not adultery: for whoso does this shall meet the reward to his wickedness.

69. Doubled to him will be the torment on the Judgment Day, and he will continue therein in disgrace;

70. Except him who repents and believes and does good works—these, for them will God change their evils into good; for God is forgiving, compassionate.—

71. And whoso turns and does good, verily he turns to God repentant.

72. And they who bear not false witness, and when they pass by a vain discourse, pass it by with dignity,

73. And who, when they are reminded by the signs of their Lord, fall not down deaf and blind thereat;

74. And who say, Our Lord, give us in our wives and offspring the joy of our eyes, and make us patterns to the pious.

75. These will be rewarded with high places, for that they steadfastly persevered, and they shall meet therein with greeting and salutation:

76. For ever shall they continue therein : excellent Home and abode.

64. 'The ignorant,' who have no proper conception of their

duty to God or to men.

'Peace;' it expresses the perfectly harmless way it is the duty of every man to adopt with regard to those who are not in his way to achieve social or spiritual advantages.

65. 'Standing up,' *i.e.,* to pray.

67. See Surah xvii. 31.

68. 'Unless by right.' See Surah v. 35.

'Adultery;' it includes fornication as well.

'The reward,' etc. See Surah xxiv. 2.

70. 'Who repents,' *i.e.*, of his evil action. See Surah iv. 21, 22.

71. The truly penitent turns from his evil ways and ever afterwards does good.

72. 'With dignity,' worthy of their character as the servants of God.

73. 'Fall not down,' etc. That is, whose hearts are open to hear truths about God; whose lusts have not cast a veil over their hearing and their sight.

74. The earnest longing of the faithful servants of God is to see their wives and children striving in the way of piety with themselves.

Principal Contents

God, His power, 47-52, 55; His true servants, 64-76.

Judgment Day, the, a terrible reality, 28.

Quran, the, 1; its revelation gradual, 34.

Miracles demanded. 8-10, 22, 23.

SURAH XXVI.—THE POETS.

(Mecca.)

A mention of the Poets in verse 224, give the Surah the title it bears.

The Prophet : His Despondency :

1. T.S.M. These are the verses of the plain Book,

2. Haply thou dost worry the life out of thyself for the that they believe not.

3. If We please, We can send to them from heaven a sign to which their necks will humbly submit.

4. But there comes to them no admonition from the merciful God, but they turn aside from it.

5. And call it a lie!—but a message shall come to them which they shall not laugh to scorn.

6. Do they not see the earth—how We grow therein all noble kinds of vegetables?

7. Verily herein is a sign: but most of them will not believe!

205. Even if We suffer them to enjoy for some years,

206. And there come upon them what they are told,

207. What will their enjoyments avail them?

214. And warn thy relatives of nearer kin,

215. And lower thy wing to the believers who follow thee;

216. And if they do not obey thee, say thou, I am clear of what ye do:

217. And trust in the mighty, the compassionate God,

218. Who sees thee when thou dost stand up,

219. And thy behaviour among those who worship;

220. Verily He is the hearing, the knowing.

5. 'A message;' the Judgment Day which is stern reality, and which they can ill afford to ignore.

206. 'What they are told;' namely, the punishment due to their actions.

215. 'Lower thy wing;' that is, behave themselves with meekness.

218. 'Stand up;' *i.e.*, to pray.

The Devils and Their Associates :

221. Shall I tell you upon whom the devils descend?

222. They descend upon every lying, wicked person.

223. They impart what they have heard, but most of them are liars.

222. Only the liars and wicked people are under the influence of the devils, See also notes on Surah ii. 13.

223. The character of the wicked people is here strongly put forth.

The chief characteristics of the Arab poets described here and in the two succeeding verses are : 1. Extravagant language; 2. Vain imaginings: and 3. Lies.

Poets : Good and Bad Among Them :

224. The poets do those follow who err,

225. Dost thou not see how they wander distraught in every valley,

226. And that they say what they do not ?

227. Except those who believe and do good and remember God most,

228. And who defend themselves after that they have been wronged. And those who wrong will by and by know what a change will come over them !

225. 'They wander distraught.' etc. Their compositions being as wild as the actions of a distracted man; for most of the ancient Arab poetry was full of vain imaginations; as fabulous stories and descriptions, love-verses, flattery, extravagant praises of their patrons, and as excessive reproaches of their enemies, incitement to vicious actions, vainglorious tauntings, and the like.

227. That is, such poets as believe in God, whose works, far from the profaneness of the former, run chiefly on God, and contain exhortations to obedience and other religious and moral virtues, without any satirical invectives, unless as excepted in the following verse.

228. 'Defend themselves.' That is, unless against such as have

given just provocations, by having first attacked them with invectives.

Principal Contents

Devils, and their associates, 221-3.

Poets, good and bad among them, 224-8.

Judgment a stern reality, 5.

SURAH XXVII. — THE ANT.

(Mecca.)

This Surah takes its name from the word which occurs in verse 8.

The Quran :

1. T.S. These are the verses of the Quran, and the plain Book,

2. A guide and glad tidings to the believers, who are steadfast in prayer and give alms, and of the Hereafter they are sure.

The Ungodly :

3. Verily those who believe not in the Hereafter, We have made fair-seeming to them their works, and they are bewildered.

4. These are they for whom is an evil punishment, and in the Hereafter they shall — yea, they shall — lose terribly.

God : His Power :

60. Say thou, Praise to God, and peace upon His servants whom He has chosen ! Is God good, or what they join with Him ?

61. Is not He who made the heavens and the earth, and sent down to you rain from heaven whereby We grow luxuriant groves ? It is not in your power to make the trees spring up. What ! A God with

God ? Nay, these are a people who transgress.

62. Is not He who has set the earth firm, and made the rivers flow in its midst, and put a barrier between the two seas ? What ! A God with God ? Nay, most of them do not know.

63. Is not He who answers the oppressed when they cry to Him, and takes off their ills, and has made you to inherit the earth ? What ! A God with God ? How few consider !

64. Is not He who guides you in the darkness of the land and the sea, and who sends the winds as the forerunners of His mercy ? What ! A God with God ? Far be God above what they join with Him !

65. Is not He who created at first, and then restores it, and who gives you food from heaven and earth ? What ! A God with God ? Say thou, Bring your proofs, if ye are of those who speak the truth.

66. Say thou, None in the heavens and the earth knows the secret beside God;

67. And they know not when they shall be raised.

63. 'To inherit.' That is, to take the place of the older generations long gone by.

The Quran :

78. Verily this Quran declares to the children of Israel most of that wherein they disagree.

79. And it is certainly a guide, and mercy to the believers.

95. . . . . And say thou, Praise to God ! He will show you His signs, and ye shall know them; and thy Lord is not regardless of what ye do.

Principal Contents

Believers, 2.

God, His power, 61-5; His knowledge, 66.

Quran, the 1, 78, 79.

Ungodly, the, 3, 4.

SURAH XXVIII. — THE STORY.

(Mecca.)

This Surah takes its title from verse 25, where Moses is said to have related the story of his adventures to Shoeib.

God : His Power :

56. Verily thou canst not guide whom thou wilt, but God guides whom He will; and He best knows the rightly guided.

70. And He is God : there is no God but He ! His is praise in this world and the Hereafter, and His is the command, and to Him they shall be gathered !

71. Say thou, What think ye ? If God should cover you with one long night until the Judgment Day, what God beside God would bring you light ? Will ye not yet consider ?

72. What think ye ? If God should make it one long day for you until the Judgment Day, what God beside God would bring you night that ye might rest therein ? Don't ye see ?

73. And of His mercy is that He made for you the night and the day, that ye may rest therein and that ye may seek of His abundance, and that ye may give thanks.

73. 'Seek of His abundance;' namely, by commerce.

The Future Abode :

83. That is the Home of the Hereafter : We make it for those who seek not to exalt themselves in the earth or to do wrong; and the happy issue is for the pious.

88. And call not with God any other God. There is no God but He; all things shall perish, except His Face. His is the command, and to Him shall ye return.

Principal Contents

God, His power, 56, 70-72; His mercy, 73.

Hereafter, the, 83.

SURAH XXIX. — THE SPIDER.

(Mecca.)

A transient mention of this insect in verse 40 gives it the name it bears.

Life A Severe Trial :

1. A. L. M. Do men imagine that they will be left alone to say, We believe, and not be proved ?

3. Do they who work evil think that they shall escape Us ? How ill they judge !

7. We have enjoined upon men to be good to their parents; but if they strive with thee to join with Me that of which thou hast no knowledge, then obey them not : to Me will ye return, and then will I tell you what ye have done.

8. And those who believe and do good, We will surely introduce them among the upright.

1. The life of the believer, according to Islam, is a severe trial. Sincere work is considered more essential than were lip-service.

7. 'Strive with thee,' i.e., Use their influence with thee.

'That of which,' etc. Namely, to associate with God things against thine own conscience.

The Polytheists :

40. The likeness of those who take patrons beside God, is as the likeness of the spider which makes herself a house; but surely the frailest of all houses is the house of the spider. Did they but know !

40. The ground upon which those who take to themselves lords beside God is as weak as the web of the spider in protecting itself against the least trouble.

Prayer : Its Effect :

44. Recite what has been revealed to thee of the Book, and be steadfast in prayer; verily prayer keeps a man from filthy actions and evil; and the remembrance of God is a great thing; and God knows what ye do.

44. The natural effect of prayer on the life of man is thus summed up : 'verily prayer keeps a man from filthy actions and evil.'

Mild Exhortation in Preaching :

45. Dispute not with the people of the Book unless in the best way, except those who wrong you; and say ye, We believe in what has been revealed to us, and what has been revealed to you : and our God and your God is one God, and after Him we strive.

Miracles Demanded :

49. They say, Unless a sign is sent down to him from his Lord, ... Say thou, Signs are in the power of God alone, and I am only a plain warner.

50. Is it not enough for them that We have sent down to thee the Book to be read to them ? Verily herein

is mercy and a reminder to people who believe.

Principles to Be Held Unshaken :

56. My servants who believe, Verily My earth is vast; Me therefore, yea serve Me.

57. Every soul shall taste of death: then to Us ye shall return.

69. And those who strive after Us, We will guide them in Our ways, and verily God is with the doers of good.

56. 'My earth is vast;' that is, if ye find one place too bad for you to practise your religion take refuge in a place where thou mayest practise your religion freely:

Principle Contents

Emigration recommended, 56.

Miracles demanded, 49, 50.

Polytheists, their likeness, 40.

Prayer, its effect on life, 44.

Preaching by mild exhortation, 45.

Religion, a most serious thing, 1.

SURAH XXX.—THE GREEKS.

(Mecca.)

The Surah takes its name from the first verse where the defeat of the Greeks is mentioned. The burden of the Surah is that truth will at last prevail.

The Greeks and Persian:

1. A.L.M. The Greeks have been defeated

2. In a near land; but after their defeat they shall defeat

3. In a few years. God's is the command in the past and the future. And on that day shall the faithful rejoice

4. In the help of God: He helps whom He will; and He is the mighty, the compassionate.

5. This is the promise of God; surely God will not fail in His promise; but most people do not know.

6. They know the outside of the life of this world, and of the Hereafter they are unmindful!

1. A.L.M. See note to Surah ii. 1.

'The Greeks.' In Arabic 'ar-Rum;' by which the later Greeks, or subjects of the Constantinopolitan Empire, are here meant.

'Have been defeated,' etc. By the Persians.

This refers to the wonderful success of Khusrau Parwiz, Kesra of Persia, who carried on a terrible war against the Greek Empire, to revenge the death of Maurice, his father-in-law, slain by Phocas, which continued in an uninterrupted course for two-and-twenty years, until in A.C. 615, about the seventh year of Mohammed's mission, they made themselves masters of Palestine, and took Jerusalem.

The news of this victory of the Persians over the Greeks was turned by the Meccans as against Mohammed, who even so early entertained such high hopes regarding the success of his mission. They tauntingly pointed out that Mohammed's mission could have no chance, for as the fire-worshipping Persians had gained the victory over the Christians who held much the same views as Mohammed, so the Arab polytheism will always have the better of Islam.

2. 'A near land;' namely Palestine.

3. 'In a few years.' This came true in A.C. 625 when the Persians were defeated by Heraclius.

6. 'The outside,' etc. The outward appearance of the present life.

God : His Signs :

19. And of His signs is, that He has created you of dust, and lo! ye are men spread abroad.

20. And of His signs is, that He has created for you,

out of yourselves, wives, that ye have comfort among yourselves, and love and compassion between you. Verily herein are signs to people who reflect.

21. And of His signs is the creation of the heavens and the earth, and the variety of your languages and colour. Verily herein are signs to the worlds.

27. He sets forth to you an instance from yourselves. Have ye among those whom your right hands have possessed a partner in what We have provided you, so that ye share alike? Fear ye them as ye fear one another?

28. Nay; but those who do wrong follow their own lusts in their ignorance;

20. The principle of marriage is here distinctly laid down. It is 'to have comfort among yourselves, and love and compassion between you.'

The Standard Religion :

29. Set thy face steadfast in religion as one upright, the constitution of God whereon He has constituted men;—there is no change in the creation of God. That is the standard religion, but most people do not know.

30. And be ye turned to Him, and fear him, and be steadfast in prayer, and be not of the polytheists.

31. Of those who have divided their religion and become sectaries; every party rejoice in what they have.

29. 'Steadfast in religion; ' *i.e.,* follow not your own lusts. See verse 28, above.

'One upright.' See note on Surah ii. 129.

'The constitution of God,' etc. That is, the immutable law, or rule, to which man is naturally disposed to conform, and which every one would embrace, as most fit for a rational creature, if it were not for the prejudices of education.

According to Islam, religion is a straight, natural law, for men to follow, wherein is no perplexity or ambiguity. Mohammed himself taught that all the children of men would follow the same straight way were it not for the corrupting influences of their guardians, who consciously or unconsciously set an unnatural example by their way of life for their little folks to follow. In fine, religion was to Mohammed the natural bent of a free, unbiassed mind. See Surah ii. 209.

'There in no change;' etc. All are made equally capable of receiving truths and reducing them to practice.

The Standard Religion is here defined as 'the constitution of God whereon He has constitution men.'

'But most people do not know.' See Surah vi. 116.

30. See Surah xcviii. 3, 4.

31. Regarding sectarianism, see Surah vi. 160.

Perseverance Enjoined :

35. When We cause men to taste mercy, they rejoice therein; but if evil befall them for what their hands have sent before them, they despair!

40. Disorder has appeared by land and by sea for what men's hands have acquired, that it might make them taste something of what they have done, that haply they might turn back.

60. But do thou steadfastly persevere: verily the promise of God is true, and let not those unsettle thee who are not sure.

40. See also Surah ii. 150-52.

60. 'The promise of God,' namely, regarding the success of the truth. See verses 3 and 4, above.

'Who are not sure;' that is, who are not persuaded of the success of truth at this stage of Mohammed's mission.

Principal Contents

Disorder, the result of evil-doing, 40.

God, His signs, 19-21,

Religion, the standard, 29-31.

SURAH XXXI.—LOKMAN

(Mecca.)

The Surah has its name from the celebrated fabulist and philosopher (sometimes identified with the Æsop of the Greeks) mentioned in verse 11.

God : His power :

26. If whatever trees are in the earth were pens, and the sea should He swell into seven seas, the words of God would not be exhausted. Verily God is mighty, wise.

27. Your creation and your quickening is but as that of one being. Verily God hears, sees.

26. This is as against the Jewish belief that all knowledge was contained in their Law.

The Judgement Day:

32. Ye people, fear your Lord, and dread the day when a father shall not atone for his son, nor shall a son atone for his father at all.

33. Verily the promise of God is true: let not then the life of this world deceive you, neither let the deceiver deceive you concerning God.

34. . . . No being knows what it shall earn on the morrow, neither knows a being in what land it shall die. Verily God is knowing, informed.

32. 'The day;' the Day of Judgment.

Principal Contents

God, His power, 26, 27.

Judgment Day, the, 32.

SURAH XXXII.—ADORATION

(Mecca.)

The title is taken from verse 15, where the word casually occurs.

The Believers :

15. They only believe in Our signs, who, when warned thereby, fall down worshipping, and celebrate the praise of their Lord, and are not big with pride;

16. They rise from their beds, calling on their Lord with fear and desire, and of what We have given them do spend.

16. 'They rise,' etc. Literally, 'their sides are raised.'

Their Reward :

17. No being knows what is reserved for them of the joy of the eyes, as a reward for what they have done.

17. 'Being;' literally, 'soul.'

'The joy of the eyes;' that is, complete satisfaction.

Mohammed is also reported to have said : 'God has prepared for His righteous servants, what eye has not seen, nor has ear heard, nor has it entered into the heart of man to conceive.'

The Judgment Day :

28. They say, when is this decision to come, if ye are true ?

29. Say thou, On the day of decision, the faith of those who disbelieved shall not avail them, nor shall they be respited.

30. Therefore, avoid them, and wait thou, verily they also do wait.

Principal Contents

Believers, the, 15, 16; their reward, 17.

Judgment Day, the, 28, 29.

SURAH XXXIII. — THE CONFEDERATES
(Medinah.)

Part of this Surah treats of the combined attack, upon the Moslems at Medinah, of several Jewish tribes and of the inhabitants of Mecca, Nejd, and Tehamah, at the instigation of the Jews of the tribe on Nazir; hence the title of this Surah.

Divorce and Adoption :

1. O Prophet, fear thou God, and obey not the unbelievers and the hypocrites : verily God is knowing, wise.
2. But follow what is revealed to thee from thy Lord : verily God is informed of what ye do.
3. And trust in God, surely God suffices for a guardian.
4. God has not given a man two hearts within him; neither has He made your wives whom ye divorce to be as your mother, nor has He made your adopted sons as your sons. These are your words in your mouths.
5. Call them after their fathers : this is more just with God. And if ye know not their fathers, then are they your brothers in religion, and your companions; and it is no crime in you that ye err in this, but what your hearts purposely design. Surely God is forgiving, compassionate.
6. .... Those who are related by blood are nearer the one to the other in the Book of God, than the believers and the refugees, unless ye show kindness to your friends. That is written in the Book.

4. 'Whom ye divorce,' etc. This refers to the ancient custom of the Arabs, that of divorcing their wives on a sudden provocation, by saying to the woman, 'Thy back be to me as the back of my mother !' after which words pronounced

he abstained from her bed, and regarded her in all respects as his mother, and she became related to all his kindred, in the same degree as if she had been really so.

'Your adopted sons,' etc. This was another custom of the ancient Arabs, that of holding their adopted sons to be as nearly related to them as their natural sons, so that the same impediments of marriage arose from that supposed relation, in the prohibited digrees, as it would have done in the case of a genuine son.

5. Adoption is thus out of the question in Islam.

6. See Surah viii. 73, 76.

Mohammed's Offer of His Wives :

28. O Prophet, say to thy wives, If ye desire the life of this world, and its adornment, come, I will make a provision for you, and I will dismiss you with an honourable dismission.

29. But if ye desire God and His apostle, and the Home of the Hereafter, then truly has God prepared for those of you who do good a great reward.

28. After the promulgation of Surah iv. 3, the Moslems were given the alternative of either separating themselves from their wives whose number exceeded that of the law, or retaining them all. In this and the succeeding verses the wives of Mohammed are offered separation.

The Believers :

35. Verily the Moslems, men and women, and the believers, men and women, and the devout, men and women, and the true, men and women, and the persevering, men and women, and the humble, men and women, and the charitable, men and women, and the fasting, men and women, and those who preserve their modesty, of men and women, and who remember God frequently, of men and women, for them has God prepared pardon and a great reward.

59. O Prophet, speak to thy wives and to thy daughters, and to the wives of the faithful, that they let their wrappers fall low. That is more proper, that they might be known, and not affronted. . .

70. Ye believers, fear God, and speak words well-meant;

71. That He may bless your works for you, and pardon you your sins. And whoso obeys God and His apostle, is surely blessed with a great bliss.

59. In this verse the out-door dress of Moslem women is fixed.

Faith : A Responsibility :

72. Verily We proposed faith to the heavens and the earth and the mountains, but they refused the burden and shrank from it; but man undertook it; but verily he is unjust and foolish.

73. That God may punish of the hypocrites and polytheists, both men and women, and that God may turn to the faithful men and women; surely God is forgiving, compassionate.

72. By faith is here understood entire obedience to the law of God, which is represented to be of so high concern (no less than the future destiny of man depending on the observance or neglect thereof), and so difficult in the performance, that if God should propose the same on the conditions annexed, to the vaster parts of the creation, and they had understanding to comprehend the offer, they would decline it, and not dare to take on them a duty, the failing wherein must be attended with so terrible a consequence; and yet man is said to have undertaken it, notwithstanding his weakness and the infirmities of his nature. Some take the passage literally throughout.

Principal Contents

Adoption not as natural, 4, 5.

Believers, the, 35.

Divorce, a special form of it, 4.
Faith, a responsibility, 72, 73.
Women, their out-door dress, 59.

SURAH XXXIV.—SABA

(Mecca.)

This Surah is named after the people of Seba, in Arabia Fe lix, (three days' journey from Sanaa,) mentioned in verse 14.

God : His Power :

1. Praise to God ; His is the Heavens and the earth, and His is praise in the Hereafter; and He is the wise, the informed !

2. He knows what enters into the earth, and what issues out of it, and what comes down from heaven and what goes up to it; and He is the compassionate, the forgiving!

The Judgment Day :

3. And those who disbelieve say, The Hour will not come upon us; say thou, Nay, by my Lord! it will surely come to you. Knower of the secret ! not the weight of a mite in the heavens and the earth is hidden from Him, nor a thing small or great, but is in the plain Book.

4. That He may reward those who believe and do good : for them is pardon, and a mighty provision.

24. Say thou, Ye shall not be asked as to what lies against us, nor shall we be asked as to what ye have done.

25. Say thou, Our Lord will gather us together, then will He judge between us with truth; surely He is the judge, the knowing.

35. Say thou, Verily my Lord provides liberally for

whom He pleases, and is also sparing; but most men do not know.

3. 'The Hour;' that is, of the Judgment.

Principal Contents

God, His power, 1, 2.
Judgment Day, the, 3, 4, 24, 25.

XXXV.—THE CREATOR

(Mecca.)

The word from which this Surah takes its name occurs in verse 1. Some call it 'The Angels.'

God : His Greatness :

11. Whoso desires greatness, surely God's is all greatness; to Him rises the good word, and the good work does He exalt. But those who devise evils, for them is a severe torment; and their devices, surely there are vain.

16. Ye people, Ye are but as beggars before God; and God, He is rich, praiseworthy!

17. If He please, He can take you away, and bring forth a new creation;

18. And neither is this difficult with God.

11. The plain meaning is, In God's hand is all greatness; let those who seek it seek from Him by good words and actions which He is sure to reward.

'The good word.' Such as calling men to God and to the performance of their duties towards each other. See Surah iv. 114; also xli 33.

The Responsibility of Man:

19. And no burdened soul shall bear the burden of another; and if one burdened cries for its burden, it shall not be helped, even by a relative... Whoso purifies himself, surely purifies himself for his

own soul; and to God shall all be gathered.

29. And We have given the Book an heritage to there of Our servants whom We have chosen: of them is he who wrongs himself and of them who keep to the mean, and of them is he who excels in good works by the permission of God. That is the great blessing.

37. He it is who has made you vicegerent on earth; whoso then disbelieves, upon him is His unbelief.

39. Verily God holds the heavens and the earth, or they would pass away: and if they passed away none could hold them back but He; surely He is mild, gracious.

41. O their wickedness on earth, and their devices! But the devices of evil will only encompass the people thereof.

19. 'Burdened soul;' that is, with sins.

'Purifies himself;' that is, by good thoughts and mental habits.

29. 'Who wrongs himself,' that is, by committing sins, which make him liable to punishment.

'Who keeps the mean;' that is, who means well, and performs his duty for the most part, but not perfectly.

Principal Contents

God, His greatness, 11, 16, 17.

Man, his responsibility, 19.

Wickedness encompasses the doer thereof, 41.

SURAH XXXVI.—Y.S.

(Mecca.)

The initial marks at the beginning of the Surah give it the title it bears.

The Ungodly:

29. O the misery of men! No apostle comes to them but they laugh him to scorn!

30. Do not they see how many generations We have destroyed before them?

31. Then return not to them.

32. But all together shall be gathered before Us.

36. Glory to Him who made pairs of all, of what the earth grows and of themselves, and of what they do not know.

30. 'Destroyed before them;' *i.e.,* for their own evil works.

31. 'To them;' that is, to the other gods whom they worship besides God.

God : His Signs :

37. And a sign to them is the night : We withdraw the day from it, and lo! they are wrapped in darkness.

38. And the sun hastens to his place of rest: that is the ordinance of the mighty, the wise God.

39. And the moon, We have fixed stations for it until it becomes like an old palm branch.

40. It is not for the sun to overtake the moon, nor the night to outsrip the day: but each does swim in its sphere.

71. Do not they see that We have created for them out of what Our hands have made, cattles of which they are the masters?

72. And that We have subjected these to them? Some are for their riding, and of them they eat.

73. And for them therein is benefit and drink.

74. Will they not yet be thankful?

75. And they have taken Gods beside God that they might he helped!

76. But no power have they to help them; yet they are for them an army at their service.

80. Who gives you fire from a green tree? and lo! ye burn from it.

82. His command when He wills a thing is to say to it, Be and it is.

83. Wherefore glory to Him, in whose hand is the Kingdom of all things; and to Him ye shall return.

38. 'The sun hastens,' etc. That is, the hastens to run his daily course, the setting of the sun resembling a traveller's going to rest.

'Place of rest.' Some copies vary in this place, and instead of 'Limustakarrin laha,' read with a slight variation in vowel points, 'la mustakarra laha;' according to which the sentence should be rendered, 'The sun hastens, and has no place of rest.'

39. 'Stations.' Namely the twenty-eight constellations through one of which the moon passes every night.

'An old palm branch.' For when a palm branch grows old, it shrinks, and becomes crooked and yellow, not ill representing the appearance of the new moon.

80. 'Fire from a green tree.' The usual way of striking fire in the east is by rubbing together two pieces of wood, one of which is commonly of the tree called Markh, and the other of that called Afar : and it succeeds even though the wood is green and wet.

Principal Contents

God, His sings, 37-40, 71-3, 80.

Ungodly, the 29-32.

SURAH XXXVII.—THE RANKS
(Mecca.)

This Surah derives its name from the word which occurs in verse 1.

Truth: Its Success:

171. Our word has gone forth that Our servants the apostles.

172. Should surely be helped, and that Our armies should gain the victory for them.

173. Wherefore turn aside from them for a time,

174. And see, for they also do see.

180. Glory to thy Lord, Lord of greatness, above what they say!

181. And peace upon the apostles,

182. And praise to God, Lord of the worlds.

174. 'And see.' That is, watch how God in His wisdom chooses to guide the affairs in the way of achieving His purpose. See verses 171 and 172, above.

'They also do see.' They are watching to see if it could be in accordance with their own desires.

Principal Contents

Truth, its success, 171, 172.

SURAH XXXVIII.—S

(Mecca.)

The Surah takes its name from the initial letters at its beginning.

God's Ways:

1. S. By the Quran full of warning! those who disbelieve are in pride and contention!

2. How many generation have We destroyed before them!—and they cried out, but it was no time to escape.

26. We have not created the heaven and the earth and what is between them in vain: that is the opinion of those who disbelieve; but woe to those

who disbelieve because of the Fire !

27. Shall We do with those who believe and do good, as with those who do evil in the earth? Shall We do with the pious as with the wicked?

26. See Surah lxvii. 2.

A Warning :

65. Say thou, Verily I am only a warner; and there is no God but God, the one, the supreme,

66. Lord of the heavens and the earth, and what is between them; the mighty, the forgiving.

67. Say thou, It is a weighty message,

68. But ye turn aside from it!

86. Say thou, I ask not of you for this a reward, and I am not of the meddlesome.

87. It is only a reminder to all creatures;

88. And ye shall know its message after a time.

27. See Surah v. 100.

Principal Contents

Creation on purpose, 26.

Evil and good not the same, 27.

God, His ways, 1, 2.

SURAH XXXIX.—THE TROOPS

(Mecca.)

The title of this Surah is taken from verse 71, where it said the wicked shall be sent to Hell. and the righteous admitted into Heaven by troops.

The Quran:

1. The revelation of the Book is from God, the mighty, the wise.

2. We have sent down to thee the Book in truth;

therefore serve God being sincere in religion to Him.

2. 'In truth;' that is, to some practical end.

'Sincere in religion to Him;' that is, not with a view to make a show of it.

Religion to God:

3. Is not sincerity in religion due to God?

9. If ye are ungrateful, surely, God is rich without you; yet He likes not ingratitude in His servants; yet if ye are thankful He will be well-pleased with you. . .

3. All religious feeling should be exhibited to God alone.

The Pious:

13. Say thou, O My servants who believe, fear your Lord: for those who do good in this world, is good; and surely vast is God's earth; verily for those who steadfastly persevere is a reward without measure.

14. Say thou, I am commanded to worship God, being sincere in religion to Him, and I am commanded to be the first of the Moslems.

15. Say thou, Verily I fear if I rebel against my Lord the punishment of the great Day.

16. Say thou, God will I serve, being sincere in religion to Him.

The Ungodly:

17. But ye serve what ye choose beside Him. Say thou, Verily the losers are those who lose themselves and their families on the Judgment Day; is not that a plain loss?

19. And those who shun the worship of Taghut and are turned to God, for them are glad tidings: give

glad tidings then to My servants, who hearken to My word and follow the good thereof. These it is whom God has guided and these it is who have hearts.

23. . . . But woe to those whose hearts are hardened against the remembrance of God! these are in plain error.

17. See the idea of a Moslem Heaven in Surah xiii. 13.

19. 'Taghut.' The word properly signifies an idol: hence anything worshipped besides God.

The Quran :

24. God has revealed the best discourse, a Book consistent, and teaching by iteration: the skins of those who fear their Lord do creep at it; then do their skins grow soft and their hearts also, at the mention of God; that is the guidance of God: He guides by it whom He pleases. . .

Of Older Generations:

26. Those who have been before them called it a lie; but a punishment came upon them from where they did not expect.

27. And God made them taste shame in the life of this world, but the punishment of the Hereafter is greater; did they but know!

28. We have struck for men in this Quran every parable, that they might consider.

29. An Arabic Quran without crookedness, that they may fear to do wrong.

30. God strikes forth the parable of a man with partners at variance among themselves, and of a man who strives for a man; are these equal? No, praise to God! but most of them do not know.

30. This passage represents the uncertainty of the polytheist, who is distracted in the service of different masters; and the one satisfaction of mind which attends the worshipper of the only God.

The Judgment Day:

31. Thou shall die and they shall die;

32. Then surely on the Judgment Day ye shall dispute before God.

40. Say thou, Ye people, do your part, and I also am doing; by and by shall ye know.

45. Say thou, God's is the intercession altogether: His is the kingdom of the heavens and the earth; then to Him shall ye return.

48. And if those who do wrong had all that is in the earth altogether, and with it another like it, surely they would ransom themselves with it from the pain of the punishment on the Judgment Day, and there shall appear to them from God what they never could imagine:

49. And there shall appear to them evils which they have acquired, and what they had mocked at shall encompass them.

32. For the prophet will represent his endeavours to reclaim them from their evil ways, and their obstinacy, and they will make frivolous excuses, as that they obeyed their chiefs, and kept to the religion of their fathers, etc.

God's Mercy:

54. Say thou, O My servants who have transgressed against your own souls despair not of the mercy of God; verily God forgives sins, all of them; surely He is the forgiving, the compassionate.

67. And they esteem not God as is His due; and on the Judgment Day the whole earth will be but His handful.

The Judgment Day:

68. And there will be a blast on the trumpet, and all in the heavens and the earth will expire, unless those whom He shall please; then there will be another blast on it, and lo! they shall rise up and look on.

69. And the earth shall shine with the light of her Lord, and the Book shall be set, and the prophets and the martyrs shall be brought up, and the judgment between them shall be given with truth, and they shall not be wronged.

70. And every soul shall be fully paid what it has done; surely He knows what they do.

69. 'The Book,' i.e., of men's actions.
'With truth,' or 'with justice.'

Principal Contents

God, His mercy need not be despaired of, 54.
Judgment Day, 68-70.
Quran, the 1, 2, 24.
Pious, the 13.
Sincerity in religion to God, 2, 3.
Ungodly, the 17.

SURAH XL.—THE FAITHFUL
(Mecca.)

The title is taken from verse 29, wherein mention is made of one of pharaoh's family who believed in the mission of Moses.

The Quran:

1. H.M. The revelation of the Book is from God, the mighty, the knowing.

2. Forgiver of sins, and accepter of repentance, severe to punish, full of forbearance:

3. There is no God but He; and to Him shall ye be gathered.

The Judgment Day :

18. Warn them of the approaching Day, when hearts shall rise up to their throats choking them.

19. And the wrong-doers shall have no friend or intercessor to help them;

20. He knows the deceitful of eye, and what their bosoms hide.

21. And God will decide everything with truth; . . .

Of Apostles:

78. And We have sent apostles before thee: of some We have told thee, and of others We have told thee nothing.

83. And when their apostles came to them with evidences, they exulted in what knowledge they had; but what they mocked at encompassed them.

78. See Surah ii. 3, notes.

83. 'They exulted,' etc. Being prejudiced in favour of their own views, and despising the instructions of the prophets.

Principal contents

Apostles, numerous, 78.

Judgment Day, the, 18-21.

Quran, the , 1, 2.

SURAH XLI.—WORSHIP

(Mecca.)

It is so called because the ungodly are herein exhorted to worship God alone as their Lord and Master.

The Quran :

1. H.M. Revealed from the merciful, the

compassionate God:

2. A Book the verses whereof are explained; an Arabic Quran for a people who understand;

3. Bearing glad tidings and warning; but most of them do turn aside and hearken not.

4. And they say, Our hearts are veiled from what thou dost call us to, and in our ears is a deafness, and between us and thee is a curtain: act therefore, we also will act.

1. 'H.M.' See Surah ii. 1, note.

The Apostle:

5. Say thou, Verily I am only a man like yourselves: it is only revealed to me that your God is one God; go straight then to Him, and ask pardon of Him: but woe to the polytheists,

6. Who give not alms, and in the Hereafter disbelieve!

7. But they who believe and do good, for them is a reward that fails not.

5. See Surah xviii. 110.

The Unity of God:

30. Verily those who say, Our Lord is God, and then keep straight, there shall descend upon them angels, saying, Fear not, neither be ye grieved, but rejoice in the Gardens which ye are promised;

31. We are your friends in the life of this world and in the Hereafter; and for you therein is what your souls desire and for you therein is what ye ask for,—

32. A present from the forgiving, compassionate God.

30. See also Surah xlvi. 12, 13.

A Good Word:

33. And who speaks better than he who calls to God and does good, and says Verily I am of the Moslems?

34. Good and evil shall not be held equal: resist evil with what is better, and lo! between whom and thyself was enmity shall become as it were thy warmest friend; but none will attain to this unless the patiently persevering, and none will attain to this unless the most highly favoured.

33. See also Surah iv. 114.

The Quran:

41. . . . Verily it is a mighty Book.

42. Vainity approaches it not, either from before it or from behind it: it is a message from the wise, praiseworthy God:

46. Whoso does good it is for his own soul, and whoso does evil it is against it; and thy Lord is not unjust to His servants.

49. Man is not tired of praying for good, and if evil befall him, he desponds and despairs.

52. Say thou, What think ye? If it is from God, and ye disbelieve in it, who is more misguided than he who is wide away from it.

Promise of Success:

53. By and by We will shew forth Our signs to them in countries and among themselves until it is plain to them that it is the truth. It is not enough for thee that thy Lord is witness of all things?

54. Are not they in doubt as to the meeting of their Lord? Does not He encompass all things?

53. 'We will shew forth,' etc. By the rapid progress of Islam among other nations as well as among themselves.

Principal Contents

Apostle only a man, 5.

God, His unity, 30.

Good word, 33, 34.

Quran, the 1-3, 41, 42.

Success, its promise, 53.

Ungodly, the, 4.

SURAH XLII.—COUNSEL

(Mecca.)

The title is taken from verse 36.

God: His Commandment:

14. Call thou, and go straight on as thou art commanded, and follow not their desires, and say thou, I believe in what God has sent down of the Book and I am commanded to do justice between you; God is our Lord and your Lord: for us are our works and for you your works: there is no dispute between us and you: God will gather us together, and to Him shall we return.

Believers : Their Character:

34. Whatever things are given you are a provision of the life of this world: but what is with God is better and more enduring for those who believe and in their Lord do trust;

35. And who avoid heinous and filthy crimes, and when they are angry to forgive;

36. And who hearken to their Lord, and are steadfast in prayer, and their affairs are guided by consent among themselves, and of what We have given them do they spend;

37. And who, when a wrong is done them, redress themselves:

38. And the reward of evil is evil like it—but whoso forgives and is reconciled, His reward is with God; surely He loves not the wrong-doers.

39. And whoso redresses himself after his wrong, surely against these there is no way;

37. See Surah xvi. 127.

38. Forgiveness is here inculcated in a most effective way. See Surah xli. 34; also xvi. 127, 128.

The Ungodly :

40. Verily there is only a way against those who wrong men and act insolently in the earth without right: for them is a painful punishment.

41. And whoso endures patiently and forgives, verily that is a bounden duty.

50. It is not for man that God should speak to him unless by inspiration or from behind a veil;

51. Or, He sends an apostle to reveal by His permission what He will; surely He is high, wise.

Principal Contents

Believers, their character, 35-8.

God, His commandment, 114.

Ungodly, the 40.

SURAH XLIII.—GOLD ORNAMENTS

(Mecca.)

The word chosen for the title of this Surah occurs in verse 34.

Jesus: An Apostle :

59. Jesus is only a servant whom We favoured, and We made him an example to the children of Israel.

81. Say thou, If the merciful God had a son, then first would I be to serve him.

82. But no. Glory to the Lord of the heavens and the earth, Lord of the Throne, above what they say!

89. Therefore avoid them and say, Peace, by and by shall ye know.

59. 'Favoured.' *i.e.,* with the gift of prophecy.

89. 'Peace;' see Surah xxv. 64, notes.

Principal Contents

God has no son, 81.

Jesus, an apostle, 59.

SURAH XLIV.—SMOKE

(Mecca.)

The word from which this Surah takes its name occurs in verse 9.

God's Purpose in Creation:

38. We have not created the heavens and the earth and what is between them in sport,

39. But We have only created them in truth, though most of them do not know.

58. And We have only made it easy in thine own tongue, that they may consider.

59. And wait thou, verily they also do wait.

58. 'Made it easy;' refers to the message of the prophet.

59. Impatience is condemned and patience enjoined.

Principal Contents

God, His purpose in creation, 38, 39.

Quran, the, made easy, 58.

SURAH XLV.—THE KNEELING

(Mecca.)

The word which forms the title of this Surah occurs in verse 27.

The Believers:

13. Speak to those who believe, that they forgive those who hope not for the days of God, that He may reward people according to what they have acquired.

14. Whoso does good it is for his own soul, and whoso does evil it is against it, then to your Lord shall ye return.

13. 'The days of God,' the prosperous success of the Moslems, with which was to come the religion of God.

The Judgment:

20. Do the workers of iniquity imagine that We will do with them as with those who believe and do good, that their lives and deaths be equal? Ill do they judge!

21. God created the heavens and the earth in truth that He may reward every soul for what it has acquired, and they shall not be wronged.

The Ungodly:

22. What thinkest thou? He who makes God of his lust and whom God misleads knowingly, and whose hearing and heart has He sealed up, and over whose sight He has put a covering, who will guide him after God? Will ye not consider?

Principal Contents

Believers to forgive the unbelievers, 13.

Judgment, the, 20, 21.

Reward according to works, 14.

Ungodly, the, 22.

SURAH XLVI.—AL AHKAF

(Mecca.)

The title of this Surah is the name given in verse 20 to the territory in the province of Hazramaut where the ancient Adites lived.

The Apostles:

8. Say thou, I am not singular among the apostles, neither do I know what will be done with me or with you: verily I follow only that which is revealed to me; and I am only a plain warner.

8. 'I am not singular,' etc. That is, I do not claim for myself a privilege above the other prophets.

The Faith :

12. Verily those who say, Our Lord is God, and then keep straight: there is no fear for them, neither shall they grieve.

13. These are the people of the Gardens, to continue therein for ever,—as a reward for what they have done.

18. And for all are grades according to what they have done, that God may repay them their works, and they shall not be wronged.

12. See also Surah xli, 30.

Principal Contents

Apostle, his human character, 8.

Faith, the, 12.

Reward according to grades, 18.

SURAH XLVII.—MOHAMMED

(Medinah.)

This Surah is named after the prophet mentioned in verse 2.

Captives: Their Treatment:

4. When ye encounter the infidels, strike off their heads until ye have made a great slaughter among them, and bind fast the bonds;

5. Then either a free dismissal or a ransom, until the war has laid down its arms. This do;—and if it pleased God He could take vengeance upon them: but He would prove the one of you by the other. . .

This World:

38. Verily the life of this world is only a play and a pastime; but if ye believe and fear to do wrong, He will give you your rewards, neither does He ask of you your riches.

39. If He were to require these of you and press you, ye would be niggards, and it would call forth your grudges.

40. Behold! ye are they who are called to spend in the way of God, and some of you are niggards; but whoso is niggardly is niggardly to his own soul, and God is rich, but ye are poor; and if ye turn back, He will bring another people in your place, who will not be like yourselves.

5. In pre-Islamic Arabia as in most other ancient peoples the captives of war were sold into slavery; whereas by this provision they may be either freely dismissed or held as hostages, in which case they might be ransomed by their people. Their mutilation was discountenanced, and only in war could they be slain (as stated in verse 4).

Principal Contents

Captives, their treatment, 4, 5.

World, this, 38.

SURAH XLVIII.—THE VICTORY

(Medinah.)

The Surah has its name from the first important word with which it opens.

God: His Apostle :

28. He it is who has sent His apostle with guidance and the religion of truth, that He may exalt it above all religions; and God suffices for a witness.

29. Mohammed is an apostle of God, and those who are with him are severe to the ungodly, and full of tenderness among themselves, Thou mayest see them bowing down and worshipping, seeking the grace of God and His goodwill. . . . God has promised to those who believe and do good among them, pardon and a great reward.

28. 'Above all religions'; that is, above all sectarianism.

29. See also Surah xxv. 24, etc.

Principal Contents

Mohammad, and apostle, 29.

Promise of future good, 29.

SURAH XLIX.—THE APARTMENTS

(Medinah.)

The word from which this Surah takes its title occurs in verse 4.

Rumours to be Inquired Into:

6. Ye believers, if there come to you a wicked man with news, inquire into it, lest ye hurt people through ignorance, and then have to repent of what ye have done.

Believers: Their Differences:

9. If two bodies of the faithful fight, do ye make

peace between them; and if one of them transgress against the other, fight against the one who transgresses, until they return to the judgment of God : and if they do return, make peace between them with equity, and do justice; verily God loves the equitable.

10. Verily the faithful are but brothers : wherefore make peace between your brothers; and fear God, that ye may have mercy.

11. Ye believers, let not men laugh other men to scorn who may possibly be better than themselves; neither let women laugh other women to scorn who may possibly be better than themselves. Neither defame one another, nor call one another names; an ill name is wickedness after faith : and whoso repents not, surely these are the wrong-doers.

Suspicion A Sin :

12. Ye believers, avoid all suspicion; and verily some suspicions are a sin; and be not inquisitive; neither speak ill the one of you in the absence of the other : would any one of you like to eat the flesh of his dead brother ? Surely ye would abhor it. Then fear God; verily God is relenting, compassionate.

Natural Division of Men :

13. Ye people, We have created you of a male and a female, and have made you into peoples and tribes that ye might know. Verily the most honourable of you to God is the most pious of you; surely God is knowing, informed.

Faith and Religion :

14. The Arabs of the desert say, We believe; say thou,

Ye do not believe; but say, We accept Islam; for the faith has not yet entered into your hearts. But if ye obey God and His apostle, He will not fail you in anything of your works; verily God is forgiving, compassionate.

15. The faithful are those only who believe in God and His apostle, and then doubt not, and strive with their wealth and their lives in the way of God; these are the true.

16. Say thou, Will ye teach God about your religion ? But God knows what is in the heavens and what is in the earth; and surely God knows all things.

14. The distinction between Faith and Religion is here acknowledged. The one concerns the very innermost part of men's character, while the other is a mere outward compliance with Law, which is so constituted as to lead to Faith where all formalities cease.

Principal Contents

Back-biting condemned, 12.

Believers, their differences, 9; their brotherhood, 10.

Faith and religion, 14.

Inquisition disallowed, 12.

Mocking at people disallowed, 11.

Natural divisions of men, 13.

Piety esteemed above all, 13.

Rumours to be inquired into, 6.

Suspicion a sin, 12.

SURAH L. — K.
(MECCA.)

The Surah has its title from the initial letter marks at its beginning.

God's Omniscience :

15. We created man, and We know what his soul whispers within him : and We are nearer to him than his jugular vein.

16. When the two deputies to take account, take it, one on the right, and the other on the left;

17. Not a word he utters, but a watcher is by him ready :

18. And the agony of death shall come in truth : that is what thou wouldst avoid !

16. This refers to the guardian-angels over men.

17. The intent of this passage is to exalt the omniscience of God, who wants not the information of the guardian-angels, though He has thought fit in His wisdom, to give them that employment; for if they are so exact as to write down every word which falls from a man's mouth and thoughts which he har harboured and works which he has done, how can we hope to escape the observation of Him who sees our inmost thoughts ?

Mohammed further taught that the angel who notes a man's good actions has the command over him who notes his evil actions; and that when a man does a good action, the angel of the right hand notes it down ten times and when he commits an evil action, the same angel says to the angel of the left hand, 'Forbear setting it down for seven hours, may be he will pray and repent and amend.'

The Judgment Day :

19. And there will be a blast on the trumpet : that is the promised Day.

20. And every soul shall come, and with it a driver and a witness,—

21. Thou wast careless heretofore of this, but now have We taken the veil from off thee, and thy sight is piercing this day.

44. We know what they say; and thou art not to compel them;

45. But warn by the Quran him who fears My threat.

Principal Contents

Death inevitable, 18.

God, His omniscience, 15

Guardian-angels, 16, 17.

Judgment Day, 19-21.

SURAH LI.—THE SCATTERING

(Mecca.)

The word occurs in verse 1; hence the title of the Surah.

The Judgment:

1. By what scatters with scattering,
2. And those bearing their load,
3. And those speeding lightly along,
4. And those which apportion by command!
5. It is only a truth with which ye are warned.
6. And verily the Judgment will surely come!
7. By the heaven full of tracks!
8. Verily ye widely differ in what ye say.
10. Perish the liars,
11. Who are sunk in carelessness!
12. They ask, When is the Judgment Day to come?
20. And in the earth are signs to those who have faith,
21. And in yourselves; will ye not yet see?
23. And by the Lord of heaven and earth, verily this is true, even as ye speak yourselves.

7. 'Tracks;' *i.e.*, the paths or orbs of the stars, or the steaks which appear in the sky like paths.

23. 'As ye speak,' etc. That is, without any doubt or reserved meaning as ye affirm a truth to one another.

Principal Contents

God, His signs, 20, 21.
Judgment inevitable, 6.

SURAH LII.—THE MOUNTAIN

(Mecca.)

The title is taken from the first verse of the Surah.

The Judgment Day:

1. By the mountain,
2. And the Book written,
3. On outspread scroll,
4. And the frequented House,
5. And the lofty vault,
6. And the swelling sea!
7. Verily the punishment of the Lord will surely come:
8. And none shall put it back.
9. Reeling on that Day shall the heaven reel,
10. And stirring shall the mountains stir.
11. And woe, on that day, to those who called it a lie,
12. Who wrangled for pleasure!
13. On that day shall they be driven and thrust into Hell.
14. This is the Fire which ye called a lie.

21. And to those who believe, and whose offspring follow them in the faith, We will join their offspring, and We will not fail them in anything which they have done; every man lies pledged for what he has earned.

35. Were they created by none? or were they the creators?

36. Did they create the heavens and the earth? Aye, but they will not believe!

43. Have they a God beside God? No. Glory to God above what they join with Him!

44. And if they see a fragment of the heaven falling down, they will say, A thick cloud!

45. Wherefore leave them until they come face to face with the Day when they shall swoon away;

46. A day in which their subtleties shall avail not at all, and they shall not be helped.

47. Verily for those who do wrong is a punishment beside this; but most of them do not know.

48. Wait thou patiently the judgment of thy Lord: for thou art in Our eye; and celebrate the praise of thy Lord when thou risest up;

49. And in the night-time glorify, Him, and when the stars are setting.

3. 'Outspread scroll'; it refers to the Volume of Nature before us.

21. See Surah xiii, 23.

'Every man' etc. That is, every man is pledged to God for his behaviour; and if he does well, he redeems his pledge, but if evil, he forfeits it.

Principal Contents

God, the creator, 35, 36.

Judgment Day inevitable, 7.

SURAH LIII—THE STAR

(Mecca.)

The word in the first verse gives the Surah its title.

The Prophet :

1. By the star when it sets!
2. Your companion errs not, nor is he led astray;
3. Neither speaks he out of lust.
4. It is only a revelation revealed.
5. One mighty in power taught it him,
6. Endued with wisdom.

2. 'Your companion;' refers to Mohammed, whom the Meccans so well know from a boy up. They knew his pure character and respected it, and called him 'al-Amin,' the trusty, the union of all virtues; but in his fortieth year when Mohammed stood up to preach his Mission they regarded him as one under the influence of some spirits.

Ancient Idolatry of the Arabs :

19. What think ye of Al-Lat and Al-Uzza,
20. And Manat, that other third?
21. What! shall ye have male children, and He female?
22. This were indeed an unfair partition!
23. These are only names, which ye and your fathers have named. God has not revealed concerning them any authority: they follow only an opinion and what their souls do lust. But now has come to them a guidance from their Lord.

19. 'Al-Lat,' etc. There were the three female deities which the ancient Arabs worshipped.

Judgment Inevitable:

24. Shall man have what he desires?
25. God's is the Hereafter and this life:
26. And many as are the angels in the heavens, their intercession shall be of no avail;

27. Until after God has given permission to whom He shall please and will accept.

32. God's is what is in the heavens and what is in the earth, that He may reward those who do evil for what they have done, and may reward those who do good with good.

33. To those who avoid great sins and filthy actions, but have done only smaller faults, verily they Lord will be extensive in mercy. . .

The Message of the Ancient Prophets:

37. Has he not been told of what is in the pages of Moses?

38. And of Abraham faithful to his pledge?

39. That no burdened soul shall bear the burden of another,

40 And that nothing lies against a man but what he has striven for?

41. And that his strivings shall at last be seen?

42. That then he will be rewarded for it with the fullest reward?

43. And that to thy Lord is the end?

44. And that He it is who makes to laugh and to weep?

45. And that He it is who makes to die and makes alive?

51. And that He it is who destroyed the ancient Ad,

52. And Samud, and left not any;

53. And the people of Noah before them, for that they were most unjust and wicked.

54. And He it was who overthrew them upside down,

55. So that what covered them covered them.

56. Then which of thy Lord's benefits wilt thou question?

58. Then Inevitable draws nigh: there is none but God to reveal it.

59. Is it at these sayings ye marvel?

60. And that ye laugh and weep not?

61. And that ye are triflers?

62. Rather worship God, and serve Him.

58. 'The Inevitable,' refers to the Judgment Day.

Principal Contents

Ancient Idolatry of the Arabs, 19-23.

Judgment Day inevitable, 24-6, 32, 37-43.

SURAH LIV.—THE MOON

(Mecca.)

The word occurs in verse 1 ; hence the title of the Surah.

The Judgment Day :

1. The Hour is at hand, and the moon is cleft asunder!

2. But if they see a sign, they turn aside, and say, A powerful charm!

3. And they call it a lie, and follow their own lusts; but everything is fixed,

4. And now has come to them a message wherein is prohibition—

5. Wisdom perfect—but warners avail not!

6. Wherefore avoid them. The Day the crier shall call to a stern fact,

7. With downcast eyes shall they come forth from their graves, like as scattered locusts,

8. Hastening to the crier. The ungodly shall say, This is a day of distress.

1. 'The Hour;' the Judgment Day.

Examples From Ancient History:

9. Before them, the people of Noah called it a lie...

16. Then how was My punishment and My warning?

18. Ad called it a lie, but what was my torment and warning?

23. Samud called the warning a lie,

30. And what was My torment and warning?

33. The people of Lot called the warning a lie,

39. And early in the morning a fixed punishment came upon them!

41. Then came to the people of Pharaoh the warning,

42. They called all Our signs lies: wherefore We seized them as with a mighty, powerful grip.

52. Everything which they do is in the Books;

53. All small and great noted down.

54. Verily the pious shall be amid Gardens and rivers,

55. In the Seat of Truth, before the King almighty.

52. 'The Books,' that is, of men's actions.

Principal Contents

Examples from ancient history, 9-42.

Judgment Day, the 1-8.

SURAH LV.—THE MERCIFUL
(*Mecca.*)

The word which gives name to the Surah occurs in the first verse.

God: His Works:

1. The Merciful has taught the Quran,
2. Created man,
3. Taught him speech,
4. The sun and the moon have their rules;
5. And the plants and the trees bend humbly,
6. And the heaven, He raised it, and set up the balance,
7. That ye transgress not in the balance.
8. And weigh with a just balance, and stint not the measure,
9. And the earth, He has made for living things:
10. Therein are fruits, and palm-trees with clusters sheathed,
11. And the grain with its husk and fragrant flowers,
12. Then which of the bounties of your Lord will ye twain deny?
13. He created man of clay like the potter's,
14. And created the Jinn from pure fire:
16. Lord of the two easts,
17. And Lord of the two wests!
19. He has let loose the two seas which meet together,
20. Yet between the two is a barrier they cannot pass!
22. From them are taken forth pearls, great and small,
24. And His are the ships towering in the sea like mountains.
26. All that is herein will pass away.

27. But there shall abide the Face of thy Lord, full of majesty and glory.

29. Him do ask all who are in the heavens and the earth; every day He is at work.

78. Blessed the name of thy Lord full of majesty and glory!

6. 'Balance;' or justice and equity in mutual dealings.

12. 'Ye twain.' This refers to the two species of rational creatures, men and genii, the verb and the pronoun being in the dual number.

The verse is intercalated, or repeated by way of burden throughout the whole Surah no less then thirty-one times.

14. The 'Jinn.' See Surah vi. 100, notes.

16, 17. 'The two easts,' etc. The original words are in the dual number, and signify the different points of the horizon at which the sun rises and sets at the summer and winter solstices.

19. 'The two seas.' Of salt water and fresh. See Surah xxv. 55.

24. 'His are the ships;' *i.e.*, they are at His mercy.

Principal Contents

God, His gifts, 1-14, 19, 20-24,

Justice towards each other, 6-8.

SURAH LVI.—THE INEVITABLE

(Mecca.)

The word occurs in the first verse.

The Judgment Day:

1. When the Inevitable is come,
2. None shall call its coming a lie.
3. Abasing, exalting!
4. When the earth is shaken by a shock,

5. And the mountains crumble to pieces,

6. And are scattered dust,

95. Verily this is a certain truth;

96. Wherefore praise the name of thy Lord, the great God.

1. 'The Inevitable,' refers to the Judgment Day. "The original world, the force whereof cannot well be expressed by a single one in English, signifies a calamitous accident, which falls surely and with sudden violence, and is therefore made use of here to design the day of judgment".—George Sale.

3. 'Abasing' some, and 'exalting' others.

Principal Contents

Judgment Day, 1-6; a reality, 95.

SURAH LVII.—IRON

(Medinah.)

The word occurs in verse 25.

God : His Power:

1. All in the heavens and the earth praise God: and He is the mighty, the wise.

2. His is the kingdom of the heavens and the earth: He gives life and puts to death; and He is mighty over all things.

3. He is the first and the last, and the manifest and the hidden; and He knows all things.

8. And what has come over you that ye do not believe in God, and the apostle calls you to believe in your Lord, and He has received your covenant if ye believe.

8. 'He has received your convenant.' That is, ye are obliged to believe in Him by the strongest arguments and motives.

Almsgiving:

10. And what has come over you that ye spend not in the way of God? and God's is the heritage of the heavens and the earth.

11. Who is it that will lend to God a good loan? He will surely double it to him, and for them is a mighty reward.

21. Hasten emulously for pardon from your Lord, and the Garden, vast as the heaven and the earth, prepared for those who believe in God and His prophet; that is the grace of God: He gives it to whom He will; surely God is full of unbounded grace.

Monasticism:

27. Moreover We made Our apostles to follow in their footsteps, and We made Jesus the son of Mary to follow them, and We gave him the Evangel and We put into the hearts of those who followed him kindness and compassion; but monasticism, they invented it themselves. We only prescribed to them the desire to please God, but they observed not this as was its duc; and to such of them as believe Wc will give them their reward; but most of them are transgressors.

Principal Contents

Almsgiving, 10, 11.

God, His power, 1-3, 8.

Monasticism, 27.

SURAH LVIII.—SHE WHO PLEADED
(*Medinah.*)

The Surah has its title from this word occurring in verse 1.

An Old Form of Divorce Questioned:

1. Now has God heard the word of her who pleaded with the against her husband and made her complaint to God; and God has heard your mutual discourse; verily God is the hearing, the seeking.
2. Those of you who put away their wives—they are not their mothers: they only are their mothers who gave them birth; and they certainly say a wicked thing and a lie:
3. But truly God is gracious, forgiving.
4. And those who put away their wives, and then repair what they say, shall free a slave, before they touch one another. This is what ye are warned; surely God is informed of what ye do.
5. And whoso cannot, shall fast two months consecutively before they touch one another. And whoso is not able shall feed sixty poor men.

1. 'The word of her,' etc. This was Khaula, wife of Aus b.as-Samat, who, being divorced by her husband by a form in use among the pre-Islamic Arabs, by saying to her, 'Thy back be to me as the back of my mother,' came to ask Mohammed's opinion whether they were necessarily obliged to a separation; and he told her that it was not lawful for her to live with her husband any more: to which she replying, that her husband had not put her away, the prophet repeated his former decision, adding that such form of speaking was by general consent understood to imply a perpetual separation. Upon this the women being greatly concerned because of her little children, went home, and uttered her complaint to God in prayer: and thereupon this passage was revealed, allowing a man to take his wife again, notwithstanding his having pronounced the above mentioned form of divorce, on doing certain acts of charity or mortification, by way of penance
2. 'They only,' etc. And therefore no woman ought to be placed in the same degree of prohibition, except those

who whom God has joined with them, as nursing mothers, etc.

4. 'Repair.' This seems to be here the true meaning of the original word, which properly signifies 'to return,' and is variously expounded by the commentators.

God: His Omnipresence:

8. Hast thou not seen that God knows what is in the heavens and what is in the earth? There is no private talk among three persons, but He is the fourth of them; nor among five, but He is the sixth of them, nor fewer nor more, but He is with them, wherever they are. Then He will tell them what they have done on the Judgment Day; verily God is informed of all things.

10. Ye believers, when ye talk privately together, talk not of wickedness, and hatred, and sin against the apostle, but talk of goodness and piety; and fear God to whom ye shall be gathered.

Principal Contents

Divorce, a special form of it revoked, 1-5.

Evil talk prohibited, 10.

God, His omnipresence, 8.

SURAH LIX.—THE EMIGRATION
(Medinah.)

The word occurs in verse 2; hence the title of the Surah.

The Judgment Day:

18. Ye believers, fear God; and let every soul look to what is sends on before for the morrow; and fear God; verily God is informed of what ye do.

19. And be not as those who forget God, and whom He makes to forget their own souls; these are the wicked.

18. 'Fo·· the morrow;' that is, for the next life, which may caıled so, as the present life may be called 'this day.'

The Quran: Its Effects:

21. If We had revealed this Quran on a mountain, thou wouldst surely have seen it humble itself, and cleave asunder for fear of God. These parables We strike out for men that they may consider.

21. This refers to the most effective impression of the Quran upon the hearts of man.

God: His Names:

22. He is God beside whom there is no God: knower of the manifest and the hidden; He is the merciful, the compassionate.

23. He is God beside whom there is no God: the King, the Holy, the Peace, the Faithful, the Guardian, the Mighty, the Supreme, the Most High! Glory to God above what they join with Him.

24. He is God, the Creator, the Maker, the Fashioner; His are excellent names. Whatever is in the heavens and the earth praises Him; and He is the mighty, the wise.

Principal Contents

God, His names, 22-4

Judgment Day to be regard, 18, 19.

Quran, the; its effects upon human hearts, 21.

SURAH LX.—SHE WHO IS TRIED

(Medinah.)

This Surah bears the title from verse 10, by which the women who desert and come over from the unbelieving people are to be examined, and tried whether they are sincere in their profession of the faith.

Intercourse with the Unbelievers:

1. Ye believers, take not My enemy and your enemy for friends, showing kindness towards them, while they believe not in the truth which has come to you, having turned out the apostle and yourselves, for that ye believe in God your Lord. . .

8. God does not forbid you to act with goodness and equity towards those who have not warred upon you for religion, nor turned you out of your homes; verily God loves the equitable.

9. God only forbids you to make friends of those who have warred upon you for religion, and turned you out of your homes, and have aided in your expulsion; and whoso makes friends of them, surely these are the wrong-doers.

1. This passage was revealed on account of one Hatib, who under standing that Mohammed had a design to surprise Mecca, for its violation of the Treaty of Hodeibiyah wrote a letter to the Koreish, giving them notice of the intended expedition, and advised them to be on their guard: the letter being intercepted, the Prophet asked Hatib how be came to be guilty of such an action? To which he replied that it was not out of faithlessness, or a desire to return to his old ways, but merely to induce the Koreish to treat his family, which was still at Mecca, with some kindness; adding that he was well assured his intelligence would be of service at all to the Meccans, because he was satisfied God would take vengeance on them. Whereupon Mohammed received his excuse and pardoned him; but it was thought proper to forbid any such practices for the future.

The Pledge of Women:

12. O Prophet, when believing women come to thee and pledge themselves that they will not join anything with God, nor steal, nor commit whoredom, nor kill their children, nor come with

a calumny which they have devised between their hands and their feet, nor disobey thee in what is reasonable, then pledge thou thy faith to them, and ask pardon for them of God; verily God is forgiving, compassionate.

12. 'Whoredom,' fornication or adultery.

'Kill their children.' This refers to the custom of female infanticide or the other practice of offering a male child to the idols from each family.

'Come with a calumny.' That is, calumniating women, or laying their spurious children to their husbands.

Principal Contents.

Unbelievers, intercourse with them, 1, 8, 9

Women, their pledge of faith, 12.

SURAH LXI.—BATTLE ARRAY
(Medinah.)

The Surah takes its name from verse 4, where the world pitched on for the title occurs.

God: His Power:

1. Whatever is in the heavens and whatever is in the earth praises God; and He is the mighty, the wise.

Mere Words An Abomination:

2. Ye believers, why say ye what ye do not?
3. Most hateful to God is that ye say what ye do not.
4. Verily God loves those who fight in His way drawn up in battle array as though they were a solid wall.

2. Insincerity is strongly condemned by Mohammed.

4. See Surah ix. 1-12.

Principal Contents

Words, mere, an abomination, 2, 3.
Work, earnest, required, 4.

SURAH LXII.—THE ASSEMBLY
(Medinah.)

The word occurs in verse 9; hence the title.

God: His Goodness:

1. Whatever is in the heavens and the earth praises God, the King, the Holy the Mighty, the Wise.

2. He it is who has raised up amidst the illiterate people an apostle from among themselves, to recite to them His signs, and to purify them, and to teach them the Book and wisdom, whereas before they were surely in a plain error.

5. The likeness of those who are charged with the Law, and then observe it not, is as the likeness of an ass laden with books.

The Friday Service:

9. Ye believers, when ye are called to prayer on the day of the Assembly, hasten to the commemoration of God, and leave merchandizing. That is the best for you, did ye only know!

10. And when the Prayer is ended, then disperse yourselves through the land and seek the bounty of God; and remember God most, that ye may be happy.

9. 'The day of Assembly;' refers to Friday.

10. By returning to your commerce and wordly occupations, if ye think fit; for the Moslems do not hold themselves obliged to observe the day of their public assembly with the same strictness as the Jew and Christians to their

respective Sabbath; or particularly to abstain from work, after they have performed their devotions.

Principal Contents

Apostles, their mission, 2.

Congregational service, 9, 10.

God, His goodness, 1, 2.

Neglect of law, 5.

SURAH LXIII.—THE HYPOCRITES
(Medinah.)

The word occurs in the first verse of the Surah.

The Hypocrites:

1. When the hypocrites come to thee, they say, We bear witness that thou art the apostle of God; and God knows that thou art His apostle; and God bears witness that they hypocrites are certainly liars.

2. They have taken their oaths for a cloak, and they turn aside others from the way of God. Evil is what they do.

9. Ye believers, let not your wealth and your children keep you from the remembrance of God: whoso does this,—surely these are the losers!

2. 'For a cloak;' that is, which they conveniently throw aside.

Principal Contents

Hypocrites, their character, 2.

SURAH LXIV.—MUTUAL DECEIT
(Medinah.)

This Surah has its name from the mention, in verse 9, of the judgment Day as one on which it will be found that if the just had been wicked they would have taken the place of the reprobates, while the reprobates will see that if they had been just persons they would have gone to the abode of bliss.

God: His Power:

1. Whatever is in the heavens and the earth praise God: His is the Kingdom, and His the praise; and He is mighty over all things!
2. He it is who created you; and of you is one infidel, and another a faithful; surely God sees what they do.
3. He created the heavens and the earth in truth, and fashioned you, and gave you the best forms: and to Him ye shall be gathered.
4. He knows what is in the heavens and the earth, and He knows what ye hide, and what ye manifest; surely God is informed of the inmost part of breasts.

11. No misfortune befalls them but by the permission of God; and whoso believes in God, He will guide his heart; and God is informed of all things.
12. And obey God, and obey the apostle, but if ye turn back, surely Our apostle is only bound to preach publicly.
13. God! there is no God but He: and in God let the faithful trust.

A Trial for Men:

14. Ye believers verily in your wives and your children ye have an enemy; wherefore beware of them; but if ye pass over, and pardon and forgive them, surely God is forgiving compassionate.
15. Your wealth and your children are only a trial; but God—with Him is a great reward.
16. Fear God then with all your might, and hearken to Him, and obey, and give alms: it is better for yourselves; and whoso is saved from the

covetousness of his soul,—surely these are the happy.

17. If ye lend to God a good loan, He will double it to you, and will forgive you; and surely God is grateful, mild.

18. Knower of the secret and the manifest: the Mighty, the Wise.

14. 'An enemy.' For these are apt to distract a man from his duty, especially in time of distress: a married man caring more for the things of this world.

'Pass over,' etc. Considering that the hindrances they may occasion you proceeds from their affection, and their ill bearing your sacrifices for conscience sake.

17. 'Lend to God,' etc. That is, contribute towards the success of the mission.

Principal Contents

God, His power, 1-4, 11; His fear enjoined, 16.

Trial for men, 14, 15.

SURAH LXV.—DIVORCE

(Medinah.)

The Surah takes its name from the first verse. It is a supplement to Surah ii. 228.

Divorce: Some Rules:

1. O Prophet, when ye divorce women, divorce them at their appointment term; and compute the term; and fear God, your Lord. Turn them not out from their houses, neither let them go, unless they have come in for filthy actions openly. And these are the bounds of God, and whoso transgresses the bounds of God, surely he wrongs his own soul. Thou knowest not whether God will make something new to pass after this.

2. And when they have fulfilled their term, keep

them with humanity, or part from them with kindness; and take witnesses from among you men of integrity, and stand steadfast to witness before God;—this is an admonition to you, for whoso believes in God and the Hereafter: and whoso fears God, for him will He make a way out.

4. . . . But those who are with child, their term is, until they are delivered of their burthen.

6. Keep them wherein ye dwell according to your means; and distress them not by putting them to straits. And if they are with child, spend on them, until they are delivered of their burthen. And if they suckle for you, give them their due, and consult among yourselves, with equity; and if ye find difficulty herein, then let another suckle for him.

7. Let him who has plenty spend out of his plenty, and whoso has a scanty provision, let him give out of what God has given him. God obliges not a soul but according to what He has given him. God will surely bring ease after a difficulty.

6. 'And if they suckle,' etc. See Surah ii. 233.

Principal Contents

Divorce, some rules regarding it, 1, 2, 4, 6, 7.

SURAH LXVI.—PROHIBITION
(Medinah.)

The Surah is named from a word in the first verse.

And Innocent Pleasure :

1. O Prophet why holdest thou that to be prohibited which God has allowed thee, seeking to please

thy wives? Surely God is forgiving, compassionate.

1. See notes in the Addenda.

Principal Contents

Pleasure, innocent, allowed, 1.

SURAH LXVII.—THE KINGDOM

(Mecca.)

The word occurs in the first verse of the Surah.

God: His Power and Mercy:

1. Blessed is He in whose hand is the Kingdom; and He is mighty over all things;

2. Who created death and life to prove you which of you is best in actions; and He is the mighty, the forgiving;

3. Who has created the seven heavens, one above another: thou canst not see in the creation of the Merciful God a defect. Then repeat thy gaze again, dost thou see a flaw?

4. Then repeat thy gaze again twice, thy sight will recoil to thee dazzled and dim!

15. He it is who has made the earth level for you: wherefore walk through the regions thereof, and eat of His provision; and to Him is the return.

16. Are ye sure that He who is in the heaven will not cleave the earth with you; and that then it shall quake?

17. Or, are ye sure that He who is in the heaven will not send against you a sandstorm?—then shall ye know what was My warning.

19. Do they not look at the birds above them expanding their wings and drawing them in?—

none does hold them but the Merciful God: verily He sees all things.

20. Who is it that will be a host for you if not the Merciful God?—verily the ungodly are only in a delusion.

21. Or, who is it that will provide for you if He held back His provision?—yet they persist in pride and running away.

29. Say thou, He is the Merciful God: we believe in Him and in Him we trust; by and by shall ye know who is in plain error.

30. Say thou, What think ye? If at early morn your waters should sink away tomorrow, who is it that will bring you running water?

1. 'The Kingdom,' *i.e.,* of all that is.

Principal Contents

God, His power, 2-4, 15; His mercy, 16, 17, 19-21, 30.

SURAH LXVIII.—THE PEN
(*Mecca.*)

The word occurs in the first verse of the Surah.

God: His Judgment:

7. Verily thy Lord well knows who errs from His way, and He knows the rightly guided.

42. The day when the leg is made bare, and they are called upon to worship, but they shall not be able:

43. Their looks cast down, shame covering them, for that they were called to worship while they were yet safe.

44. Wherefore let me alone with him who calls this message a lie. By and by We will lead them down by what they know not.

45. But I will bear long with them; surely My plan is sure.

48. And wait thou patiently for the judgment of thy Lord, and be not like the Fellow of the Fish, when he cried out inwardly vexed.

51. It wants little but that the ungodly strike thee down with their looks, when they hear the warning; and they say, Surely he is possessed.

52. Yet is it only a warning to the worlds.

42. 'The leg is made bare.' The expression is used to signify a grievous and terrible calamity: thus they say, 'War has made the leg bare,' when they would express the fury and rage of battle.

'They shall not be able.' Because the time of acceptance shall be past.

48. 'Like the fellow of the Fish;' impatient and pettish as Jonas proved he was.

Principal Contents

God, His knowledge, 7; His ways 44, 45.

Judgment Day, 42, 43.

SURAH LXIX.—THE INEVITABLE

(Mecca.)

The original word 'al Hakkat,' the Inevitable, is one of the names given in the Quran to the Judgment Day. The root from which it is derived signifies 'to be' or 'come to pass of necessity.'

The Judgment of God:

1. The Inevitable!

2. What is the Inevitable?

3. And what shall made thee know what is the Inevitable?

4. Samud and Ad called the Striking a lie;

5. Wherefore Samud were destroyed by a crash,

6. And Ad were destroyed by a roaring tempest.
7. He assailed them with it seven nights and eight days together: thou couldst have seen the people therein laid law, as though they were trunks of hollow palm tress;
8. And couldst thou see one of them left?
49. And We well know that there are of you those who call it a lie;
50. But it will surely be a cause of sighing to the ungodly.
51. And surely it is the certain truth,
52. Wherefore praise the name of thy Lord, the Most High.

1. 'The Inevitable,' See notes above.
4. 'The Striking,' or that which will strike terror into the hearts of men; the Judgment Day is so named in the Quran, See Surah ci. 1.

Principal Contents

God, His Judgment inevitable, 1-8.
Inevitable, the 1.

SURAH LXX.—THE STEPS
(Mecca.)

The word occurs in verse 3 of this Surah.

The Judgment of God:

1. One called for punishment
2. To the ungodly: there is none to avert it
3. From God. . .
5. Be thou patient then with graceful patience;
6. They see it at a distance;
7. But We see it nigh.

8. The Day the heaven shall be as molten brass,
9. And the mountains as carded wool,
10. And friend shall not ask a friend,
11. Though they see one another. The wicked would wish to redeem himself from the punishment of that day by his children,
12. And his wife, and his brother,
13. And his relatives who were kind to him,
14. And all who are in the earth; and that it might deliver him.
15. Never!
42. Wherefore let them wrangle, and amuse themselves, till they come face to face with what they have been warned;
43. The day they shall come out of their tombs in haste like as they were rallying to a standard:
44. There eyes cast down, disgrace covering them.—That is the day with which they are warned.

1. One Nazr b. al-Haris, a chief of the Meccans, came to Mohammed and challenged him to bring down upon him God's vengeance if he were wrong.

Principal Contents

God, His Judgment, 1-3, 6, 7, 43, 44; its terror, 9-15.

SURAH LXXI.—NOAH

(Mecca.)

The name of the prophet appears in the first verse.

Of Noah :

1. We sent Noah to his people, saying, Warn thou thy people ere there come up on them a painful punishment;

21. But they devised a great plot,

24. And they led astray many. . .

25. And for their sins they were drowned. . .

26. And they found none to help them against God.

Principal Contents

Noah, His message, 1.

Unbelievers, their plots against Noah, 21, 24; their punishment, 25, 26.

SURAH LXXII—THE JINN

(Mecca.)

The word occurs in the first verse of the Surah.

Some doctors do not take the Jinn here mentioned to be the same as genii; they think that the word here refers to a people known by that name who came from Nisibin and Nineveh in Mesopotamia. A party of these people accepted Islam at Nakhlah, where Mohammed had fled from the persecution of the people at Tayif. See Surah xlvi. 28, 29.

Of God:

20. Say thou, I only call upon my Lord and I do not join anything with Him.

21. Say thou, Verily I have no power over what may hurt or benefit you.

22. Say thou, Verily none can protect me against God,

23. Neither shall I find a refuge beside Him.

Principal Contents

God, His power, 20, 22, 23.

Prophet powerless against God, 21.

SURAH LXXIII.—THE WRAPPED UP

(Mecca.)

This Surah takes its name from the word which occurs in the first verse.

Of God And His Judgment:

8. And commemorate the name of thy Lord, and cleave to Him with entire cleaving.

9. Lord of the east and the west: there is no God but He: take Him then for your patron.

10. And endure patiently what they say, and depart from them with a graceful departure.

11. And let Me alone with those who call it a lie, and are rich in blessings, and bear with them a little.

17. And how will ye escape if ye believe not on the Day which shall made children grey-headed?

18. The heaven shall be rent by it: and the threat shall be carried out.

19. Verily this is a warning: let him who will take to his Lord a way,

8. 'And cleave,' etc. Sale translates it, 'And separate thyself unto him, renouncing worldly varities.'

17. 'Shall make children grey-headed;' in fact, all children are considered sinless in Islam, but it refers to the terror of the Judgment in men; for if the sinless are so concerned, how much more the men who have attained to age and done things on their own responsibility?

18. 'The threat,' i.e., of the Judgment.

Good Works in This Live:

20. . . . Be steadfast in prayer and give alms, and lend to God a good loan: and what of good ye send before for your souls, ye shall find it with God; this is the best and highest reward. And ask pardon of God; verily God is forgiving, compassionate.

20. 'This is the best,' etc. That is, the good which ye shall do in your life time will be much more meritorious in the sight of God, than what ye shall defer till death, and order by will.

Principal Contents

God, His power, 9; His devotion inculcated, 8.

Good works done in this life, 20.

Judgment belongs to God, 11; inevitable, 17, 18.

SURAH LXXIV.—THE ENWRAPPED
(Mecca.)

The word from which the Surah has its title occurs in the first verse.

This is generally allowed to be the second Surah revealed after the ninety-sixth which is the first.

The Prophet:

1. O thou wrapped up,
2. Arise and warn,
3. And thy Lord magnify,
4. And thy raiment purify,
5. And abomination shun.
6. And bestow not favours to gain increase,
7. And for thy Lord wait.

1. 'Thou covered.' Apparently the prophet was sharply reviled by certain of the Koreish for his recent thoughts on religion, and was sitting in a melancholy and pensive posture, wrapped up in his mantle when he is thus addressed.

5. 'Abomination,' *i.e.,* of idolatry.

Judgment Day:

8. When there shall be a trump on the trumpet,
9. That will be a day of distress
10. To the ungodly, devoid of ease.
11. Let Me alone with him whom I have created,
12. On whom I have bestowed vast fortunes,
13. And children dwelling before him,

14. And for whom I have smoothed things down,
15. And who desires that I should yet add more.
16. By no means: because he is to Our signs an opponent.
17. I will lay grievous woes upon him.
35. . . . By the moon,
36. And the night when it retreats,
37. And the morn when it brightens,
38. Verilv this is one the most terrible calamities,
39. A warning to men,
40. To him among you who desires to press forward, or to lag behind.
41. Every soul lies in pledge for what it has earned, except the people of the right hand—
42. In Gardens asking of the wicked:
43. What has brought you into the scorching fire?
44. They will say, We were not of those who prayed,
45. And we fed not the poor,
46. And we wrangled with those who wrangled,
47. And we called the Day of Judgment a lie,
48. Till the certainty did come upon us.—
49. And the intercession of the intercessors shall not avail them.

11. 'Him whom I have created.' The person here meant is generally supposed to have been Walid b. al-Mogheirah, a principal man among the Koreish.

13. Being well-provided for, and not obliged to go abroad to seek their livings, as most others of the Meccans were.

17. Or, as the words may be strictly rendered, 'I will drive him up the crag of a mountain.'

41. See Surah lii. 21, note.

'Except the people,' etc. That is, the blessed, who shall redeem themselves by their good works. Some understand this of such as die infants and under age, who are all regarded as sinless in Islam.

48. 'The certainty,' Obviously means death.

49. See Surah ii. 45, 117: also lxxx. 17-9.

Principal Contents

God, to Him belongs the Judgment, 11-7.

Judgment Day, 8-10, 35-8.

Prophet urged to persevere, 1-7.

Ungodly, the 43-9.

SURAH LXXV.—THE JUDGMENT DAY

(Mecca.)

The word occurs in the first verse of this Surah.

Judgment Day:

1. I will not swear by the Day of Judgment,
2. Neither will I swear by the soul which condemns itself!
3. Thinks man that We cannot re-unite his bones together?
4. Aye, We are able evenly to replace his fingertips.
5. But man chooses to be wicked hereafter.
6. He asks, When is the Day of Judgment?
7. But when the sight is dazzled,
8. And the moon is eclipsed.
9. And the sun and the moon are joined together,
10. On that day shall man cry, Where to fly to?
11. Aye, no place to fly to.
12. With thy Lord on that day is the refuge!

13. On that day shall man be told what he has done first and last.

14. Yea! a man is evidence against himself:

15. And though he put forth his plea. . .

20 Aye, but ye love the transitory!

21. And ye neglect the Hereafter:

22. Faces on that Day shall beam with light,

23. To their Lord looking on;

24 And faces on that day shall be gloomy:

25. They shall think that a crushing calamity will befall them.

26. Aye! when the soul comes up to the throat,

27. And they shall cry, Who will bring a charm?

28. And he thinks it his departure,

29. And leg presses upon leg,

30. To thy Lord on that day he shall be driven!

31. And he believed not, nor did he pray,

32. But he called it a lie and turned back,

33. Then he joined his people walking in a haughty mien.

34. It is nearer to thee and nearer,

35. Again, it is nearer to thee and nearer!

36. Does man think that he shall be left alone?

1. 'I will not swear,' because what is here asserted is too manifest to need the confirmation of an oath; or, the particle 'la' may be taken to be intensive in this place, in which case it must be translated, 'I swear.'

2. 'Which condemns itself;' Being conscious of having offended, and of failing of perfection, notwithstanding its endeavours do its duty.

13. 'Has done first and last.' Or, the good which he has done, and that which he has left undone.

29. 'Leg presses upon leg,' *i.e.*, in death-struggle. The words may also be translated, 'Difficulty presses upon difficulty.'

31. 'He believed not.' Or, 'He gave not alms,' or 'was not a man of veracity.'

34. Or, 'Woe to thee, woe!'

35. Or, 'And again, woe to thee woe!'

Principal Contents

Judgment Day, 1-15, 22-5; man an evidence against himself, 14, 15.

Death, 26-30.

SURAH LXXVI.—MAN

(Mecca.)

The word occurs in the first verse.

The Origin of Man:

1. Did not there pass over man a period, during which he was a thing unmentioned?

2. We created man from the germ of both sexes, that We might prove him: and We made him hearing and sight.

3. We have guided him in the way, whether he is thankful or unthankful.

1. It refers to the gradual evolution of man.

2. 'Prove him,' *i.e.*, 'which of you is the best in actions.' See Surah lxvii. 2.

'Made him hearing,' etc. That he might be capable of receiving the rules and directions given for his guidance; and of meriting reward or punishment for his observance or neglect of them.

3. 'We have guided him in the way.' God has put every man in the way, whether he proves thankful for His favours, or denies them.

The Quran:

29. Verily this is a reminder: whoso wills let him take to his Lord a way;
30. But ye shall not will unless God pleases; verily God is knowing, wise.
31. He leads whom He will into His mercy; but the wrong-doers—He has prepared for them a painful punishment.

Principal Contents

Quran, the, a reminder, 29.

Man, his origin, 1,; purpose in his creation, 2; guided in the way by God, 3.

SURAH LXXVII.—THE SENT

(Mecca.)

The Surah takes its name from the word which occurs in the first verse.

Judgment Day:

7. Verily what ye are threatened with is inevitable.
8. When the stars are dimmed,
9. And when the heaven is cleft asunder,
10. And when the mountains are scattered,
11. And when the apostles shall be told the time
12. To what day it is fixed,
13. To the Day of Decision!
14. And what shall make thee know what is the Day of Decision?
15. Woe then on that day to those who called it a lie!
48. For when it is said to them, Bow down, they do not bow down.

49. Woe on that day to those who called it a lie!

50. In what message after this will they believe?

7. 'What ye are threatened with;' namely, the Judgment of God.

Principal Contents

Judgment Day, the, 7-15.

SURAH LXXVIII.—THE NEWS
(Mecca.)

The word occurs in the first verse of the Surah.

Judgment Day:

1. Of what do they ask one another?

2. Of the Great News

3. About which they disagree,

4. Aye, by and by they shall know!

5. Again, aye, by the by they shall know!

17. Verily the Day of Decision is fixed.

18. The day when there shall be a blast on the trumpet, and ye shall comc forth in troops,

19. And the heaven shall be opened. and be full of portals.

20. And the mountains shall move away, and melt into vapour!

2. 'The Great News;' namely the Day of Judgment.

The Ungodly:

21. Verily Hell is a place of resort,

22. The home of the transgressors,

23. Therein to abide for ages;

27. For they looked not forward to their account,

28. And they gave the lie to Our signs, calling them a lie.

29. But all things have We computed and noted down.

The Pious:

31. Verily for the pious is an abode of bliss;

35. Therein shall they hear no vain talk, nor an untruth:

36. A reward from thy Lord, gift enough!

38 The day when the spirit and the angels shall stand in order, they shall not speak, unless he whom the merciful God shall permit, and who shall speak right.

39. That is the sure day: whoso then will, let him take to his Lord a home.

40. Verily, We warn you of a chastisement at hand:

41. The day when a man shall see what his hands have sent before him, and the ungodly shall cry, O that I were dust!

Principal Contents

Judgment Day, the, 1-5, 17-20, 38-41.

Pious, the, 31, 35, 36.

Ungodly, the, 21-3, 27-9.

SURAH LXXIX.—WHO TEAR FORTH

(Mecca.)

The Surah derives its title from the word used in the first verse.

The Day of Judgment:

1. By those who tear forth the souls with violence,

2. And by those who with joyous release them,

3. And those who glide swimmingly,

4. And those who strive with the utmost striving,

5. And those who conduct the affairs,

6. On a day the trumpet-blast shall disturb it,

7. Which the second blast shall follow:

8. Hearts on that day shall quake—

9. Their looks cast down,

10. They shall say, What! shall we indeed be returned from whence we came?

11. What! when we have become rotten bones?

12. They say, This then is a return to loss!

13. Verily it will be only one sound,

14. And behold, they are on the vast Plain.

34. When the crushing calamity shall come,

35. On that day shall a man remember what he had striven after.

14. 'The vast Plain.' where the Judgment is to take place.

The Ungodly:

36. And Hell shall be in full view of all who are looking on;

37. Then whoso has transgressed,

38. And has chosen the life of this world,

39. Verily Hell,—this is his abode.

40. And whoso has feared the appearing before his Lord, and has kept his soul from lust,

41. Verily the Gardens,—that is his abode!

Principal Contents

Judgment Day, the, 1-14, 34, 35.

Ungodly, the 36-41.

SURAH LXXX.—HE FROWNED.

(Mecca.)

The Surah derives its name from the first verse where the word occurs.

The Prophet Reprimanded:

1. He frowned, and turned aside,
2. For that the blind man came to him:
3. And what made thee know that he would be cleansed,
4. Or be warned, and the warning profit him?
5. Him who is wealthy
6. Thou wast all attention:
7. Yet it was not on thee that he is not cleansed.
8. But him who comes to thee in earnest.
9. And who fears.
10. Him dost thou neglect!

1. 'He frowned,' etc. The passage was occasioned by the following incident. A certain poor blind man, named Abdullah, came and interrupted Mohammed while he was engaged in earnest discourse with some of the principal Koreish, whose conversion the had hopes of; but the prophet taking no notice of him, the blind man, not knowing he was otherwise busied, raised his voice, and said, 'Apostle of God, teach me something of what God has taught thee; but Mohammed, vexed at this interruption, frowned and turned away from him; for which he is here reprimanded. Whereupon Mohammed made ample apologies to the old man, and whenever he would see him, he would show him the greatest respect and say, 'The man is thrice welcome on whose account my Lord has reprimanded me.' And when at Medinah, he twice made him governor of the city.

Judgment Day:

11. Aye! But it is a warning:
12. Whoso is willing, he will consider.

33. When the stunning blast is heard,
34. On that day shall a man fly from his brother.
35. And his mother and his father,
36. And his wife and his children,
37. To every one on that day, his own concerns will be enough.
38. Faces on that day shall be bright,
39. Laughing and joyous!
40. And faces on that day with dust upon them,
41. Darkness covering them:
42. These are the ungodly, the wicked.

Principal Contents

Judgment Day, 33-42.
Mohammed reprimanded, 1-10.

SURAH LXXXI.—THE FOLDING UP
(Mecca.)

The title is taken from a word in the first verse.

Judgment Day:

1. When the sun is folded up,
2. And when the stars fall,
3. And when the mountains are moved away,
4. And when the camels ten months gone with, young is neglected,
5. And when the wild beasts are huddled together
6. And the seas boils,
7. And when the souls are joined,
8. And when the female child who had been buried alive is asked,

9. For what crime she was put to death?

10. And when the scrolls are unrolled,

11. And when the heaven is moved off,

12. And when Hell is made to blaze forth,

13. And when the Garden is brought nigh:

14. The soul shall know what it has brought forth.

4. 'When the camels,' etc. The most valuable possession of an Arab. 'It neglected' in favour of a thing of much greater concern, namely, the Judgment that is to befall them.

8. See Surah xvi. 60, and notes.

10. 'The scrolls;' the register of men's actions. Surah lxxxiii. 7-9, 18-20.

The Quran :

27. Verily this is only a reminder to the worlds:

28. To whoso among you will walk uprightly;

29. But ye shall not will, unless God pleases, the Lord of the worlds!

Principal Contents

Judgment Day, 1-14,

Quran, the, 27-9.

SURAH LXXXII.—THE RENDING ASUNDER
(Mecca.)

The word occurs in the first verse.

Judgment Day:

1. When the heaven is rent asunder,

2. And when the stars fall down,

3. And when the seas are joined together,

4. And when the tombs are turned upside down:

5. The soul shall know what it has sent on before it and left behind.

5. The soul shall know what it has actually done so as to merit a reward in the Hereafter, and what example he has left behind him in this world for the people to follow; thus man has a double responsibility, of doing justice to his own soul, and to those of others who have consciously or unconsciously followed him.

Of God:

6. Ye man, what has misled thee against thy Lord, the generous,
7. Who created thee, and fashioned thee, and moulded thee aright,
8. In what form it pleased Him did He build thee.
9. Aye! but ye call the Judgment a lie!

Guardian Angels:

10. And verily over you are guardians,
11. Honourable, noting down;
12. Who know what ye do.
13. Verily the virtuous shall be amid delights,
14. And verily the wicked shall be in Hell.

10. See Surah 1, 16, 17.

God The Judge:

17. And what shall make thee know what is the Day of Judgment?
18. Again, what shall make thee know what is the Day of Judgment?
19. A Day when one soul shall have no power in anything for another soul, and the command on that day shall be God's.

19. See also Surah ii. 45, 117.

Principal Contents

God, faith in Him urged, 6-8; His command on the Judgment Day, 17-9.

Guardian-angels over men, 10-12.

Judgment Day, 1-5; God alone the Judge, 17-9.

SURAH LXXXIII.—THOSE WHO STINT

(Mecca.)

The first verse gives the Surah its title.

The Deceitful:

1. Woe to those who stint the balance!
2. Who, when they take by measure from others, exact the full;
3. But when they measure to them, or weigh to them, defraud!
4. What! do not these think that they shall be raised again
5. At the great Day?

1. 'The balance;' or justice and equity in mutual dealing.
2. Or, who wish that others should do them justice.
3. But in their own dealings they are deceitful.

4,5. See Surah ii. 279.

Judgment Day:

6. The Day when men shall stand before the Lord of the worlds.
7. Yea, the register of the wicked is in Sijjin.
8. And what shall make thee know what Sijjin is?
9. A Book distinctly written.
10. Woe, on that day, to those who called it a lie!
11. Who called the Day of Judgment a lie!
12. And none calls it a lie unless only the transgressor, the criminal.

18\. Yea, verily the register of the virtuous is in Illiyyun.

19. And what shall make thee know what Illiyyun is ?

20. A Book distinctly written.

7. 'Sijjin;' from. 'Sijn,' a prison.

18. 'Illiyyin.' The word is a plural, and signifies 'high places.'

Principal Contents

Deceitful, the, 1-5.

Judgment Day, 6-12, 18-20.

SURAH LXXXIV.—THE SPLITTING ASUNDER
(Mecca.)

The Surah takes its name from the first verse.

Judgment Day:

1. When the heaven is split asunder,

2. And obeys its Lord duteously!

3. And when the earth is spread out,

4. And has cast forth what is in her, and in empty,

5. And obeys its Lord duteously!

6. O man, labouring thou dost labour to meet the Lord, and thou shalt meet Him.

6. 'And thou shalt,' etc. Or, 'And thou shalt meet thy labour;' whether thy works are good, or whether they are evil.

The Hereafter:

16. I need not swear by the sunset radiance,

17. And the night, and what it drives,

18. And the moon when at her full,

19. That ye shall be carried onward from stage to stage.

19. 'Carried onward from stage to stage.' Refers to man's onward progress in the Hereafter according to his achievements in this life.

23. 'What they hide.' That is, their real feelings, whether they have reason to reject it or they do it in malice.

The Quran:

20. What has come to them that they believe not?
21. And when the Quran is recited to them they worship not?
22. Yea, those who disbelieve call it a lie!
23. God best knows what they hide.
24. Then give them glad tidings of a painful punishment,
25. Except those who believe and do good: for them is a reward that fails not.

Principal Contents

Hereafter, the, 16-20.
Judgment Day, 1-6.
Man, his future, 19.

SURAH LXXXV.—THE CELESTIAL SIGNS
(Mecca.)

The title of the Surah is derived from the first verse.

The Wrong-Doers:

1. By the heaven full of towers,
2. By the promised Day,
3. By the witness and the witnessed,
4. Perish the masters of the pit,
5. Of fire supplied with fuel!
6. When they sat around it,
7. Witnesses of what they inflicted on the faithful!
8. And they afflicted them only for that they believed in God, the mighty, the praiseworthy;

9. Whose is the kingdom of the heavens and the earth; and God is witness of all things.

10. Verily those who persecute the faithful, men and women, and repent not: for them is the punishment of Hell, and the torment of burning.

1. 'Towers:' the signs of the Zodiac.

4. 'Masters of the pit.' These were the ministers of the persecution raised by Zu Nowas, the Jewish king of Yemen, in A.C. 523, against the inhabitants of Najran; who, having embraced Christianity, the bigoted tyrant commanded all those who would not renounce their faith to be cast into a pit, or trench, filled with fire, and then burnt to ashes.

7. Or, as some choose to understand the words, 'Witnesses against themselves on the Judgment Day of the wrong they did to the faithful.'

Principal Contents.

Persecutors of the Faithful, 1-10.

SURAH LXXXVI.—THE NIGHT-COMER

(Mecca.)

The title is taken from the first verse of this Surah.

Guardian Angels:

1. By the heaven, and the night-comer!

2. And what shall make thee know what the night-comer is?

4. Every soul has a guardian set over it.

4. See Surah 1, 16, 17.

Patience Enjoined:

15. Verily they plot a plot,

16. And I will plot a plot:

17. Wherefore bear with the ungodly: let them alone a while.

15. This refers to the stratagems the Koriesh laid against Islam.

Principal Contents

Guardian angels over men, 4.;

Patience enjoined, 17.

SURAH LXXXVII—THE MOST HIGH

(Mecca.)

The title is taken from the first verse of the Surah.

Of God:

1. Praise the name of thy Lord, the Most High;
2. Who created and balanced,
3. Who fixed the destiny, and guided,
4. Who brings forth the pasture,
5. And reduces it to dusky stubble.

3. 'Fixed,' etc. Determined their various species, properties, ways of life, etc.

'And guided;' the rational by their reason and also by revelation, and the irrational by instinct, etc.

The Pure:

14. Blessed is he who purifies himself,
15. And remembers the name of his Lord and prays!
16. But ye prefer the life of this world,
17. Though the Hereafter is better and more enduring.
18. Verily this is in the Books of old,
19. The Books of Abraham and Moses.

18. This points to the continuity of the same revelation to the prophets in different ages and among different peoples.

Principal Contents

God: His power and wisdom, 1-5.

Pure, the, 14, 15.

Revelation, its unity, 18, 19.

SURAH LXXXVIII.—THE OVERWHELMING

(Mecca.)

The word occurs in the first verse of this Surah.

The Judgment Day:

1. Has the message about the Overwhelming come to thee?
2. Faces on that day shall be cast down,
3. Labouring and toiling,
8. And faces on that day shall be joyous,
9. Well-pleased with their strivings;—
10. In a lofty Garden.
11. No vain talk shalt thou hear therein.

1. 'The Overwhelming,' is a name given to the Judgment Day, because it will suddenly 'overwhelm' all creatures with fear, for that their works will then be judged.
3. Or, 'employing and wearying themselves,' in what shall avail them not.

Signs of God:

17. Do they not see the camels, how they are created?
18. And the heaven, how it is raised?
19. And the mountains, how they are fixed?
20. And the earth, how it is spread out?

God Alone the Judge:

21. Warn thou then, for thou art only a warner
22. Thou hast no authority over them;

23. Unless whoso turns back and disbelieves.
24. Him will God punish with a severe punishment:
25. Verily to Us will they return.
26. Then will it be Ours to take their account.

17. 'The camels.' These animals are of such use, or rather necessity, in the east, that the creation of a species so wonderfully adapted to these countries is a very proper instance, to an Arabian, of the power and wisdom of God. Some, however, think the 'clouds' (which the original word also signifies) are here intended; the heaven being mentioned immediately after; but we have preferred to keep to the former because 'clouds' are very seldom if ever seen in Arabia and Mohammed could hardly appeal to them from his desert home more suitably than to their domestic animal which they justly esteemed as the ship of the desert.

Principal Contents

God, His signs, 17-20.

Judgment Day, 1-3, 8-10, 11; God the Judge, 21-6.

SURAH LXXXIX.—THE DAYBREAK
(Mecca.)

The word from which this Surah derives its title occurs in the first verse.

Old Histories:

5. Hast thou seen how thy Lord did with Ad,
6. Of Iram, who were as pillars?
7. Whoso like has not been created in the land:
8. And with Samud, who hewed the rocks in the valley?
9. And with Pharaoh, master of the stakes?
10. Who all transgressed in the land,
11. And multiplied corruption therein:

12. Wherefore thy Lord poured out upon them the scourge of torment;

6. 'Iram;' the name of the territory or the city of the Adites.

'As pillars.' Refers to their gigantic stature. Or, it may refer to the lofty buildings and delightful gardens said to have been built by Shaddad, son of Ad, in which case however this verse should be translated, 'At Iram, adorned with pillars, or lofty monuments.'

7. If we choose the latter interpretation it should be rendered, 'Whose like has not been erected in the land.'

God: His Knowledge:

13. Verily thy Lord is in a watch-tower.

14. As to man, when His Lord proves him and honours him and is bounteous to him,

15. He says, My Lord honours me;

16. But when He proves him, and withholds his provision from him,

17. He say, My Lord despises me.

18. Nay! but ye honour not the orphan,

19. Neither do ye urge to feed the poor,

20. And ye devour the inheritance, devouring greedily,

21. And ye love wealth with exceeding love.

13. A Watch-Tower,' from where He observes the actions of men.

18. For worldly prosperity or adversity is not a certain mark either of the favour or disfavour of God.

20. Not suffering women or young children to have any share in the inheritance of their husbands or parents.

The Judgment Day:

22. Aye! When the earth is crushed with a crushing,

23. And thy Lord comes, and the angels also in order,

24. And Hell on that day is moved up; on that day shall man remember himself; but how will remembrance avail him?

25. He will say, O that I had sent something forward for my life!

27. O thou soul which art at rest,

28. Return to thy Lord, well-pleased and pleasing;

29. Enter thou among My servants,

30. And enter thou My Gardens.

27. Some expound this of the soul, which having by pursuing the concatenation of natural causes, raised itself to the knowledge of that Being which produced them, and exists of necessity, 'rests' fully contented, or 'acquiesces' in the knowledge of Him, and the contemplation of His perfections. Others, however, understand the words of the soul, which, having attained the knowledge of the truth, 'rests' satisfied, and relies securely thereon, undisturbed by doubts; or of the soul which is 'secure' of its salvation, and free from fear or sorrow.

Principal Contents

God, His knowledge, 13.

Histories, old, 5-12.

Judgment Day, 22-30.

SURAH XC.—THE SOIL

(Mecca.)

The Surah takes its name from the word occurring in the first verse.

Man: His Duty:

8. Have We not made him two eyes?

9. And a tongue, and two lips?

10. And pointed him out the two high-ways?

11. Yet he attempts not the steep one!

12. And what shall make thee know what the steep one is?
13. To free the captive,
14. Or to feed on the day of famine
15. The orphan of thy kin, or the poor that lies in the dust,
16. And finally, to be of those who believe and enjoin steadfastness on each other, and enjoin compassion on each other.
17. These are the people of the right hand.

8. 'Him,' refers to 'man' in verse 4, above.
10. 'The two high-ways;' namely, of good and evil.
17. 'The people of the right hand;' the blessed. See Surah lvi. 8.

Principal Contents

Man, his duties, 13-6.

SURAH XCI.—THE SUN
(Mecca.)

The word occurs in the first verse.

The Pure in Spirit:

1. By the sun and its noonday brightness,
2. By the moon when she follows him,
3. By the day when it brightens,
4. By the night, when it covers it,
5. By the heaven, and Him who built it,
6. By the earth and Him who spread it out,
7. By the soul and Him who balanced it,
8. And breathed into it its wickedness and its piety;
9. Now blessed is he who keeps it pure,

10. And lost is he who corrupts it!

8. That is, And inspired into it its faculty of distinguishing, and power of choosing, wickedness and piety.

Principal Contents

Pure, the, in spirit, 1-10.

SURAH XCII.—THE NIGHT

(Mecca.)

The word occurs in the first verse.

Men: Their Aims:

1. By the night when it covers,
2. By the day when it brightens up,
3. By Him who created the male and the female,
4. Verily your aims are divers!

The Pious:

5. But as to him who gives alms, and fears to do wrong,
6. And believes in the good,
7. To him will We make easy the way to happiness.

The Ungodly:

8. And as to him who is covetous and bent on riches,
9. And calls the good a lie;
10. To him will We make easy the way to misery.
11. And his wealth shall not avail him when he goes down.

The Blessed and the Damned:

12. Verily Ours is the guidance,
13. And Ours the Hereafter and this life.
14. And I warn you of the flaming Fire:

15. None shall be cast into it but the most wicked,

16. Who have called it a lie, and turned back.

17. But the pious shall be kept away from it,—

18. Who gives of his wealth to purify himself,

19. And who offers no favours to any one for a reward,

20. But only as seeking the Face of His Lord the Most High;

21. And in the end he will be will-pleased.

20. 'The Face of his Lord,' His glory. This refers to the Beatific Vision.

Principal Contents

Pious, the 5-7.

Reward of the pious, 17-21; that of the wicked, 14-6.

Ungodly, the 8-11.

SURAH XCIII.—THE BRIGHTNESS

(Mecca.)

The title is derived from the first verse of the Surah.

This and the six following Surahs are expressions of a state of deep mental anxiety and depression, in which Mohammed is assured of God's continued protection. They belong to a period when his success way very dubious, and his future career by no means clearly marked out.

Mohammed Assured of God's Protections:

1. By the noon-day brightness,

2. And the night, when it darkens,

3. Thy Lord has not forsaken thee, neither is he displeased,

4. And the Hereafter shall be better for thee than the present;

5. And in the end thy Lord will give to thee, and thou shalt he well-pleased,

6. Did He not find thee an orphan, and gave thee a home ?

7. And found thee erring, and guided thee ?

8. And found thee needy, and enriched thee ?

9. Then, as for the orphan, oppress him not,

10. And as to him, who asks of thee, chide him not away.

11. And as for the favours of thy Lord tell it abroad.

3. It is related that Mohammed had once turned away from an importunate beggar, which later on made him quite uneasy, and only when this Surah was revealed was he assured of his repentance having been accepted of his Lord.

6. Mohammed lost his father a few days before his birth, and his mother in his sixth year, when he was thrown upon the care of his grandfather, Abdul-Muttalib, in whose house he remained for another three years, after which again, on the death of his grandfather, he was taken under protection by his uncle Abu-Talib, who died at an advanced age in the third year before the Hegira.

7. From a boy up Mohammed had been a thinker intent on religious subjects, and at the age of 40, he felt confirmed in his earnest strivings after the truth.

8. At the age of 25, Mohammed was obliged to seek for his own livelihood, and was only relieved when in the same year Khadijah (a rich lady) extended her hand to him in marriage.

11. God's tender mercy and pity are all-embracing.

Principal Contents

God, His mercy and pity, 11.

Mohammed assured of God's continued protection, 1-11.

SURAH XCIV. — THE OPENING

(Mecca.)

The title is taken from the first verse of the Surah.

Mohammed Confirmed:

1. Have We not opened for thee thy breast ?
2. And eased thee of thy burden.
3. Which galled thy back ?
4. And have We not raised thy name for thee ?
5. Then verily with trouble comes ease.
6. Verily with trouble comes ease.
7. And when thou art free, then labour,
8. And to thy Lord strive.

1. By disposing and enlarging it to receive the truth, and wisdom, and prophecy; or, by freeing thee from uneasiness and ignorance.

2. 'Thy burden;' that is, mental struggle.

7. 'Labour,' that is, to serve God.

Principal Contents

Mohammed confirmed, 1-8.

SURAH XCV.—THE FIG

(Mecca.)

The word which gives the Surah its title occurs in the first verse.

Man: His Creation and Fall:

1. By the fig and the olive,
2. By Mount Sinai,
3. And this inviolate soil !
4. We have created man of the most excellent fabric,
5. Then We brought him to be the lowest of the low,—

6. Except those who believe and do good; for them is a reward unfailing.

7. What then shall make thee call the Judgment a lie after this ?

8. Is not God the best of judges ?

4, 5. That is, as the commentators generally expound this passage, 'We created man of comely proportion of body, and great perfection of mind, and yet We have doomed him, in case of disobedience, to be cast into Hell.' Some, however, understand the words of the vigorous constitution of man in the prime and strength of his age, and of his miserable decay when he becomes old and decrepit; but they seem rather to intimate the perfect state of happiness wherein man was originally created, and his fall from thence, in consequence of his disobedience, to a state of misery in this world, and becoming liable to one infinitely more miserable in the next.

Principal Contents

Man, his creation, 4; his fall, 5.

SURAH XCVI.—THICK BLOOD

(Mecca.)

The Surah derives its name from the word occuring in verse 2.

The first five verses are allowed to be the first piece of revelation vouchsafed to the prophet of Islam.

The First Call:

1. Cry, in the name of thy Lord who created—

2. Created man from blood.

3. Cry, for thy Lord is the most bountiful,

4. Who taught the use of pen,

5. Taught man what he knew not.

2. 'Blood;' in the original 'alak,' life germ,

Man: His Insolence:

6. Aye; verily man is insolent
7. At seeing himself get rich.
8. Verily to thy Lord is the return.
9. What thinkest thou of him who holds back.
10. A servant when he prays ?
11. What thinkest thou ? If he followed the guidance, or enjoined piety ?
12. What thinkest thou ? If he called it a lie and turned his back ?
13. What! does not he know that God sees ?
19. Nay, obey not him; but worship, and draw near to Him.

9. 'Of him.' This refers to Abu Jahl.

10. 'Servant,' or lit. 'slave.'

Principal Contents

Man, his insolence, 6, 7; his fate, 8-13.

Mohammed, his first call, 1-5.

SURAH XCVII.—POWER

(Mecca.)

The Surah is named from the word in the first verse.

The Quran Revealed:

1. Verily We have revealed it on the night of power.

1. 'The nigh of power.' This was the night Mohammed received his first revelations. The Moslem doctors generally place this night sometimes during the last ten nights of Ramazan, and the more accepted date is the night which falls between the 23rd and 24th days of that month.

Principal Contents

Quran, the, revealed during the month of Ramazan 1.

SURAH XCVII—CLEAR EVIDENCE

(Medinah.)

The Surah derives its name from the word which occurs in verse 3.

The Unity of Religion:

3. And those who were given the Book were not divided among themselves until after that there bad come to them the evidence:

4. And they were only commanded to serve God being sincere in religion and upright, and to be stead-fast in prayer and give alms; and that is the standard religion.

3. See ii. 209, notes.

Principal Contents

People of the Book commanded to worship God alone, 4.

Religion, the unity of, 3, 4.

SURAH XCIX.—THE EARTHQUAKE

(Mecca.)

The word from which the Surah is named occurs in the first verse.

The Judgment Day:

6. On that Day shall men come forward in distinct classes to see their works:

7. And whoso has done an atom's weight of good shall see it.

8. And whoso has done an atom's weight of evil shall see it.

Principal Contents

Judgment Day, 6-8.

SURAH C.—THE CHARGERS
(Mecca.)

The Judgment Day:

6. Verily man is to his Lord ungrateful !
7. And verily he is a witness thereof;
8. And verily, in the love of pleasure he is keen;
9. Ah ! does not he know that when what is in the tombs is laid bare,
10. And what is in the bosoms is brought forth,
11. Verily their Lord shall on that day be fully informed about them ?

8. 'Pleasure;' lit, 'good' of worldly things.

Principal Contents

Judgment Day, 9-11.

Man ungrateful, 6.

SURAH CI.—THE STRIKING
(Mecca.)

The title is derived from the first verse of this Surah.

The Judgement Day:

5. Then as to him whose balance is heavy—his will be a life well-pleasing;
6. And as to him whose balance is light—his abode is the Pit.

Principal Contents

Judgment Day, 5, 6.

SURAH CII.—DESIRE.

(Mecca.)

The first verse of this Surah gives it the title it bears.

Vain Desires:

1. The desire of increase occupies you
2. Till ye come to the graves.
3. Nay, in the end ye shall know.
4. Again; nay, in the end ye shall know.
5. Nay, if ye only knew it with certainty !
6. Ye shall surely see Hell;
7. Again, ye shall surely see it with an eye of certainty.
8. Then shall ye be asked on that day about the pleasures.

Principal Contents

Increase, desire of, 1-6.

Judgment Day, 8,

SURAH CIII.—THE AFTERNOON

(Mecca.)

The word occurs in the first verse.

The Fate of Man:

1. By the age !
2. Verily man is in loss,
3. Except those who believe and do good, and enjoin truth, and enjoin steadfastness on each other.

Principal Contents.

Man, his fate, 1-3.

SURAH CIV.—THE SLANDERERS

(Mecca.)

The word occurs in the first verse.

Slander and Backbiting:

1. Woe to every slanderer, backbiter,
2. Who hoards up wealth, and counts it over !
3. He thinks that his riches will be with him for ever !
4. Aye, he will surely be cast into the crushing Fire.

2. 'Counts,' etc. Has no better use of his wealth.

Principal Contents

Slanderers, 1

Miserly, the, 24.

SURAH CV.—THE ELEPHANT

(Mecca.)

The word occurs in the first verse.

In the year of Mohammed's birth, Abrahah, the Christian king of Yemen, had built a church at Sanaa with a design to draw the Arabs to go in pilgrimage there instead of visiting the temple of Mecca. Being disappointed in this, he determined to destroy the Kaabah, and set out against it at the head of a large army wherein was also a huge elephant, an animal quite new to the Arabians and very frightful. They reached Mecca, but the following day a pestilence broke out in their ranks, and they retreated in disgrace.

Of Abrahah's Attack:

1. Hast thou seen how thy Lord did with the masters of the elephant ?
2. Did not He make their stratagem lead them astray ?
3. And send down upon them afflictions in succession,

4. To inflict upon them punishment prescribed,
5. And make them like leaves of corn eaten down ?

3. It may also be rendered, 'And send down upon them birds in flocks;' for the word translated 'afflictions' also means 'birds.' See Surah xvii. 14, and notes thereon.

The word occurs in the first verse.

4. Or, 'To cast down upon them stones of baked clay.'

It is supposed that the pestilence was small-pox, as the word for small-pox also means 'small stones' in reference to the hard gravelly feeling of the pustules.

Principal Contents

Abrahah's attack on Mecca, 1-5.

SURAH CVI.—THE KOREISH
(Mecca.)

God's Goodness:

1. For the uniting of the Koreish,
2. Their uniting for the caravan of winter and summer,
3. Let them serve the Lord of this House,
4. Who provides them against hunger, and has made them safe from fear.

2. This refers to the custom of sending out regularly from Mecca two caravans, one in winter and the other in summer, to bring supplies of provisions from Yemen and Syria to keep off famine.

4. 'Fear.' Refers to Abrahah's Invasion.

Principal Contents

Annual caravans, 1-4.

SURAH CVII.—RELIGION.
(Mecca.)

The word occurs in the first verse.

The Infidel:

1. What thinkest thou of him who calls the Religion a lie ?
2. He it is who pushes away the orphan,
3. And urges not others to feed the poor.
4. Then woe to those who pray.
5. Who in their prayers are careless,
6. Who make a show of devotion,
7. And refuse help to the needy.

1. 'Religion;' it also means 'Judgment'.

Principal Contents

Religion, who give it the lie, 1-7.

Prayers, careless, 5; for a show, 6; without a pitying heart, 7.

SURAH CVIII.—THE ABUNDANCE

(Mecca.)

The word occurs in the first verse.

Promise of God:

1. Verily We have given thee an abundance;
2. Then pray to thy Lord, and stand upright.

Principal Contents

Promise of God, 1, 2.

SURAH CIX.—THE UNBELIEVERS

(Mecca.)

This Surah is an open declaration of faith to the unbelievers; hence its title.

An Open Declaration:

1. Say thou, Ye who disbelieve.
2. I do not worship what ye worship,

3. Nor do ye worship what I worship;
4. Neither will I worship what ye worship,
5. Neither will ye worship what I worship—
6. Ye have your religion, and I have my religion.

Principal Contents

Moslems, their position clearly defined, 1-6.

SURAH CX.—HELP

(Medinah.)

The word occurs in the first verse.

The Conquest of Mecca:

1. When comes the help of God, and the Victory,
2. And thou seest men entering the religion of God in troops,
3. Then celebrate the praise of thy Lord, and ask pardon of him; verily He is ever relenting.

1. 'The Victory;' *i.e.,* of Mecca; which happened in A.H. 9, when people flocked to accept Islam.

Principal Contents

Victory of Mecca, 1-3.

SURAH CXI.—ABU LAHAB

(Mecca.)

The word occurs in the first verse.

Abu Lahab Cursed:

1. Perish the hands of Abu Lahab, and perish he !
2. His wealth shall avail him not, nor his gains.

1. Abu Lahab was the surname of Abdul-Uzza, an uncle of Mohammed. He was a most bitter enemy to his nephew, and opposed the establishment of his new religion to the utmost of his power. When the prophet had called

together his own people and told them of his message from on high, Abu Lahab cried out, 'Perish thou ! Was it for this thou hadst called us ?' and took up a stone to cast at him; which occasicned this passage.

By 'the hands' some by a synecdoche understand his 'person;' others by a metonymy, his 'affairs' in general, they being transacted with those members; or his hopes in this world and the next.

Principal Contents

Abu Lahab cursed, 192.

SURAH CXII.—THE UNITY

(Mecca.)

This Surah is a declaration of the Islamic faith in the Unity of God; hence the title,

The Unity of God:

1. Say thou, He is the one God !
2. God the eternal !
3. He begets not,
4. And is not begotten !
5. And there is not one like to Him.

Principal Contents

God, the one, 1; has no son, 3; nor any His like, 5.

SURAH CXIII.—THE DAYBREAK

(Mecca.)

The word occurs in the first verse.

Refuge in God:

1. Say thou, I betake me to the Lord of the day-break,
2. From the evil of what He has created,
3. And from the evil of the night when it comes on,

4. And from the evil of those blowing on knots,
5. And from the evil of the envier when he envies.

2. That is, from the evils proceeding either from the perverseness and evil choice of those beings who have a power to choose, or the natural effects of necessary agents, as fire, poison, etc., the world being good in the whole, though evils may follow from these two causes.

4. 'Those blowing,' etc. The weird women, who use to tie knots in a cord, and to blow on them, uttering at the same time some magical incantations over them, in order to work on and debilitate the person they had a mind to injure.

Principal Contents

God, refuge in, from evils, 1-5.

SURAH CXIV.—MEN

(Mecca.)

The word occurs in the first verse.

Refuge in God:

1. Say thou, I betake me to the Lord of men,
2. King of men,
3. God of men,
4. From the evil of the whisperer who slyly withdraws,
5. Who whispers into the bosoms of men;
6. From Jinn and men.

4. That is, the evil spirits.

Principal Contents

God, refuge in, from evil spirits, 1-6.

ADDENDA.

Surah ii. 2. 'And observe prayer.'

Prayer is the first of the four fundamental points of religions practice in Islam. It was by Mohammed regarded so necessary a duty, that he used to call it 'the pillar of religion,' and 'the key of paradise.' Its value is set forth in Surah xxix. 44.

That this important duty might not be neglected, Mohammed obliged his followers to pray five times every twenty-four hours, at certain stated times; namely, 1. Between dawn and the sun-rise; 2. After the sun has begun to decline from the meredian; 3. In the afternoon, before sun-set; 4. After sun-set, and before the day is shut in; 5. Before the first watch of the night. These prayers are always binding upon all Moslems, but there are other prayers which are supererogatory in accordance with the practices of the Prophet.

The principal thing to be regarded in the discharge of this duty is the inward disposition of the heart, which is the life and spirit of prayer; its most punctual observance of the external rites being of little or no avail if performed without due attention, reverence, devotion, and hope. See Surah lxxxvii. 14, 15; lxvii. 12; xlii. 34, 35; vii. 54, 204; ii. 182, 239; etc.

Surah ii. 172.

Mohammed's definition of charity embraced the wide circle of kindness. 'Every good work,' he would say, 'is charity. Your smiling in your brother's face is charity; an exhortation addressed to your fellow-men to do good is equal to almsgiving; your putting a wanderer in the right road is charity; your assisting the blind is charity; your removing stones and thorns and other obstructions from the road is charity; your giving water to the thirsty is charity.'

Surah ii. 187. 'Rancour is worse than slaughter.'

The primary significance of the Arabic word 'fitnah,' translated 'rancour,' is burning with fire. It signifies a 'trial' or 'probation' and affliction, distress or hardship; and particularly an 'affliction whereby one is tried, proved, or tested.' *Vide* E. W. Lane's 'Arabic-English Lexicon,' p. 2335.

Surah ii. 230. At the same time the Prophet emphatically said :—

Cursed is the second husband who makes the wife (divorced) lawful for her first husband and cursed is the first husband for whom she is made lawful.

Surah ii. 272. The following are some of the teachings of Mohammed on the subject of education:—

To acquire knowledge is binding upon all Moslems, whether men or women.

The ink of the scholar is more holy than the blood of the martyr.

Paradise is open to him who leaves behind him his pen and his ink.

The world is supported by four things only: the learning of the wise, the justice of the great, the prayers of the righteous, and the valour of the brave.

A mind without erudition is like a body without a soul.

Glory consists not in wealth but in knowledge.

Acquire knowledge, because he who acquires it in the way of the Lord performs an act of piety; who speaks of it praises the Lord; who seeks it, adores God; who dispenses instruction in it, bestows alms; and who imparts it to its fitting objects, performs an act of devotion to God. Knowledge enables its possessor to distinguish what is forbidden form what is not; it lights the way to Heaven; it is our friend in the desert, our society in solitude, our companion when bereft of our friends; is guides us to happiness; it sustains us in misery; it is our ornament in the company of friends; it serves as an armour against our enemies. With knowledge, the creature of God rises to the heights of goodness and to a noble position, associates with sovereigns in this world, and attains to the perfection of happiness in the next.

Seek for knowledge even if it be in China.

He who leaves his home in search of knowledge, walks in the way of God.

He who travels in search of knowledge, to him God shows the way to Paradise.

One hour's meditation on the work of the Creator is better than seventy years of prayer.

To listen to the instructions of science and learning for one hour is more meritorious than attending the funerals of a thousand martyrs,—more meritorious than standing up in prayer for a thousand nights.

To the student who goes forth in quest of knowledge, God will allot a high place in the mansions of bliss; every step he takes is blessed, and every lesson he receives has its reward.

The seeker of knowledge will be greeted in Heaven with a welcome from the angels.

To listen to the words of the learned, and to instil into the heart the lessons of science, is better than religious exercises.

Him who favours learning and the learned, God will favour in the next world.

He who honours the learned honours me.

Surah ii. 274.

While inculcating charity in the widest sense of the word, the Prophet of Islam condemned beggary in unfaltering terms. I shall here instance only one. A man came to the Prophet begging alms; the Prophet said, 'Have you nothing at home ?' 'Yes,' said he, 'I have a large carpet, with one part of which I cover myself and spread the other; and a wooden cup out of which I drink water.' The Prophet said, 'Bring me the carpet and the cup.' And when the man brought them, Mohammed took them in his hands and said, 'Who will buy these ?' A man said, 'I'll buy them for one dirhem.' The Prophet said, 'Who will give more ?' This he repeated twice or thrice, until another man paid two dirhems. Mohammed gave away the carpet and the cup to that man; and taking the two dirhems gave it to the man saying, 'Buy food with one of them, and give it to your family that they may make it their sustenance for a few days, and buy a hatchet with the other, and bring it to me.' And when the man brought it, Mohammed himself put a handle to it, and giving it to the man said, 'Go thou, cut wood, and sell it, and let me not see thee for a fortnight.' The man did as he was commanded, and when after a fortnight he came to Mohammed he had already got ten dirhems. The Prophet blessed him, and said, 'Buy a garment with part of them and food with part. And verily this thy cutting wood and selling it, and making thy livelihood by it is more honourable for thee than begging.'

'Beggars shall be raised on the Judgment Day with shame on their faces !'

Surah iv. 23. The following is from the Prophet's Sermon on the Mount : —

Ye men, ye have rights; and ye women, ye have rights. Husbands, love your wives and treat them kindly. Verily, ye have taken them on the security of God, and have made their persons lawful to you by the word of God. Know that the thing most displeasing to God is divorce.

Surah iv. 40. The following are some of the Prophet's saying with regard to neighbours:—

He is not of us who eats to his full and leaves his neighbour hungry.

A man who worships God a great deal but is abusive to his neighbour, God cares not about his worship.

A man who worships little and gives but little in alms, but tries to do good to his neighbours, is one of God's best creatures.

Surah v. 7.

Marriage was, to Mohammed, a sacred relation. 'Matrimonial alliances between families and people increase love more than anything else.' 'When people marry they perfect half their religion,' 'Marry those whom you will love, and who will love you.' 'When any of you marry, let them meet each other first.' 'No woman can be married except by her own free will.' 'If she consent not, she cannot be married.'

Surah vii. 29. The following are some of the Prophet's sayings with regard to dress:—

God will not look at him who wears long garments with pride.

God will have no compassion upon him who wears long trousers with pride.

Wear white clothes, because they are the cleanest and the most agreeable.

God accepts not the prayers of those who pray in long robes.

Surah xvii. 39.

'Every one,' Mohammed used to say, 'must desist from boasting. And it you do not leave off boasting, verily you will be more hateful in the sight of God than a black-beetle. Men are but children of Adam, and Adam was made of the dust. What then can ye be proud of ?

Surah xxiv. 33.

The Quran has urged the abolition of slavery by the common rules of morality; (see Surah xc. 13; ii. 172; etc.) as also by the law; (see Surah ix. 60; iv. 93; lviii. 4; v. 91.) There was absolutely no ground for perpetuating the custom after the generation that in the time of Mohammed had practised it had passed away. See Surah xlvii. 5, and notes.

Surah xxxix. 54. Among the sayings of the Prophet on the subject are the following:—

God says, Whoso does one good act, for him are ten rewards, and I also give more; and whoso does evil, his punishment is equal to it, or else I forgive him; and he who seeks to approach Me one cubit I will seek to approach him two fathoms; and he who walks towards Me, I will run towards him; and he who cometh before Me with the earth full of sins, but joins no partner to Me, I will come before him with an equal front of forgiveness.

Thus says the Lord, Come back, come back, whatever thou art come back; hast thou denied Me or worshipped another for Me, or broken My commandments, come back. This threshold of Mine is not the threshold of despair. If thou hast forgotten thyself, turn with true penitence and come back.

Surah xli. 33.

Amr son of Abaratah relates: "I went to the Prophet and asked, 'O Prophet of God, What does Islam really consist in ?' And he said, 'It consists in purity of speech and hospitality.' I then asked, 'And what is faith ?' And he said, 'Patience and beneficence.'

Surah lxvi. 1.

One day Mohammed ate honey in the apartment of one of his wives, which so far excited the jealousy of some of his other wives that they agreed to tell Mohammed when he would come on his round of visit that they smelt he had eaten of a certain juice which though resembling honey in taste and consistence was yet the one which he hated the most; whereupon Mohammed swore off form it; which occasioned this passage. The other versions of this story have been examined in my Commentary: also my 'Life of Mohammed,' pp. 233-6. Calcutta. 1910.

Surah civ. 1. Among the sayings of Mohammed are the following :—

The best of God's creatures are those, who when they meet you, remind of God, and the worst of His creatures are those who carry tales about to do mischief and separate friends, and seek out the defects of people.

He who wears two faces in this world shall have two tongues of fire on the Day of Judgment.

It is unworthy of a Moslem to injure people's reputations, or to curse any one, or to abuse any one, or to talk vainly.

A slanderer and backbiter shall be shut out from Paradise.

The best atonement you can make for backbiting is immediately to ask pardon of him whom you have injured, and to say, 'O God, pardon me for what I have done,' and to determine not to do so again.'